Resilience

T0385461

for

A Wiley Brand

Resilience

by Eva Selhub, MD

A Wiley Brand

Resilience For Dummies®

Published by: **John Wiley & Sons, Inc.,** 111 River Street, Hoboken, NJ 07030-5774, www.wiley.com

Copyright © 2021 by John Wiley & Sons, Inc., Hoboken, New Jersey

Published simultaneously in Canada

For general information on our other products and services, please contact our Customer Care Department within the U.S. at 877-762-2974, outside the U.S. at 317-572-3993, or fax 317-572-4002. For technical support, please visit https://hub.wiley.com/community/support/dummies.

Wiley publishes in a variety of print and electronic formats and by print-on-demand. Some material included with standard print versions of this book may not be included in e-books or in print-on-demand. If this book refers to media such as a CD or DVD that is not included in the version you purchased, you may download this material at http://booksupport.wiley.com. For more information about Wiley products, visit www.wiley.com.

Library of Congress Control Number: 2021930166

ISBN 978-1-119-77341-2 (pbk); ISBN 978-1-119-77356-6 (ebk); ISBN 978-1-119-77364-1 (ebk)

Manufactured in the United States of America

SKY10024452_012521

Contents at a Glance

Table of Contents

Introduction

L ife has a way of throwing people curveballs, and how they deal with these difficult situations can make or break their lives. It seems, now more than ever, that everyone is faced with uncertainty and challenging life experiences daily in the form of pandemics, terrorist threats, job layoffs, loss of loved ones, illness, or economic instability. And yet, despite such adversity, people adapt and keep going. In addition, some individuals are even able to move forward with richer, healthier, and more rewarding lives as a result of having struggled through hardship. Is this a unique trait?

Indeed, achieving resilience isn't an extraordinary ability; rather, it's ordinary and ingrained in all of us. Humans are innately wired to adapt to difficulty. The key is to be able to tap into this wiring by developing behaviors, habits, and strategies that support us to thrive rather than dive. What is unique is that the path to resilience is different for everyone. It's a personal journey, and what works for one person may not work for another.

For this reason, this book is intended to help readers embark on their personal journey to resilience. The information within delves into a richer understanding of what constitutes resilience, the factors involved in becoming resilient, and the various strategies that can be used and developed to be able to adapt and thrive in the face of setbacks and challenges. You will find, I hope, that this book is filled with wisdom and guidance to help you cope with stress and difficulty so that you can find your way to enjoying a meaningful, happy, and healthy life.

About This Book

When I was asked to write *Resilience For Dummies*, I was thrilled to have the chance to share with readers the knowledge and practical advice that I know can guide anyone to achieve optimal resilience. This book covers all the bases when it comes to learning about how to become resilient, whether it relates to health, relationships, career, or family life or enhancing your meditation practice or spirituality. It offers you insight, easy-to-follow instructions, scientific knowledge, practical tips, and time-honored wisdom. I truly believe that knowledge is power, and with practice comes more power. For this reason, the book is filled with do-it-yourself exercises that enable you to embody the knowledge so that it becomes reality.

The best thing about this book is that it is practical and applicable to life. Explore the book and feel free to read the chapters that appeal to you or read from cover to cover. Experiment with the exercises, and take time to reflect. Read it once or several times. Bring the words into practice as you see fit. Remember that achieving resilience is a process, and, hopefully, this book has timeless information that will serve you along the way.

Foolish Assumptions

When writing this book, I made the assumption that you, like many people I know, are trying to find ways to cope with the enormous amount of stress we all face in today's world. Foolishly or not, I assumed that you don't want to struggle anymore and that, instead, you want to learn how to find ways to thrive despite adversity and find your bliss in any mess you find yourself in. Perhaps you think you can't do it, but I believe that you can — and if nothing else, I believe that you will enjoy reading, learning, and discovering that you're more resilient than you think.

Icons Used in This Book

Throughout this book, I use icons to draw your attention to particular kinds of information, exercises, or opportunities to reflect. Here's what they mean:

This icon alerts you to important insights, clarifications, or ways to do things better.

I use this icon whenever I want your attention. Please read the text associated with it for important information.

This icon asks you to take a moment to reflect on a question or several questions and see how you feel.

Beyond the Book

In addition to the material in this printed book, go to www.dummies to find a Cheat Sheet with additional tips that you can access from your computer or phone. Simply type "Resilience For Dummies Cheat Sheet" in the search box.

Where to Go from Here

The book is designed in such a way that you don't have to read the book from cover to cover. Rather, you can open the book to the chapter you're interested in. You get to decide how and what you want to learn. Of course, if you want to understand the basis of resilience and use it as the foundation from which you jump off and learn everything else, start with Part 1, in which I discuss the truth about stress and the six pillars of resilience. If you're keen on learning more about meditation, mindfulness, staying calm, and homing in on your intuition and insight, delve right into Part 2.

Take your pick, enjoy the read, and feel free to let me know how your journey goes, at www.drselhub.com!

1

Getting Started with Resilience

Chapter **1**

Embarking on the Journey to Resilience

Contrary to what many people think, resilience has nothing to do with avoiding stress, hardship, or failure in life. Instead, it's about knowing that life is filled with both joy and adversity and that when hardship happens, you'll be prepared to take it on, learn from it, and become stronger as a result. Resilience confers the ability to bounce back easily and thrive in the face of life's *many* inevitable challenges. In this chapter, I describe the factors that determine resilience, explain how it's possible to develop resilience even if your genes aren't wired that way, and set the stage for how you can embark on the journey to building your bounce back muscle and becoming stronger, wiser and feeling more fulfilled.

Resilience Is for Everyone

It's true that some people are naturally more resilient than others. These folks see challenges as opportunities, maintain a positive outlook, find meaning in the struggle, and successfully adapt to adversity. The good news is that even if it doesn't come naturally to you, you can build your bounce-back muscle. It comes down to choosing not to let adversity get you down and instead work towards using the situation to become stronger and wiser. Here are your options:

>> **Stay broken:** Succumb to stress, fall apart, and stay that way — you're unable to recover normal functioning and feel helpless.

>> **Stay weak:** Succumb to stress, get injured, and partially recover — you're week and your functioning is still subpar.

>> **Get back to baseline:** Manage the stress and bounce back to baseline, whatever that may be.

>> **Become stronger:** Reckon with the stress and grow stronger, wiser, and fitter as a result.

You can choose to feel victimized by life's hardships or choose to accept them and make the most of every situation. You'll have to make some effort to build your resilience muscle, but it's absolutely possible, especially if your choice is to thrive rather than dive.

When you're ready to choose to thrive and embark on a journey to greater resilience, this book provides you with information, tools, skills, and so much more to help you along the way.

What Determines Resilience?

At some point, most people incur some form of suffering, whether it's the death of a loved one, illness, injury, divorce, job loss, or another difficult life event. Not everyone copes with adversity in the same way, though, because it's influenced by multiple factors. Some of these factors you have no control over, like your genes, the culture you grew up in, or critical life events that may have occurred in your past. Some of these factors are within your control, such as your beliefs, behaviors, attitudes, and chosen networks of support. The question is, which of these determinants carries the most weight when it comes to resilience? Is it up to nature, or is it a result of nurture?

Though genetics does play a role, it appears that people have the ability to develop resilience despite genetics. According to a study conducted by the National Institutes of Health's National Institute of Nursing Research, led by Heather Rusch, two critically important factors associated with resilience are in your control to change:

>> **Self-mastery:** The degree to which you perceive yourself as having control and influence over circumstance.

>> **Social support:** The degree to which you perceive you are cared for and receiving help from other people.

The stronger these two factors, according to the research, the higher the likelihood that an individual will be resilient in the face of trauma or stress.

In the next several sections, I describe the different factors that determine resilience and see how it all works.

Your genes

Though it hasn't been established that a single gene or gene variation confers resilience, it has been found that genetic factors can influence how you respond to stress and deal with adversity. A range of genes has been identified that are associated with resilient *phenotypes* (how a gene expresses itself physically). Genes or variations of genes, for example, can influence the stress response, nervous system, immune system, and pathways that produce feel-good neurotransmitters like serotonin and dopamine and determine your biological response to stress. The bottom line is that science is showing that although genes play a role in determining resilience, they're only part of the story because it's now widely known that nature and nurture go hand in hand.

Your life experiences — especially early life, culture, and behaviors — influence the expression of genes and the neurobiological systems that enable adaptation to stress and resilience. Meditation, exercise, healthy nutrition, and social support are examples of lifestyle changes that can effect such neurobiological changes and, possibly, genetic expression. In short, you can influence your genes and still achieve better self-mastery and social support.

Childhood development

Early childhood experiences can positively or negatively affect the development of the stress response and how individuals subsequently learn to cope with adversity. Trauma and abuse can lead to changes in central nervous system circuits, a hyperactive stress response, more anxious behavior, and vulnerability to stress from learned helplessness, as people learn to believe that they have no control to change their circumstance or situation.

It has also been shown that when individuals realize that it's possible to change behaviors — even in the face of adversity — and feel better, learned helplessness doesn't happen. Examples might include when a child suffers bullying at school and receives a lot of love and support from family, friends, and counselors and is provided with effective coping tools. Children who gain the ability to adapt to stress develop better self-esteem, prosocial behavior, and more immunity to stress as they age.

As such, neither your genetics nor your past necessarily blocks you from being resilient. Either of these may support a tendency to adapt to stress more effectively or less effectively, but neither seals the deal on your ability to become stronger and more positive and have a better sense of self-mastery.

Culture

Individual behavior and coping styles are influenced by cultural patterns of beliefs, values, commitments, resources, and expected behaviors. Culture, therefore, can predict resilience as it shapes how people might see themselves and how they relate to others. The culture of a family can especially shape how a child develops a sense of self-concept and self-esteem. For example, a culture might value the woman's role as being quiet and docile, and subject to a man's authority, whereas another culture advocates for gender equality. Children growing up in either of these households will likely grow up to have very different self-concepts.

Culture refers not just to your ethnicity or religion but also to the culture of your family or your workplace. Cultures that promote respect, collaboration, reliance, open communication, and strong core values promote resilience within the community as well as individual resilience.

Psychological outlook

Your upbringing and environment can influence your outlook and how you see yourself and the world at large. A positive outlook has been found to be protective in the face of adversity and associated with better coping behaviors, quicker recovery times, improved health and wellbeing, and a better sense of self-mastery. The reverse is true for a negative outlook, as a negative view of oneself and the world increases the perception and magnitude of stress and reduces the sense of self-mastery and belief that challenges are manageable. A negative outlook is associated with limiting beliefs, negative self-talk, narrow thinking, and less effective coping habits.

A myriad of traits are associated with a positive outlook. Those most associated with resilience are believing that success is possible (optimism), viewing difficulties as opportunities for growth and learning, having the willingness to push forward, being able to accept change, and being open to making mistakes and learning from failures. All these traits can be cultivated with practice and also aren't purely dependent on upbringing and genetics.

Coping habits

Coping habits are habits you have developed that have helped you get through challenges or difficulties. In general, there are two types of coping habits, adaptive and maladaptive.

>> **Adaptive** habits are the behaviors that help you cope with stress that are also healthy for the mind and body.

>> **Maladaptive** habits are behaviors that might reduce anxiety and therefore help you cope but are themselves destructive to your health.

Confronting your fears head-on, appraising situations realistically, calming your emotions, and maintaining healthy behaviors — like good sleep hygiene and a balanced exercise-and-nutrition regimen — are examples of adaptive coping habits. Choosing to avoid dealing with fear and drinking alcohol, binge eating, or throwing yourself into work so that you aren't sleeping, exercising, or eating appropriately are examples of maladaptive coping habits.

Some adaptive coping habits that improve resilience are exercising, eating a healthy diet, meditating, accessing social support, connecting to spirituality, learning to reappraise thoughts and beliefs, regulating emotions, and partaking in altruistic activities. These habits can be learned and cultivated, even when maladaptive coping has been the norm.

Social support

Support comes in the form of family, intimate partners, colleagues, neighbors, friends, spiritual community members, and others. The presence of strong networks of support and the seeking of social support are both associated with resilience. Both invigorate psychological hardiness and the ability to thrive in the face of adversity. Studies show that stronger social bonds can improve quality of life, wound healing, and life expectancy. In contrast, the lack of support is correlated with more depression and a weaker sense of control.

The ability to forge healthy social bonds, be able to communicate effectively, and show value and compassion are traits that a resilient person exemplifies, enabling them to have a truly viable social support system in times of need. With help, anyone can learn to improve their ability to form healthier relationships and stronger networks of support.

Humor

Sometimes, you have to laugh to literally keep yourself from crying, and when you do, it can make you more resilient. Humor helps you release stress, and it's a conduit to strengthening social bonds while being protective against stress. A study of sojourn students from mainland China attending school at a Hong Kong university, for instance, found that the students who used humor to adjust to the new culture were able to thrive best, and that humor acted as a buffer against stress.

Humor and laughter are wonderful resources when coping with hardship, because they lighten the load emotionally as well as physiologically. Laughter especially can relax the stress response, give you more energy, and soothe tension. It has also been found that laughter can improve your immune system, relieve pain, improve your mood, and enhance a sense of wellbeing. You always have the option to make use of your funny bone during times of stress.

Spirituality

The internal belief system that guides values, ethics, social behaviors, and psychological outlook also influences resilience. Individuals who have a strong sense of purpose, a feeling of connection to a greater whole, or a feeling of connection to spirituality are more resilient. Studies show that purpose in life is a key factor in helping individuals manage traumatic events, and that low spirituality is a leading predictor of low resilience. Whether it's because you have a sense of purpose, belong to a spiritual community, partake in healthier behaviors, or have a more optimistic outlook, science confirms that spirituality confers better health.

It doesn't matter what pathways you choose to connect to spirituality, because it comes in many forms. You can follow a particular faith or religion, feel connected to a higher power, spend time in nature, read uplifting literature, or be driven by a higher purpose. How spiritual you are today may be influenced by your upbringing and culture, but it's also a factor that can be cultivated in order to build your resilience.

What Resilience Is Not

Until I was in my late 20s, I believed that if I worked hard, good things would come my way, which drove me to complete medical school and a challenging residency. I also believed that my value was wrapped up in my accomplishments. Whenever I was praised or succeeded in an endeavor, I felt confident and good about myself. If I did not succeed or did not receive praise, my sense of value plummeted. I blamed myself for not being good enough and, as a result, worked even harder — at the expense of my own health. When I finally took the time to self-examine my behavior, I came to understand that unless I succeeded or received praise, I had a pattern of feeling unworthy and victimized by the universe. I realized that I needed to work on myself, reach the source of my negative thinking, and find ways to correct it if I wanted to be a healthier and more resilient person.

REMEMBER

When you take responsibility for your behavior and learn to overcome feelings of victimization, helplessness, low self-worth, or hopelessness, you're truly on the path to resilience. I don't mean that you don't experience periods of fear, worry, or upset. Of course, you do! You're human. The key is that you don't stay in these negative states for too long because you're able to shift your perspective and use the situation to learn and grow.

The victim mindset

Life can be hard, and when it knocks you down, it's normal to fall and even to cry. *Staying* in a state of pity for too long though, can lead to a victim mindset, where you feel you're powerless to effect change and that life is totally out of your control.

When you have a *victim mentality,* you believe that life is happening to you rather than for you or with you. It's a mindset that usually develops over time, after experiencing multiple setbacks or hurts or the loss of love and support. Eventually, you decide that you have no control over life and that you're helpless to change it. As a result, you may avoid taking responsibility for yourself or your life and avoid taking risks, embracing change, improving yourself, or making hard decisions. Instead, you may live in fear, complain a lot, and tempt other people to feel sorry for you. This list describes some of the signs that indicate you're on the verge of having a victim mentality:

>> **You feel powerless.** When bad things happen to you, you believe that you have no control over the situation and that you're helpless to effect change. You believe you have no power and are therefore a victim of life's circumstances. Powerlessness can manifest as a lack of self-esteem, feelings of failure and incompetence, and low motivation.

If you find that you're feeling helpless or powerless, ask yourself, "What is it that I do have control over? Is the belief that I am powerless true?"

>> **You put yourself down.** Feeling powerless often goes hand in hand with negative self-talk and self-doubt. You question your abilities, feel you aren't worthy of success, believe you're incapable of succeeding, and often end up self-sabotaging your efforts. You regularly put yourself down and, in so doing, paint yourself as a victim.

If you find that you're putting yourself down, ask yourself, "Am I really that terrible? Is this belief even true? Can I think of times when I was successful?"

>> **You overgeneralize the negative.** When a negative event happens, you overgeneralize and view it as part of a continued pattern of negativity and ignore evidence to the contrary — that many aspects of your life, and even similar situations, have been positive. You may use the words *never, always, all, every, none, no one, nobody,* or *everyone* to support your belief that you don't, and never will, have or be enough or that a situation will forever be bad. Examples of statements you might make are "I can never win," "I am always the last to know," and "You never listen to me."

If you make these kinds of statements, ask yourself, "Are there times when this doesn't happen?" and "Is this statement really true?"

>> **You catastrophize.** When you exaggerate the importance of a problem, making it bigger than it necessarily is, you're *catastrophizing*. For instance, you might tell yourself that you absolutely cannot handle a given situation when the reality is that it's just inconvenient. In other words, you believe that even the smallest inconveniences are the end of the world. A tendency to make such problems important can indicate your underlying fears of being inadequate, unimportant, or dispensable.

If you find that you catastrophize and make mountains out of a molehill, ask yourself, "What is the worst thing that could happen? Is this statement really true?"

>> **You feel paranoid.** You regularly feel that the world is out to get you and inflict misery on you. You believe that no matter what you do, life will be miserable and always unfair and you can't count on anything, least of all other people. Life is not only happening to you but also against you.

If you find yourself feeling like life is against you, ask yourself, "Are there times when things went my way? Is this belief really true?"

Learned helplessness

Most people vacillate between feeling optimistic and feeling victimized, depending on what is happening in their lives and how they're feeling about themselves at that particular juncture. Though people don't start out feeling victimized as children, for the most part, they can eventually learn to feel this way as they incur hardships, traumas, or other difficult life events that may cause them to feel more helpless about affecting change in their lives. For some people, as they face continuous negative and uncontrollable hardships, and their efforts fail at effecting change, they eventually stop trying and give up believing that they have any power to improve their circumstances.

Is there something in your life you have tried to do and regularly failed, so you gave up trying? How did that failure make you feel?

REFLECTION

The term *learned helplessness* was coined by the psychologists Martin Seligman and Steven Maier in 1967, when they were studying how dogs behaved when experiencing electric shocks. Seligman and Maier discovered that dogs who realized that they couldn't escape the shocks eventually stopped trying, even when it was possible for them to avoid the shock by jumping over a barrier. In later experiments, Seligman studied human subjects and their response to loud and unpleasant noises. Subjects had the option to use a lever to stop the noise. Subjects whose lever was ineffective at stopping the noise gave up trying after one round.

Learned helplessness can show up in all aspects of your life. You can see it all around you if you look. People are discouraged about politics and decide not to vote, or they're discouraged about losing weight because nothing has worked, or their best friend won't leave a bad relationship because they believe that no one better is out there, or their child has decided not to study because they believe that they will fail anyway. You or someone you know might be depressed, emotionally unpredictable, unmotivated, and unwilling to change healthy habits. When you learn over time that you have little to no control over your life and life circumstances, no matter what you do, you give up hope and give up trying. It may keep you in an abusive relationship or a stressful job or keep you physically ill, even though you have options available to you to get out and change.

Here are some common signs of learned helplessness:

>> Mental health problems, such as anxiety, depression, or post-traumatic stress disorder (PTSD)

>> Inability to ask for help

>> Easy frustration and willingness to give up

>> Lack of motivation and desire to put in effort

>> Low self-esteem and lack of self-belief in success

>> Passivity in the face of stress

>> Procrastination

Hopelessness

When you feel *hopeless,* you lack hope in the possibility of a better future. This belief negatively affects how you see the world, yourself, and other people. It can lead to feeling depressed, as though darkness has descended on your life and there's no point in doing anything. You're devoid of inspiration and you have no interest in going out, seeing people, working, or engaging in normal activities. The scarcity of social connection and poor motivation to seek help then adds to feelings of isolation or abandonment, exacerbating the feeling of hopelessness.

Hopelessness is often associated with mental health issues like anxiety, depression, substance dependency, suicidal ideation, eating disorders, post-traumatic stress, and bipolar disorder. It can also show up intermittently during periods of difficulty and eventually pass when life lets up a bit. The problem is that when you fall into hopelessness, it can feel like a trap so that you lose the motivation to find help and get out, even though you have plenty of pathways to do so.

I have worked with many people who have complained of depression and described feeling this way. I personally have faced "the darkness of my soul" at critical junctures in my life, after experiencing one traumatic event after another. For my clients as well as myself, feeling hopeless was a symptom of feeling defeated, dissatisfied, and beat up by life events and feeling too exhausted to gather the energy to fight back. With time, love, and support, and reappraising my core beliefs and improving self-care, hopelessness was eventually turned back into hope.

REMEMBER

If you're having difficulty getting out of the trap, I cannot stress enough how important it is to seek help from a therapist, counselor, or trusted friend. You aren't on this journey alone, and you have available options to feel better, as both I and my clients discovered.

Here are some signs that you're starting to feel hopeless:

>> Your situation will never improve.

>> It's too late for you to change.

>> No one can help you.

>> You will never be happy again.

>> You will never find love.

>> You have no future.

>> Success isn't possible.

Breaking the Victim Cycle

The first step to breaking the victim cycle is to first accept that you're human and that it's normal to feel stress, fear, anxiety, grief, and loss. You want to accept that when you feel negative emotions and are overcome by stress, it's natural for your brain to trigger a fight-or-flight response and to cause you to feel more fear or overwhelm. The next step is to *choose* not to stay there.

When you make the choice to shift your mindset away from the victim mentality, you choose to remember that you have the ability to view yourself and your life differently; you have the ability to access resources to not only survive difficulty but also to come out better and stronger. Once you have made the choice to shift, you can then access the tools that will support you to attain a more resilient mindset and eventually stay there.

You will see in this book how to recognize negative and self-sabotaging thoughts and then take responsibility for them, realizing that you have the power to shift them to a more positive narrative. You will see how to connect with and regulate your emotions, develop positive beliefs and a more optimistic outlook, uphold behaviors that will support you to thrive, and cultivate strong social support networks. Embarking on this journey ultimately requires that you take responsibility for your life; take ownership for your actions, thoughts, and feelings; and do a bit of work to design your life in a way that empowers you to be at your best. When you make the choice to do so, you break the victim cycle.

If you're ready to become a master of your life, you're ready to build your six pillars of resilience.

Cultivating the Six Pillars of Resilience

Over the past 30 years, I have worked toward better understanding what makes a person more resilient. It has been both a personal journey as well as a process that I have guided thousands of patients and clients through. I have discovered that developing resilience and ultimately *fitness,* or the ability to bounce back from hardship even stronger and wiser than before, involves cultivating these six major pillars of resilience:

>> Physical hardiness

>> Emotional equilibrium

>> Mental clarity and toughness

>> Spiritual connection

>> Loving relationships and strong social connections

>> Influential leadership within your community

Developing physical hardiness

Physical hardiness can facilitate resilience and protect you from the negative effects of stress. If you think about it, it makes sense that feeling physically fitter would help you be more resilient. It also makes sense that when you feel physically sick or weak, life feels that much harder. It's impossible to think clearly, work effectively, or fully enjoy life when your body is sick, tired, inflamed, and not functioning at its best. Whether it's caused by lack of sleep, exercise, or proper nutrition or by poor work conditions, hectic scheduling, or negative thinking, inflammation and a lack of proper fuel will leave you lacking fighting power when stress comes your way.

Improving physical vitality requires that you perceive everything in your life as something that is either enriching your health or hurting it; providing you with fuel that will enhance your life force or taking fuel away that will diminish your life force. Whether it's by improving your quality of sleep, developing an exercise routine, abiding by a healthy nutrition plan, or developing a meditation practice, the key is to challenge the body physically yet also fuel it appropriately so that you can thrive instead of dive.

Achieving emotional equilibrium

Positive emotions serve as fuel, in that they fuel you to feel strong, capable, and confident — as though you can conquer challenges. Negative emotions, on the other hand, if persistent, align you with fear-based thinking and behaviors and can lead you through the victim cycle. Studies show that resilient individuals are emotionally balanced; they not only maintain positive emotions in the face of stress but also use them to bounce back from negative experiences as they remain confident, optimistic, and open.

The path toward improving resilience involves learning how to become more self-aware, mindful, and relaxed so that you can regulate your emotions, find your equilibrium, and shift into a more positive state. The path involves learning to use negative emotions as signals and opportunities for growth and change, thus controlling them instead of letting them control you. Through mindfulness practices, self-observation, and techniques that help you release your negative emotions, you learn to quiet your emotions, find harmony within yourself, and have access to optimism and positive belief.

Boosting mental clarity and toughness

When fear takes over, the stress response is activated, releasing stress hormones into your brain and body and causing feel-good neurotransmitter levels to drop and fear-related behaviors and thinking to preside. Your ability to think clearly and make good decisions diminishes. A person who is more resilient has the capability to override this physiological change and maintain clarity of mind, objectivity, and rational thinking. Rather than fall apart, they keep it together, work through the stress, and persevere.

Being able to boost your mental clarity and stay mentally tough in the face of hardship requires that you be self-aware, calm, open to change, and comfortable with not having all the answers, in the belief that, come what may, you have what it takes to prevail. It involves maintaining a positive and optimistic mental attitude, no matter the circumstance, and having the grit and stamina to keep trying, even when you experience setbacks.

Enriching spiritual connection

A growing body of evidence is showing that a spiritual outlook makes humans more resilient to trauma. The literature also shows that possessing a sense of meaning and purpose in life is positively related to quality of life and improved health and functioning. People with greater spirituality partake in healthier behaviors, maintain a more positive world view, are more connected to a community, and feel a greater sense of belonging — all factors that strengthen resilience.

Enhancing your connection to spirituality can take many forms. You can awaken and harness this pillar of resilience via meditation or nonreligious prayer, practicing mindfulness, spending time in nature, joining a spiritual community, reading uplifting literature, volunteering, or working toward a greater understanding of your higher purpose. Experiencing resilience with a spiritual lens helps you stay more positive and optimistic, find meaning in difficulty, express more gratitude, discover stronger social support, employ healthier behaviors, and improve your coping skills.

Establishing healthy relationships

Humans are social creatures. They have an innate desire to belong and to be together. Numerous studies show that social support is essential for maintaining physical and psychological health. Not all relationships, unfortunately, are created equal. Quality relationships can support your resilience, and unhealthy ones can break it. Though healthy, high-quality relationships can buffer stress and can help you live longer, heal faster, and improve behaviors, unhealthy relationships can lead to physical and emotional distress, self-sabotaging behaviors, and loss of self-confidence and self-mastery.

To build your resilience, you therefore want to establish loving and healthy relationships that support you to thrive. This requires taking a deeper dive into yourself, uncovering your core values and feelings of worth, learning to accept and love yourself, and committing to knowing that your relationships will help you learn and grow. It involves examining your current relationships, assessing your levels of commitment and investment, improving your sense of compassion, and learning how to effectively communicate, express gratitude, see value, and receive as well as give.

Belonging to a community and becoming a leader

When you understand that you're part of a community and you cultivate this network of support, you enhance your resilience. Knowing that you belong and that a group of people have your back helps you know that you have assistance and resources to mitigate uncertainty. It supports you to stay optimistic and feel secure, encourages you to work well with others as a team, enhances your sense of trust and confidence that success is possible, and helps you find purpose in difficult times.

The more cohesive and resilient the community, the better off you are. Studies show that people who are affiliated with communities that are prepared and have resources to manage adversity are more resilient than those individuals who lack such an affiliation. Building this pillar of resilience thus involves strengthening your networks of support and helping your community become more resilient itself. It involves knowing that, to some extent, even if you aren't a CEO, a captain of a team, or someone's boss, you still have influence on the people around you and you have a choice of whether you want that influence to be positive or negative.

Building this pillar involves working through blocks and negative mindsets that might keep you alienated, isolated, or unable to seek support, and also learning to find value in the virtues and efforts of people around you. It entails becoming aware of the influence you have on others; communicating more effectively; remaining clearheaded, authentic, and insightful; and being a positive and resilient leader who inspires others to do the same.

Ultimately, the path toward optimal resilience differs from one individual to the next because everyone has different genetic tendencies, backgrounds, and life circumstances, and some individuals are more fit in one pillar over the other. The beauty is that there is no single right way to get there, because many tools and many paths lead to the same place, where, eventually, stressful challenges become opportunities and life indeed becomes more joyful, successful, and rewarding. Are you ready to embark on the journey to resilience?

response

Chapter **2**

The Basis of Resilience: Harmony Versus Stress

Resilient people have the ability to think clearly and find solutions to complex situations, even under duress. They are able to maintain adaptability and flexibility in the midst of change, stay open to support and learning, culti-vate optimism, dedicate themselves to person renewal, and, ultimately, thrive in the face of adversity. Resilient people not only resist succumbing to stress but also find a way to adapt to it and become stronger, wiser, and get better at a given task as a result.

In this chapter, you can learn about what stress is, how the stress response affects the mind and body, why perception is half the battle, and how it's possible to improve your ability to not only manage the stress in your life but also use it to your advantage on your path to resilience.

Without Stress, You Would Be Dead

Stress is part of life. You can't get around it. You actually *need* stress in order to live. If anyone claims they have no stress, I would guess they are dead.

Feeling tired? Stress. Feeling hungry or cold? Stress and stress. Low blood pressure? Stress again. Worried about a deadline, the world economy, or whether your child will perform well in school today? Yep. Stress again.

Stress isn't always bad. It's often just the state of things. Your blood sugar will eventually fall, and at some point you will want the answer to a question. Not knowing or understanding something is, of course, stressful.

Stress motivates you to find food, climb the corporate ladder, innovate, seek information, and find new ways to become more comfortable or travel somewhere faster. Without stress, you wouldn't get out of bed in the morning, procreate, leave for work on time, put food on the table, or shift positions when you're uncomfortable. Without stress, you wouldn't be motivated to obtain food, put on warm clothing when it's freezing outside, find a partner to make babies with, or get a job. Think about it: If you freeze to death, go hungry, and skip having babies — there goes the human species or, well, at least your genetic lineage.

The Perpetual Quest for Harmony

Stress can manifest as mild feelings of discomfort about real-life threatening challenges or hidden stressors such as having the gene for breast cancer, harboring low feelings of self-worth, or discovering mold in your bedroom. The brain doesn't care, because the brain simply wants harmony. Anything that challenges your state of harmony (or *homeostasis*, in scientific terms) qualifies as stress. The brain doesn't care whether it's physical, psychological, or environmental; real or imagined; microscopically small in your body; or a major event happening in the world. If it's challenging your state of harmony, it's also challenging your livelihood — or your value as a human being, according to your brain. In response, your brain activates a series of responses to motivate action in an attempt to adapt to the stress and regain your harmony. The process of achieving harmony or stability by way of change or adaptation is *allostasis*. The brain drives this process until it finds harmony, and as far as you're concerned, this happens when you feel better.

When you're uncomfortable, what do you do? You shift positions. You go from feeling achy to feeling at peace. When you don't understand something, what do you do? You "google it." You go from feeling confused to feeling smart. When you're anxiously awaiting a call after a job interview or a date, how do you feel when you finally receive the call and it's good news? You're relieved and happy!

And there you have it — every one of your actions, habits, or behaviors is built on the desire to find relief and happiness.

Take a moment to think about why you're driven to make more money or maintain the perfect relationship or become thin or eat your favorite meal. What do you receive at the end? Satisfaction? Peace? Joy? Happiness?

No matter what you believe is driving you, in the end, deep within the wiring of your brain, you're driven to feel at peace and be happy. This desire is hard-wired into your nervous system and driven by the stress response.

Examining the Stress Response Feedback Loop

The stress response, or the physiological response to stress, exists for good reason: It gets you out of bed in the morning, to meet your nutritional needs, to prepare your body to fight infections and heal wounds, to maintain blood pressure and survive traumas, to solve difficult problems, and to allow energy to be expended in response to a wide range of signals so that you can adapt to an ever-changing environment and survive.

Fight-or-flight

Walter Cannon, a Harvard physiologist, coined the term *fight-or-flight* in the 1930s to describe the inborn defense response to threat or danger that ultimately ensures survival. When faced with danger, we humans are catapulted into action by stress hormones such as adrenalin and cortisol. As we became heavily focused and hyperalert, our pupils dilate and our peripheral vision is blocked, forcing our focus on reaching safety. Our muscles tense, our heart rate increases, and we breathe faster to economize on oxygen consumption. Energy stores from the liver, fat cells, bones, and muscles are released into the bloodstream, and our digestive system shuts down so that this energy can be dedicated toward fighting like mad or running like there's no tomorrow (literally because, if you die, there will be no tomorrow).

Here's a rundown of the stress response and its effect on your body:

>> The **pupils** dilate.

>> **Blood vessels** constrict in the hands and feet and gut.

>> The **gastrointestinal tract** shuts down, causing slower movement of the colon and other organs.

>> The **reproductive system** shuts down.

>> **Muscles** become tense, especially the back, neck, jaw, and shoulders.

>> The **immune system** suffers more inflammation, clotting, and allergic reactions (over time, causing poor immunity against infections or cancers).

>> The **cardiovascular system** experiences an increase in heart rate and blood pressure.

>> The **respiratory system** experiences an increase in breathing rate and inflammation.

>> The **metabolic system** shifts to *catabolism,* or breakdown. The liver releases glucose stores. Fats are broken down to fatty acids. Proteins from muscle stores are broken down into amino acids. Bones are broken down for minerals.

>> The **brain** experiences less complex thinking, and more fear-related behaviors are initiated, causing hyper-alertness and arousal.

>> Your **mood** is affected by a loss of serotonin, and other neurotransmitters cause depression, anxiety, and other mood disorders.

>> In your **mind,** higher-thinking centers are shut down, as are big-picture thinking and judgment to enable focus (causing more myopic thinking).

The feedback loop

Once out of danger, the built-in turn of the switch in your brain turns off the stress response. Stress hormone levels drop, your heart rate, blood pressure, and breathing slow down, your muscles relax, your digestive system starts working, and blood flow resumes to your fingers and toes, as the parasympathetic nervous system (the one that creates calm) is activated, and the sympathetic nervous system (the one that creates hyperalertness and hyperactivity) is turned down. Happy chemicals, like dopamine and morphine-like substances, fill your brain as adrenalin levels wear off, giving you the feeling of euphoria and calm. This is considered a *positive feedback loop*, or when the message is received by the brain that the outcome is positive (stress gone), so it turns off the stress response switch.

Here's an example, which shows how you go from hangry (the combination of *hungry* and *angry*) to happy:

1. Your blood sugar drops.

2. The body picks up the imbalance and sends an alert to the brain.

3. The stress response is activated, stress hormones are released, the heart rate increases, and the intestines contract.

4. You notice the aches in your belly — that you're feeling a bit weak and dizzy and that you're irritable.

5. Your conscious brain understands that you're hangry.

6. Your conscious brain remembers that eating food will help you feel better.

7. You eat.

8. Your blood sugar goes back to normal.

9. The message travels to the brain.

10. The brain turns off the stress response as dopamine, serotonin, and endorphins flood your brain.

11. The result of all this activity is that you now feel happy and satiated.

To continue with this scenario, if you can't manage to find food, the stress of having low blood sugar doesn't get fixed. In fact, the problem grows worse, as do your symptoms, so the stress response keeps firing. This causes your blood pressure and heart rate to remain high, as stress hormones fly through your body and muscles remain tense. And, this is in addition to the fact that you're starving. This is considered a *negative feedback loop*.

Aside from your dying of hunger, an unchecked stressed response that results from a perpetual negative feedback loop can also be problematic. If left unchecked, physiological responses that are meant to be beneficial in the short term can become harmful as they rage on. Heightened blood pressure can turn into heart disease; muscle tension, into fibromyalgia; negative mood, into dysphoria and depression; heightened inflammation, into a wide variety of immune disorders; and focused thinking, into myopia and an inability to make sound decisions.

The reason I explain this concept to you is that this negative feedback loop, and an unchecked stress response, happens *all* the time and most people don't even realize it. They don't realize that they're living in constant disharmony until one day they find that their body has to fight a virus, recover from an accident, or withstand the stress of moving homes — and their body can't handle it. They get sick.

Living in Disharmony: The Real Stress

You might be starting to understand the real problem with stress: It's not just the stress that is problematic but also the stress response itself. Disharmony breeds more disharmony, which leads to a bigger stress load, which weakens the mind and the body.

To make matters worse, the brain can't tell the difference between one stress and another. It can't distinguish between running for your life and running late to work or between having your life threatened and your self-esteem challenged.

In the 1950s, Hans Selye expanded on Cannon's work and explained that you don't have to be chased by a raging animal for the fight-or-flight response to be mounted and that this heightened reaction occurs regardless of whether the challenge at hand is life threatening. You might be physically ill or worried about paying your bills, getting fired, or surviving after your spouse leaves you. You might worry about an event that is happening now or one that might happen in the future. The physiological response is the same.

When a threat is ongoing — like a constant worry, a deep feeling of unworthiness, the presence of an abusive family member, or chronic pollution exposure — the negative feedback loop persists and the stress response doesn't shut down. As a result, an overactive stress response can lead to a host of physical problems as well as a negative state of mind, belief, and mood. Ultimately, when your brain perceives that you're continually under threat and that there's no end in sight, feelings of helplessness or hopelessness can take over.

REMEMBER

In other words, if you frequently worry, get upset, feel anxious or frustrated, or become wracked with self-doubt, your brain receives messages that your world is extremely threatening and that you're weak and lack the capacity to handle it, which makes the brain continue firing the stress response. The more the response fires, the more stress hormones rage, while happy chemicals like serotonin drop and fear-related and nonsocial behaviors are activated, causing you to lash out or withdraw socially.

In contrast, when you see your world as manageable and any stress as not threatening but rather as a challenge to be reckoned with, the stress response is activated for short periods that motivate you into action, positive feelings and moods are maintained, and resilience is assured.

Expecting a Good Outcome Is the Key

The key to keeping the stress response under control is expecting good, or the belief that a positive outcome is possible. If your brain perceives a particular situation to be manageable, it fires the stress response only long enough to motivate the necessary action, like an athlete who is motivated to compete and win a race.

Positive expectation reflects a state of inner certainty or trust in success or manageability of a particular endeavor or challenge. Negative perception, in contrast, indicates a mental state of lower self-appraisal and a negative worldview. The brain sees this negative perception as disharmony and a stress in itself, which triggers the stress response and the associated response or reactions.

For example, you may agonize over what to do about a work project. You worry that you'll make the wrong decision, one that your boss will disapprove of. You worry that if you make a mistake, you'll be raked over the coals. You agonize night and day over this issue. You worry about getting fired, even though you have never given your boss reason to fire you. You worry about it anyway. You lose sleep. You drink too much coffee during the day and too much alcohol at night, in an attempt to calm your nerves. You can feel your heart rate increase and your blood pressure rise. You feel tired and achy and overwhelmed now by the demands of your life, and you simply don't think you can handle much more. You argue with your spouse and honk the car horn repeatedly at the driver in front of you. You dislike the way you're behaving, but you can't seem to help it. Your life is falling apart and so are you. A negative expectation has bred a negative outcome.

If you were able to change your mindset to believe that whatever choice you make, you would be okay, the scenario would likely play out quite differently. You might, for instance, feel confident about your ability to make choices and truly believe that there's no such thing as a wrong choice because every choice brings opportunity for growth and learning. You might expect a good outcome no matter the situation, which in turn influences how your body responds. You have that much control!

Believing in Possible

Have you heard of the placebo and nocebo effects? The *placebo effect* is a term normally used in medical research to test the validity of a procedure, medication, or herb by comparing it to an inert therapy, like a sham procedure or sugar pill. The placebo effect occurs when a person feels better or symptoms improve, whereas the nocebo effect transpires when a person feels worse or experiences side effects. In research, if findings show that the inert therapy provides similar improvements as the procedure or drug, the person often attributes the effect to placebo. If the inert therapy induces negative side effects, the person attributes the effect to nocebo.

Whether a procedure or a drug works or is useless is less interesting to me than this notion: Your beliefs can affect the physiology of your body. It's truly incredible!

The incredible power of belief has led many a scientist to try to better understand the power of the mind and the associated complex physiological mechanisms. Note the difference, for example, between the effects of positive versus negative expectations.

Positive expectation, or the placebo effect, has these characteristics:

>> The brain's dopamine and opioid systems are activated.

>> The release of dopamine, opiates, and opioid-like substances normally induces feelings of euphoria and positivity.

>> These chemicals also slow down or turn off the stress response and influence other processes in the body, including immunity and pain regulation.

In contrast, negative expectation, or the nocebo effect, has these characteristics — it is associated with

>> The same brain centers as anxiety

>> Increased activity in regions associated with the stress response

>> An increased experience of pain

For example, a patient who is confident in his or her surgeon and believes a surgical procedure will go well might require less pain-and-calming medication. Compare this to someone who is worried that the surgeon might make a mistake or that the procedure will not achieve a positive result, and then might require larger doses of anesthesia and analgesia.

The point here is that your beliefs have a direct effect on physiological responses, how you feel, and, ultimately, how you behave. When you perceive stress to be manageable, you exemplify positive expectation, which evokes a more controlled stress response, an improved mood, a healthier body, continued access to higher and logical thinking, and, ultimately, better decision making and behaviors that help you adapt to life's hardships.

Coping to Adapt, or Not

Generally, coping means we have managed to adapt to a given stress and feel better. If you're hungry, you cope by eating. If you're tired, you cope by sleeping. Or maybe you don't? Maybe you drink caffeine instead so as not to be tired. Hm. Does this latter scenario count as coping?

In a way, yes, it does count as coping. It's just not *adaptive*, which means it's not good for you. And, rather than support your body to ultimately thrive, it's more likely to cause you to dive — at some point, anyway.

All of our human behaviors and habits are learned ways of coping with stress. We developed them early in life, when we learned that doing something in a certain way leads to feeling good. We also learned to avoid doing other things, because they caused us to feel badly.

The problem is that feeling better doesn't necessarily translate into managing a given stress or the body actually being in harmony. For example, you may have learned that asking for help leads to being rejected, so you avoid doing so. Working hard and getting a job done yourself makes you feel valued and accomplished, so you keep doing it, and at 150 percent effort. You may have learned to cope with sleep deprivation by drinking caffeine and to cope with your anxiety by eating ice cream.

What's wrong with this picture? All these actions, behaviors, and habits help you cope and temporarily feel better, and probably enable you to be more successful at your job, but in reality you aren't fully addressing all your stress. You have neither addressed your fear of rejection nor listened to your body and taken care of its needs. You're coping, but it's *maladaptive.* Adaptive coping would involve you addressing your fears, creating work–life balance, sleeping when you're tired, and nurturing your body with the right kind of fuel or food.

Maladaptive coping

Maladaptive coping usually has negative consequences and is often counterproductive, working in the short term but causing trouble in the long run. Here are some examples:

» Avoidance

» Substance use

» Addictions

» Emotional eating

» Workaholism

» Impulsive decision-making

» Rumination (continuously thinking the same thoughts)

» Risk-taking

» Self-harm

Adaptive coping

Adaptive coping has positive consequences and enables a more resilient body and happy life. Here are some examples:

>> Facing difficult situations head-on

>> Asking for support or advice

>> Meditating

>> Regulating emotions to find calm

>> Addressing negative beliefs and hurtful memories from the past

>> Exercising

>> Fueling the body with nutrient-rich food

>> "Sleeping on it" to clear your mind

>> Being patient

>> Maintaining a positive outlook and looking for meaning and opportunities for learning and growth

REFLECTION

How do you cope when life throws you curveballs, and it feels like you're being punched in the gut? Do you ruminate, avoid the situation, drink yourself silly, binge-watch TV, or stuff your face with food? Or, do you face the situation head-on and see it as a chance to learn and grow, gather advice, meditate on the problem, give it some time to unfold, and take good care of yourself because you know you'll need it?

In life, you'll invariably experience hardship or negative emotions, be stressed by life's curveballs and by relationships, and face decisions that are hard to make. You'll also always have the power to make choices that will support you to function at your best at all times — choices that enable you to be truly resilient.

Harmonizing Stress and Becoming Resilient

The environment is constantly changing, and so are you, which means that you can influence any change in a positive or negative direction by the choices you make. You have the power to transform your mind and improve the functioning of your body, if you choose.

If you do make the choice, the work is logical and involves three foundational steps that I will review in the following order as the quieter your mind is, the calmer you are, the more open you can be to learn and take in new information. With this information, you can be better equipped to create a framework for yourself and your life that supports you to thrive:

1. Quiet the stress response.

2. Remain open to learn and understand.

3. Build and restore your supporting infrastructure.

Quieting the stress response

When you quiet the mind and limit the stress response, you reduce negative chatter and gain better access to your intelligence, and your rational and positive mindset, while helping keep in check the physiology of your body. Whether you choose to take deep breaths, meditate, take a mindful walk, or stretch, quieting the stress response helps you

>> Think more clearly

>> Make wiser decisions

>> Listen attentively

>> Maintain a positive outlook

>> Encourage positive expectation and a belief in a good outcome

>> Keep the stress response effects beneficial rather than harmful in that the stress response is only active for short periods

>> Be more social and friendly, enabling you to seek support when necessary

>> Shift out of a negative mood or state

Being open to learn and understand

When you view difficult challenges as opportunities for learning, growing, and gaining wisdom, you stay curious, ask questions, and remain open — traits that are consistent with emotional resilience. The desire to seek a better understanding and to see everything as a mystery for you to unfold can give you a better sense of control, which invariably also better keeps the stress response in check. Being open, therefore, helps you

>> Make more informed decisions

>> More easily solve problems and find solutions

>> Become curious and playful

>> Feel more in control

>> Seek help or advice

>> Examine your motivations and behaviors more deeply

>> Develop better self-awareness

>> Be more positive, more imaginative, and more likely to believe in new possibilities

Building and restoring

Who supports you, what supports you, where you feel most supported, and how you support yourself all influence the stress response and your physical, psychological, mental, and spiritual health. This infrastructure of support includes such factors as your social support network and relationships, the physical environment where you spend most of your time, and your self-care practices, such as restful sleep, exercise, a nutrient-rich diet, meditation, time spent in nature, play, and being involved in spiritual practices of one kind or another. Building and restoring your infrastructure helps you

>> Enhance physical and mental health

>> Maintain a strong social support network

>> Recognize that you belong to a community

>> Improve your sense of spirituality or your sense that you belong to something even greater than you can imagine

>> Keep the stress response in check by ensuring that needs are met

>> Support a positive self-image and self-belief

REMEMBER

You have the ability to create a life and a mindset that support you to thrive and live your best possible life. You can do so by improving your physical health, balancing your emotions, developing a resilient mindset, enhancing your sense of spirituality, cultivating quality relationships, and building a resilient community. You can build your six pillars of resilience. Read on and learn more!

Chapter **3**

The First Pillar: Physical Vitality and Flexibility

If you aren't physically well, your ability to handle challenges, think clearly, stay positive, and ultimately bounce back from adversity and illness diminishes. Resilient people tend to be physically strong and flexible. They are able to recover quickly from injury and don't easily succumb to health problems. They take care of themselves and ensure that they're well fueled to be able to withstand long days and stay focused.

Ensuring physical vitality and flexibility is the first pillar of resilience. A strong and flexible body translates into having more physical and mental energy to handle and recover from hardship, and it gives you better protection from the potential negative consequences of stress. This chapter explores what physical vitality has to do with being resilient and focuses on the variety of ways your body needs to be fueled.

What Fitness Has to Do with Resilience

When you're feeling sick, how well do you function at work? How much energy do you have just to get through the day? Indeed, studies show that physical fitness can facilitate resilience and protect individuals and their families from the negative effects of stress. (Physical Fitness and Resilience, Sean Robson). The more robust and flexible your body, the more energy and flexibility you will have in, and for, life!

Improving physical vitality requires that you begin to perceive everything in your life as something that will fuel your body to thrive and enable continuous personal renewal. Whether it's by improving quality of sleep, developing an exercise routine, abiding by a healthy nutrition plan, or developing a meditation practice, the key to being resilient is to challenge the body physically, fueling it appropriately and allowing time for rest, recovery, and play. As you read on, you will understand why.

What Good Is Success If You're Sick or Dead?

When I lecture to a group of high-performing executives and professionals, I often ask my audience to raise their hands to indicate who believes that they are well, sick, or fit. Invariably, the majority of people claim that they are well. I show them the bell-shaped curve (see Figure 3-1) that represents the model for health. Then I show them that wellness can fall on either end of the bell-shaped curve and that most people vacillate on the part of the curve that's closer to sickness than fitness.

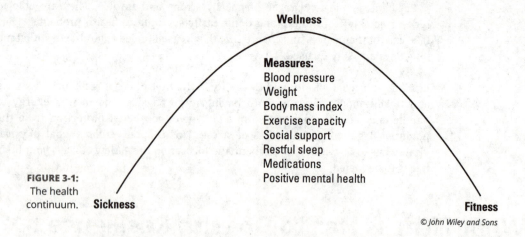

FIGURE 3-1: The health continuum.

Wellness

Measures:
Blood pressure
Weight
Body mass index
Exercise capacity
Social support
Restful sleep
Medications
Positive mental health

Sickness

Fitness

© John Wiley and Sons

I ask them, "If or when a virus like COVID-19 invades your community, how well are you to fight it and come out still well?"

Ask yourself these questions:

- ➤ How well am I?

- ➤ If I were to catch a virus, would I have symptoms? Would I be able to recover quickly?

- ➤ If I were to undergo surgery or get in an accident, would I recover quickly? Would I suffer from a lot of pain? How quickly would I get back to normal?

- ➤ Where do I land on the curve?

It's impossible to think clearly, work effectively, or fully enjoy life when your body is sick, tired, inflamed, and not functioning at its best. Success and wealth are irrelevant when you have no fighting power to beat life's challenges.

Wouldn't you rather be on the side of the health curve near fitness? I mean, what good is all the wealth and success you achieve if you're dead?

Taking Survival of the Fittest for What It's Worth

Did you ever stop to think that your fittest ancestors survived because they could run the fastest when it came to getting away from a predator or running toward capturing their next feast? The fittest could climb higher, walk farther, lift more, survive poor weather conditions, and win the battle for land. The fittest were also the most flexible and capable of adaptive and inventive new ways to find food, shelter, or warmth. Without a brain that is capable of making new neural connections, those ancestors wouldn't have invented fire or any similar assets people use today.

In today's modern world and living conditions, people don't need to think about being fit to survive — they can drive everywhere, order in, turn on air conditioning or the heating system, or send emails if they need to communicate. People have become increasingly more sedentary, in many ways lazy, and very much disconnected from their bodies. And so, when adversity does happen — whether it's natural disasters or stressful events that happen in their own lives, many get sick. The immune system simply isn't strong enough to take the beating.

Of course, your human ancestors didn't live long because of the harsh living conditions and lack of resources and hygiene. But think about it now: If you were to incorporate just a little of what your ancestors did — move your body more, eat only what's organically available, incorporate periods of fasting, sleep when the sun goes down, take time to appreciate and be in nature, meditate and pray, and exist as part of a social infrastructure — how resilient you could be!

Using It or Losing It

The human body (and mind) is truly magnificent. Every part of you has a purpose, from the pinkie on your left hand to the lens in your eye. The brilliant design of your human body is that each part makes up part of the whole and that a network of nerves, blood and lymphatic vessels, hormones, and a slew of other chemicals enables each part to communicate and collaborate with one another. When you take care of your body, all parts work together like musicians playing in a concerto so that you flourish and thrive. The problem is that if you don't exercise your muscles or fuel your body, you lose your ability to flourish. It's like having a few musicians who haven't been practicing play out of tune with the rest of the group at the final recital.

REFLECTION

Think about all the different functions of the brain. It regulates your mood, thoughts, and cognition and every one of your bodily functions. It also activates your behaviors and actions, like breathing, solving problems, or choosing a romantic partner. It remembers what you have done before so that you don't have to figure it out again in the future, and it anticipates the future so that it can come up with new solutions and innovations. It constantly changes its shape as nerve cells form new connections, every time you have new experiences, which allows you to adapt to life's twists and turns.

Amazing, right?

The ability of the brain to reshape itself and grow new nerve connections is called *neuroplasticity*. Every time you engage a new muscle group in an activity, nerve connections grow or get strengthened in the brain. Every time you relax, rest, or sleep, the neurons and working synapses grow stronger and flexible, as they get a chance to rest and recover. It's this very process of neuroplasticity that enables you to be wiser, smarter, happier, stronger, and, ultimately, more resilient. Evidence suggests, in fact, that improved diet, exercise, and sleep routines improve neuroplasticity and cognition as you age

On the flip side, if you don't engage in new experiences and stay active physically and mentally, you don't end up stimulating these neural connections and, in the end, you lose them. You literally can become duller and lose your mind, as you can see in the cognitive decline that comes with aging. You don't snooze or move — you lose! The same is true for all the parts of your body, including your immune system.

Fueling Your Immune System

Your immune system, like your brain, is working 24/7, acting as your security system and keeping your body strong and healthy as it defends your body against incoming toxins, bacteria, viruses, or other invasion. This security system roams around your body, looking for things that don't belong, and gets rid of them without your even knowing. It is that good!

Like any employees, your security guards want to be nourished and supported. When you do, you're likely to experience vibrancy as immune cells seek out and neutralize the bad guys. When your immune system is overtaxed, however, your employees cannot work effectively or efficiently, making you more susceptible to getting sick with infections and more prone to developing other health problems, like heart disease, depression, and inflammatory or autoimmune disorders.

Take the aging process, for instance. As your body endures the trials and tribulations of life as it ages, it's like a car that's exposed to varying extreme weather and rough terrain over time: Without good care, the car is prone to the oxidation process called *rusting*. Oxidation also occurs in the human body as you're exposed to stress — whether it's cigarette smoke, processed foods, or poor sleep — whereby oxygen molecules that are missing an electron (*free radicals*) are formed. These molecules then go roaming around the body, without aim or direction, looking for something to fill the empty spot left by the electron and bumping into the other cells of the body, inducing sparks, general mayhem, and ultimately, damage such as rust. Yes, that's right: If not taken care of, your body can rust, just like a car does.

This is where your immune system comes in. *Antioxidants* are your body's natural security guards that toss out the free radicals and keep you free of rust. Your body can make antioxidants, or you can get them from the fuel or food you eat.

The point is that your immune system is influenced by what happens in your life and how you support your body to get through your life. Stress, poor food choices, lack of exercise, lack of sleep, and other negative lifestyle choices tax the immune system's capacity to function well and increase inflammation and oxidative stress. Healthy lifestyle choices, on the other hand, support the immune system to not be overworked and provide nutrients and fuel for the system to thrive.

Assembling the Components for Physical Hardiness

Everything that you put in your body or that you do in your life is either a fuel or a toxin. When you put fuel in your car, do you put in high-octane oil, or do you put in vegetable oil?

Whether it's lack of time or knowledge or sheer laziness, you may be like most people and not realize that everything you put in your body, surround yourself with, or do for yourself is a form of fuel. Toxic thoughts, foods, or environments all can have the effect of causing damage to your brilliant human body. The more toxins you're exposed to, the harder your body has to work to maintain its vital energy. The higher octane in the fuel you give your body, the more energy it builds and maintains.

You have the ability to support your body to thrive wherever you find yourself today on the health spectrum. The key to physical hardiness is following these five guidelines:

>> Sleep restfully.

>> Eat a nutrient-rich diet.

>> Engage in physical activity.

>> Relax and meditate.

>> Spend time in nature.

Of note, for further evaluation of your sleep quality and my recommendation for useful tips to improve sleep, go to Chapter 16, where I discuss ways to fuel your body in more detail.

Sleeping restfully

Sleep is essential for your physical, psychological, and emotional well-being. A lack of sleep has many negative consequences other than just causing you to feel more tired. It can wreak havoc on your immune system, hormones, weight, muscle and bone mass, brain function, heart, and even your DNA — and this isn't even the entire list. When you sleep, your brain, your nervous system, and the rest of your body get to rest. While you sleep, your stress system is turned down, your cortisol levels drop, your immune system grows stronger, your brain consolidates memory and everything you have learned, and your body naturally releases hormones, including *growth hormone*, a protein hormone that plays a major role in metabolism and influences energy levels, muscle mass, weight, mood, and libido.

When clients complain to me of feeling anxious or depressed, or of having a lot of body aches, I find out more about their sleep and sleep habits. I ask them if they feel rested upon awakening, if they awaken frequently at night, if their bed and bedroom are comfortable, if they have good habits before going to sleep, and if they ingest small amounts of caffeine or other stimulants. Invariably, when they fix their sleep habits, their symptoms improve drastically.

For sleep to be fuel, the quality of the sleep outweighs the quantity. For example, note how rested you feel upon awakening or how tired-versus-energized you feel in the middle of the day.

REFLECTION

Think about a time when you were sleep-deprived. How much energy did you have to handle stress? How much physical energy did you have to just get through the day?

Now think about a time when you had luxurious sleep. Can you describe your mood the following day? How about your physical energy?

What you need to understand is that your body cycles four or five times through different stages of sleep. Each stage has different qualities that enable your brain and body to be restored, and how many times you cycle through these stages varies by the person and the circumstance.

>> **Stage 0, wakefulness:** Occurs right before you start falling asleep and the period after you awaken. It also includes the times you awaken during the night.

>> **Stages 1 and 2, light sleep:** Occurs as sleep is initiated and you're transitioning into deeper sleep. At this stage, your body is relaxing and slowing down, as reflected by more relaxed muscles, a slower breathing rate, and a lower heart rate.

>> **Stages 3 and 4, deep sleep:** Occurs when your brain and body truly have a chance to be rejuvenated and renewed. It is during this time that your blood pressure drops, tissues grow, cells are repaired, blood flow to your muscles increases, brain waves slow down, and waste is removed from the brain.

>> **Stage 5, REM sleep:** Occurs so that your brain can reenergize and renew. It is during this stage that you dream, memory is consolidated, and new learning occurs. Your stress response slows down, leading to a slower heart rate and respiratory rate, your muscles become immobile, and your brain activity increases, which is why you might have more vivid dreams. This stage generally occurs in later dream stages and can be shortened when you don't get enough sleep.

Your sleep quality and the vitality of your brain and body can be negatively affected when any one of these stages is disturbed. Stimulants, for instance, can keep you from falling asleep, shortening your sleep time and therefore keeping you from getting more REM sleep.

The key to ensuring that you fully cycle through these stages when you sleep includes the following seven components:

» **Avoid ingested stimulants.** Try not to drink too much alcohol, caffeine, or sugar, especially in the evening.

» **Implement stimulus control.** Remove all electronic, work-related, or other objects that stimulate your brain. Your bedroom is a place for sleep and sex only.

» **Set a schedule.** Go to bed and wake up at the same time every day so that your body gets into a rhythm. Avoid napping unless you have lost sleep time at night and need to catch up.

» **Exercise your body during the day.** Physical exercise helps regulate cortisol levels and other neurochemicals, helping you get more restful sleep at night. Hard workouts tend to improve deep sleep.

» **Calm your mind.** Your mind must be calm and quiet so that you can go into deep sleep. You can meditate before going to sleep, and definitely avoid working or watching the news for at least an hour, if not more, before going to sleep.

» **Eat early.** You don't want your digestive system having to work hard while you're trying to sleep. Neither do you want your body to be hungry. Have a nourishing meal that isn't too heavy several hours before bedtime.

» **Optimize your sleep environment.** Make your bedroom quiet and dark, and make your bed comfortable. These types of disturbances may be keeping you from reaching deep and restorative sleep.

Eating a nutrient-rich diet

Do you pay attention to what you eat and how different foods make you feel? Maybe you have noticed that eating too much sugar or white flour leaves you achy, tired, and irritable the following day or that drinking more than one cup of caffeine a day, especially late in the day, increases anxiety levels and keeps you up at night. The truth is, what you eat and when you eat greatly influence your ability to fully perform in your life.

Indeed, your body is designed to get fuel from the bounties of nature. Nature offers you a variety of foods that help the body break down fat into energy, improve metabolism, increase sensitivity to insulin, reduce inflammation, strengthen the immune system, and decrease oxidative stress. Called *functional* foods, these nutrient-dense foods contain enzymes, vitamins, minerals, proteins, fats, and complex carbohydrates that fuel the mind and body to enhance their functions. These foods not only have the ability to treat and prevent a whole host of ailments and diseases like diabetes, cardiovascular disease, autoimmune problems, and metabolic syndrome, but they can also enable improved cognition and mood as you age.

Adherence to diets like the Mediterranean diet, for example — which involves a substantial intake of fruits, vegetables, and fish and a low intake of sugars, red meat, and dairy — has been shown to improve mood and cognition as you age.

Unfortunately, at least in the Western part of the world, most people tend to follow the Western diet, which is loaded with refined sugars, saturated and hydrogenated fats, little fiber, and even less-healthy fats. Here are some examples of these processed foods:

>> Refined grains like those found in white bread

>> Potato chips

>> Frozen pizza

>> Packaged baked goods

>> Packaged snacks

>> Soft drinks

>> Candy

>> Fried fast food

The other problems are twofold: One problem is that most people eat without paying attention to what they're eating — eating on the run and often barely chewing their food. The other issue is that people have forgotten that food is fuel. They look at it as good or bad and use it to reward themselves when they feel down or are celebrating or deny it from themselves when they feel they should be punished.

REMEMBER

Food is fuel. It's meant to nurture and fuel your brain and body so that you have the energy to get through the day and your brain and body have the energy to complete their functions. Food is either nutrient-dense and supportive of your bodily functions or it's nutrient-poor and toxic to your bodily functions.

This list describes the six key components you need in order to make sure your food is fuel:

>> **Practice mindful eating.** If you're like most people, you eat without tasting, smelling, or noticing whether the foods you're consuming are fueling you to thrive or slowly causing you to dive. Being *mindful* means paying attention and noticing the tastes, smells, textures, and qualities of the foods you eat. Mindful eating translates to eating more slowly, appreciating your food, and making healthier choices. Studies also show that mindful eating may help individuals overcome compulsive eating and promote healthier eating behaviors. It also suggests that mindfulness encourages a slower, more thoughtful way of eating; can help with weight problems; and maybe steer some people away from processed food and other, less-healthful choices.

>> **Eat healthy fats.** Your body and brain need fat to thrive. Nutrient-dense or healthy fats are broken down efficiently into fuel and therefore help your metabolism, your brain function, your energy levels, and your weight control. Examples of these fats are avocado, coconut products (oil, butter, flakes, flour, and milk) and the omega-3 oils that you can get from borage, cod liver, krill, or salmon. By far, the worst kinds of fats are the man-made trans fats, which are essentially fats that have been put through a hydrogenation process that changes the chemical structure of the fat, giving it a longer shelf-life in the grocery store. Trans fats are often ingredients in fast food, frozen pizzas, chips, cookies, and other unhealthy snacks.

>> **Consume five to ten servings of fruits and vegetables every day, as recommended by the USDA.** Vegetables provide you with essential vitamins and minerals, fiber, and antioxidants and are also low in sugar and fat. How many servings do you consume? (No, pizza doesn't count.)

>> **Eat complex carbohydrates.** Carbohydrates are necessary for your metabolism, energy, and vitality. They make up the larger proportion of calories on your plate — normally, up to 50 percent. Requirements vary for each person, depending on their activity level and health issues. Some people do better with a low carbohydrate diet, and others thrive with a lot. The key is to pay attention to your choice of carbohydrates, leaning toward complex carbohydrates that have a low *glycemic index* (they don't cause insulin spikes), such as vegetables, fruits, whole grains (quinoa or oats, for example), nuts, seeds, legumes, and tubers like sweet potatoes, while avoiding refined sugars and flours.

>> **Ingest good sources of protein.** Proteins are vital for the building, support, and repair of tissues, bones, and muscles. They're important for multiple functions in the body that ultimately affect your immunity, energy level, mood, and cognitive abilities. The key is to avoid processed meat and choose lean (preferably grass-fed) meats, fish, hormone-free poultry, eggs, and plant-based proteins derived from such foods as legumes, nuts, vegetables, and whole grains.

>> **Support your friendly gut bacteria.** A healthy gut means having trillions of good bacteria living, digesting, absorbing, and promoting a healthy immune system. Eating processed and fast foods and having high stress, little sleep, and multiple rounds of antibiotics usually results in the loss of this microflora and an imbalance or disharmony in the natural gut world, allowing disease-causing bacteria to thrive, inflammation to abound, and nutrient absorption to plummet. You therefore want to increase your intake of probiotic foods, like kefir, miso soup, microalgae, pickles, sauerkraut, kimchi, and kombucha tea.

Engaging in physical activity

REMEMBER

Physical activity includes more than aerobic activities. It can also include such activities as walking, yoga, bowling, dancing, and gardening, and anything that also improves flexibility and balance, like stretching and tai chi.

The bottom line is that your body is meant to move, not sit for extended periods. And as I've mentioned, if you don't use it, you lose it. Literally, your muscles can atrophy while your brain cells take a permanent nap!

Exercise boosts strength and flexibility, builds up cardiovascular health, expands cognitive function, raises the levels of good cholesterol (HDL), and improves bone density; exercise decreases the risk of diabetes and certain cancers (like colon and breast cancer) and reduces symptoms of depression as effectively as antidepressants. A sedentary lifestyle, on the other hand, contributes to massive health problems, including diabetes, heart disease, obesity, and — let's face it — for the most part, a lot of flab.

Doing different activities engages a variety of muscle groups. You may choose to jog one day, practice yoga another, and garden the next. Walking outdoors where the terrain is not so predictable, for example, not only revs up your cardiovascular engine but also forces your brain and body to work on balance, coordination, and navigation.

Are you someone who is physically active, or do you tend to sit on your butt most of (or all of) the day? Whatever your fitness level, you have the opportunity to improve.

When you combine the following nine ingredients, you have the recipe for improving your physical fitness:

1. **Assess your fitness level.** Whether you're just getting started or embarking on getting fitter, assess your fitness level when you're physically active. You can easily check your heart rate before and after a workout, see how long it takes you to walk a mile, or track how many squats you can do in a minute. You can create a set of measures that you can check every month or so to monitor your progress.

2. **Set a goal.** I find that my clients are more motivated when they set goals and then work toward reaching them. You can set a goal, like wanting to learn a new movement or skill or ride a bike or complete a pull-up or run a 5K marathon.

3. **Make the exercise fun.** If you don't like it, you won't do it. Find something you enjoy and will likely continue doing. Try different activities and stick to the ones you like. Find a friend or join a group if you think that will motivate you and keep you accountable.

4. **Mix up your activities.** To ensure that you avoid boredom and activate a variety of muscle groups (and thus brain cells), engage in a variety of physical activities. You can jog one day and kayak another and do yoga a third. You can do high-impact training one day and low-impact the next. Nor do you want to fatigue your muscles — you want to give them time to recover, so mixing it up will help you avoid overworking the same muscle group.

5. **Check the intensity.** Different levels of intensity have different effects on your body. If you're starting out or have injuries, you will want to start slowly and build the level of intensity as tolerated. For most adults, the recommendation is to do some kind of *moderate* aerobic activity (you can still have a conversation) for 150 minutes a week or *vigorous* activity (if you talk, you might pass out) for 75 minutes a week, or do a combination of both.

6. **Add resistance training.** Because it's especially important to build muscle mass, you will want to add in some kind of resistance training at least two days a week, with light or heavy weights or simply by using your body mass to engage in movements like push-ups, air squats, or yoga postures.

7. **Work up to your goal.** Many people make the mistake of becoming overzealous and excited to work out and then either get injured or burn themselves out after a few days.

   Slow and steady wins the race! Stay connected with your fitness level, and adapt your body slowly to the strain of the exercise.

REMEMBER

8. **Make exercise part of your daily life.** Physical activity can be incorporated into your daily life by walking more instead of driving, taking the stairs instead of the elevator, and standing more often instead of sitting. You can dance when you're watering the plants or do some air squats while talking on the phone. Get creative!

9. **Take time to recover.** Your muscles need time to recover, so pay attention to your body and take some rest days. Pay attention to pain, and listen when you need to ease up.

Relaxing and meditating

The brain needs time to be quiet, and the body time to relax for you to function at your best. Unfortunately, the fast-paced, must-get-it-done-now lifestyle has led most people to burn out and feel exhausted. Research suggests that lack of time for rest and recovery is a big factor in predicting occupationally induced fatigue and other health complaints. What this tells you is that constant work and being on the go without breaks and time for relaxation and sleep will eventually cause you to dive rather than thrive. And if you're dead — that's right — what good is working so hard?

You don't have to take a lot of time to relax — it's just a good idea to do it. In fact, if you give yourself a little break, you might find that you're more productive because you have put some fuel in your tank.

Making time for solitude and recovery can be as easy as allowing yourself 20 minutes to meditate, stretch, take a mindful walk in nature, or even nap. Relaxation techniques stop the stress cycle. When you meditate or practice mindfulness, you elicit the *relaxation response,* a state of deep rest brought about by focused attention to a simple mental stimulus, first described by Dr. Herbert Benson in 1971.

Numerous studies have confirmed that the relaxation response lessens chronic pain and reduces levels of anxiety and depression and dependency on sleep medication. The relaxation response improves postoperative recovery, blood pressure, and insomnia, and it increases the synchronization of brain alpha waves, which are associated with clearer thinking and creativity, and theta waves, which have been associated with a state of maximal awareness, deep insights, and intuition.

Throughout this book, you can read about different techniques that will help your mind and relax your body. Know that there is no right or definitive way to relax or even meditate. What matters is that the chatter inside your head is quieted, your muscles have a chance to relax, your stress response is slowed, and your entire body has the chance to recover and renew.

Different practices can bring you closer to calm and relaxation. These are the seven key practices:

>> **Mindfulness meditation:** Promotes the nonjudgmental awareness of the present moment while calmly accepting feelings, sensations, thoughts, or experiences.

>> **Guided imagery:** Helps you cultivate the ability to be relaxed and at ease by engaging all your senses as well as your imagination.

- » **Progressive muscle relaxation:** Requires first tensing a particular muscle group, like the forehead or neck, for several seconds and then allowing those same muscles to relax for about 30 seconds while noticing how your muscles feel as you relax.

- » **Practicing gratitude and awe:** Allows you to "feel lucky," by taking you out of the negative feedback loop of victimization and negative thinking and bringing you into the present moment.

- » **Diaphragmatic breathing:** Involves a simple breathing technique that activates the diaphragm and allows the abdomen to expand and contract with the in-breath and out-breath, respectively, allowing for slowing of the breath and a larger volume of breathing in.

- » **Movement meditation:** Puts meditation in motion, such as yoga or tai chi, when you perform a set of movements that aim to improve balance, flexibility, focus, and relaxation.

- » **Immersing your senses in nature.** Induces, for many people, relaxation and a sense of peace. When you immerse your senses in the experience of being in nature — noticing sights, sounds, smells, textures, or tastes — you can remain in the present moment, turn off the stress response, and enjoy the benefits of nature.

Aligning with nature

If you're like most North Americans, you spend the majority of the day indoors, in a car, in an office, at a computer, or on your smartphone, and this was before COVID-19 *forced* you to stay inside and on Zoom and Facebook all day long. You rarely get out into nature.

Are you aware that research points to a strong correlation between more screen time and higher incidences of depression and anxiety, poor performance, and attention deficit? For an even more interesting question, did you know that, in contrast, in studies involving adults, a walk in a rural (rather than urban) setting significantly improved mood and cognition?

Consider these health benefits of nature exposure:

- » People who live closer to green space have fewer health complaints and better health outcomes.

- » Green space itself is a stress buffer, helping people cope better with life's adversity.

- >> Invisible chemicals in some trees, called *phytoncides,* can reduce stress hormones, lower anxiety, and improve blood pressure and immunity.

- >> Being outdoors provides the benefits of getting natural sunlight, providing the much-needed vitamin D and stabilization of melatonin levels, which are offset when you spend a lot of time sitting at the screen.

- >> Something as simple as having a view of nature from your window has been shown to improve cognitive performance and fatigue symptoms.

- >> People who lived closer to or near forests had significantly lower rates of lung, breast, uterine, prostate, kidney, and colon cancers.

- >> A weekend camping trip can help regulate your circadian rhythm so that you sleep better.

- >> Exercising in the great green outdoors is associated with increased physical activity, lower levels of perceived exertion, higher stress reduction, and improved mental performance, mood, and self-esteem.

Do you need more proof?

Whether you spend more time in nature or bring it into your home, having more nature exposure supports you to thrive. To bring nature into your life, you need the following seven ingredients:

- >> **Take some mindful nature time.** Spend 20 minutes a day in nature — hiking, walking, gardening, sitting, or meditating. Without your knowing it, you'll be exposed to unseen elements that are positively affecting your brain and body, like negative ions, that improve your immune system and relax your body — as opposed to positive ions that are emitted from electronics that can wreak havoc on your system. Whatever you choose to do, be in nature mindfully. Spending time in nature, engaging all your senses, and nonjudgmentally observing and appreciating everything around you brings your body and mind into a state of calm, reducing stress and stress hormones.

- >> **Buy some plants.** Put a plant in your office or wherever you spend a lot of time. A plant in a room can improve cognition and energy and can even decrease pain. In this latter case, studies found that placing a plant in a hospital room reduced hospital stays, decreased the need for pain medication, and reduced the negative comments that nurses wrote on patients' charts.

» **Find a room with a view.** Individuals heal faster in hospitals and have more energy and better cognitive abilities at work when they have a view to nature, versus bricks or the urban concrete jungle. If possible, try to spend the majority of your time when in your home or office in the room that provides you with views of green. If this isn't possible, you can also hang photos of nature in your line of vision and add a beloved photo of nature as a screen saver on your computer or smartphone.

» **Get away to nature and, better yet, attend a wellness retreat.** Getting away, relaxing with dear friends or family or even alone, and spending time being in nature, meditating, eating healthy, and sleeping deeply are sure to help you feel rested and renewed and get back on track. A study published in the January 2017 issue of the *Journal of Psychosomatic Research* reported that meditation retreats are moderately to largely effective in reducing anxiety, depression, and stress and improving quality of life

» **Eat nature.** Well, this one is obvious: If it doesn't come from the earth but rather from a synthetic chemical, your body will react — and not well, whether you realize it or not. Think about bringing nature into your body, especially if you can't get out to nature. Eat foods that are naturally available. Shop in the outside perimeter of the grocery store, buying vegetables, fruits, lean and hormone-free protein, wholesome grains, and nuts and seeds. Join a food co-op or farm or, even better, if you can, plant your own vegetables. You get the benefit of eating healthy, spending time in nature, and getting some exercise.

» **Exercise green.** When you exercise outdoors, you gain the benefits of being in nature like at any other time, and you gain the benefits of being able to enjoy the process more as well as feel less fatigue or pain. Studies have shown, for instance, that jogging in the woods results in faster completion times of an 1800 meter run, and on the psychological realm, more satisfaction, more enjoyment, and less frustration versus running open laps. Jogging in the woods decreases the perceptions of fatigue and physical symptoms that might otherwise interfere with exercise adherence. Outdoor running versus the treadmill at an equivalent duration is associated with less fatigue, diminished anxious thoughts, less hostility, more positive mental thoughts, and an overall feeling of invigoration. (For more on this topic, check out the book *Your Brain on Nature,* by myself and Alan Logan, ND [Naturopathic Doctor], and published by Harper Collins).

» **Live near green space or, if you can't, get away to green space as often as possible.** As I mentioned, studies all over the world are showing that the closer you live to green space, the better your heath and the lower your stress. Green space can include neighborhood parks, gardens, and green areas, so you don't have to drive far to a nearby forest or mountaintop. Research your own neighborhood to find where the parks are, and spend some time there or start your own garden.

Chapter **4**

The Second Pillar: Developing Mental Toughness and Clarity

Your thoughts — positive and negative — also serve as fuel for your body and mind. When you're under duress, positive beliefs, confidence, and the ability to think clearly can falter, largely a result of fear and anxiety taking over, along with a cascade of stress hormones like adrenaline and cortisol. This doesn't happen often to the resilient person. Studies show that resilient individuals are more likely to remain confident, optimistic, and open in the face of change. They have a certain mental toughness that enables them to push through hardship, knowing that they will come out stronger and wiser.

This chapter explores the why's and the how's of the second pillar of resilience: mental clarity and toughness.

What Kind of Mindset Do Resilient People Have?

If you were to take two objects, one made of rubber and the other made of glass, and throw them on the ground, what would you expect to happen? The glass breaks, the rubber bounces. One you can glue back together, but it's never quite the same, and the other is as good as new.

Resilient people manage adversity in the same way. They bounce back as good as new, if not stronger and better. As a result, they possess a confident mindset, one that is self-assured, optimistic, tenacious, and mentally tough. Bouncing rather than breaking, they're flexible and adaptable — and usually calm under pressure — and they embrace change and challenges.

A resilient mindset isn't always easy to come by. Life has a way of knocking people down, and it hurts. Once hurt, people tend to shy away from being hurt again, believing that they're weaker than they truly are.

I personally had to learn how to be more mentally tough. You see, before I learned true resilience, I didn't like to fail or to appear weak. I had a fear of not being good enough, of looking stupid, especially when it came to athletic endeavors. I wasn't convinced of my own self-value and sought approval outside of myself.

In my late 40s, in my effort to address my chronic back pain from a car accident when I was 15 years old, I made myself start a rigorous exercise program. I was scared out of my mind, of not only failing but also ending up in pain and having to head back to physical therapy. Through the support of excellent coaches and friends, and by listening to my body's needs, I pushed through my fears and slowly grew stronger and more agile. I developed muscles I never knew I had, including the ones in my mind. The stronger and more flexible my body became, the more I started looking at life's challenges as manageable. Whether it was a strenuous workout or a challenging life event, I found myself saying, "Well, this might be difficult. But I got this."

The truth, as I learned, is that the human brain and body are quite resilient — and that you have the ability to develop a mindset that sees hardships as challenges to be reckoned with and as opportunities to grow and learn. You can cultivate a resilient mindset by first recognizing the traits that make people resilient.

Resilient people

>> **Foster a growth mindset.** They believe that life constantly provides them with opportunities to learn and grow, even when challenging. They don't feel

victimized by life's circumstances, in other words, they believe that they're the co-creators of their destiny.

>> **See failures as opportunity.** They refuse to give up after failing. Rather, they view setbacks as opportunities to innovate, create, and grow.

>> **Avoid taking things personally.** They don't see failures as a representation of their value, and they don't blame or shame themselves when situations go awry.

>> **Embrace change.** They're excited about change, seeing it as a chance to learn something new, gain new perspectives, and challenge themselves.

>> **Choose to commit and persevere.** They're committed to achieving their goals, purpose, relationships, and beliefs, and they persevere despite obstacles.

>> **Maintain a positive self-image.** They know their value and don't feel victimized by their circumstances or seek value externally, like worrying about what other people think.

>> **Think optimistically.** They believe that a positive outcome is possible.

>> **Keep an open and objective mind.** They stay open to opportunity and remain level-headed to enable better decision-making.

>> **Envision success.** They have insight and vision that enables them to respond to challenges decisively and often quickly.

Fixed Versus Growth Mindsets When It Comes to Resilience

Carol Dweck, in her book *Mindset: The New Psychology of Success*, identifies two mindsets: fixed and growth. A *fixed* mindset is "believing your qualities are carved in stone," and a *growth* mindset is "the belief that your basic qualities are things you can cultivate through your efforts."

With a fixed mindset, your beliefs in your own abilities are self-limiting, and you see the road ahead filled with negativity, hardship, and challenges. You tend to feel more victimized by life, believing that life is happening *to* you. You often feel self-doubt and feel easily discouraged or defeated, letting your insecurities, failures, or negative beliefs define you and hold you back from learning and growing.

With a growth mindset, on the other hand, you perceive opportunities for growth and learning everywhere. You view failures not as defeats but rather as chances to learn and develop new skills. You see the silver lining in difficult situations and maintain an optimistic attitude. You keep moving no matter the setback, adapting to change and believing in the myriad of possibilities ahead. You believe that life is happening with you and that you're the co-creator of your destiny.

Most people vacillate between mindsets depending on the situation and sometimes the day. My client John, for example, was an astute businessman who ran a successful company. He felt confident about his work and didn't blink an eye if he had a difficult client or was called away to solve a big problem at the office. He wasn't working with me to help him manage his stress with work, however. Insecure when it came to relationships, he was 48 years old and still single, and he pretty much threw himself into work and avoided intimacy. His belief was, "I fail at relationships. It will never work. I don't know why I bother."

If you break down this sentence, you can pick out the negative terms that reflect a fixed and limited mindset, like "I fail" and "It will never work" and "why bother?" None of these phrases motivate action or reflect openness for growth. The statements reflect a fixed mindset.

Having said that, John was seeking my help to work to overcome whatever was blocking his ability to be intimate. That act of seeking help showed that he was indeed interested in learning and changing. I asked him to try changing his words this way: "I have had challenges with intimate relationships in the past, and I am hoping to learn more about why this has been the case so that I can heal and grow as a person. I am looking forward to having a healthy relationship someday." After stating these words, he felt less defeated and more confident about his future.

REFLECTION

Perhaps you can repeat John's two statements to yourself. Do you notice the difference? Which motivates, and which defeats? Which opens the door to new opportunities, and which slams the door in your face?

You might feel confident in one area of your life and insecure in another. No matter how you feel, when you decide that all experiences present chances to learn and grow, you begin to adopt the resilient mindset.

Developing Mental Toughness

When you let go of your limiting assumptions and the fixed mindset, setbacks don't keep you from pushing forward. The most resilient people don't drop out when the going gets hard. Rather, they have grit, so they push back just as hard and keep going. They're mentally tough.

Wikipedia defines *mental toughness* as a measure of individual resilience and confidence that may predict success in sport, education, or the workplace. Achievers and high performers face setbacks all the time — from failure to fatigue, stress, and burnout — yet they keep going and don't stop until their goals are met. They have grit, meaning they can sustain interest in and effort toward long-term goals. Their grit is their drive.

Ian Turner and his colleagues developed a scale called MTQ48 Psychometric Tool to measure mental toughness. They described *the 4Cs*, which are the four important traits on the scale that, when combined, form mental toughness:

>> **Control:** Addresses how much control you feel you have in your life and how much self-control you have over your emotions. It reflects your inner confidence and self-value as well as your ability to remain calm during trying times.

>> **Commitment:** Looks at how committed you are to achieving your goals. When you're fully committed, you delay gratification, stick with your plan, and work hard, no matter the obstacles.

>> **Challenge:** Assesses the degree to which you embrace change and challenges as opportunities to learn and grow rather than see them as threats. When you embrace challenges, you're more willing to take risks and push way beyond your comfort zone.

>> **Confidence:** Involves your self-belief, in your own abilities to manage through adversity and in knowing that, come what may, you have the strength to stand your ground and succeed.

Resilient people don't take falls or failures personally. They don't define their value according to their successes, either. Rather, they have an inherent confidence in their value, worth, and ability to reach their goals.

Getting in control

People who are resilient are able to weather hardships because they are certain in their life's purpose and feel that they have a sense of control in their life and their emotions. They don't feel victimized by circumstances — rather, they believe that they have a role to play in their destiny and therefore have the ability to effect change. They're comfortable with who they are, and they don't allow negative thoughts or feelings to run them over. Rather than fall prey to anxiety or fear, resilient people remain calm and objective, able to listen to their gut instincts, weigh in on information as it unfolds, and make sound decisions.

The opposite of this is someone who lacks a sense of self-control over emotions and feels like they aren't in control of their life. They feel more victimized by life circumstances, believing that they are trapped and have no ability to create change. More prone to being overrun by fear and anxiety, they're less capable of making decisions under duress. Indeed, science indicates that difficulties in decision-making are associated with both anxiety and depression.

REFLECTION

How do you rate when it comes to feeling or being in control? Are you confident in your ability to influence change? Can you rein in your emotions and stay calm when you're nervous, angry, or frustrated?

Everyone has had to face uncertainty and instability at some point, whether it's a pandemic, an unstable economy, the loss of a loved one, or global warming. It's not so unusual to feel anxiety, helplessness, or hopelessness. It's up to you to decide how you want to respond to life's events. You can lose your cool or stay calm, withdraw or stay engaged, argue to prove your point or have an open discussion to gain clarity. Neither response is wrong or right. One of the responses is simply more conducive to a resilient life, and it's your choice to make. The good news is that it's possible to develop these four components of getting in control (which you can see throughout this book) to feel more in control of your life and your emotions:

» **Quieting your mind:** Calming your mind allows you to feel a better sense of control and gain a bigger perspective. People who are able to achieve this sense of calm are better able to gain insight, wisdom, and a positive outlook; maintain their sense of well-being; and stay clear-headed regardless of the situation. You too can find calm through a variety of techniques, including meditation and mindfulness practices, physical exercise and other movement, or sleeping and journaling, to name a few.

» **Regulating your emotions:** You can also use a variety of methods to better regulate your emotions to find your sense of calm, and they all involve improving your self-awareness and being attuned with the beliefs and thoughts that are exacerbating your feelings of helplessness or hopelessness, and anger or resentment. When you lessen the emotional charge, your stress levels diminish and you're better able to detach from the situation and remain objective and clear-headed.

» **Building your self-worth:** As you build your resilience, you develop a strong sense of self-value and self-belief. You rarely experience the self-doubt that disables your ability to move forward, because you believe in your inherent capacity to adapt and be at your best. You don't look outside of yourself to feel worthy, and you don't assess your value according to accomplishments or failures. It is this knowing of your value that allows you not to judge yourself when you fail or make mistakes.

>> **Being optimistic:** The ability of resilient people to bounce back from hardship and maintain their emotional balance is predicated on the ultimate belief that a positive outcome is possible and that, invariably, they are valued and worth having this outcome. They're optimistic, in other words. Optimism enables them to transform negative feelings and thoughts into positive ones. A fascinating study evaluating the longest-detained American prisoners of war in Vietnam confirmed this finding and confirmed which factors most influenced that ability to exhibit intact psychological functioning despite the trauma, or *resilience*. After analyzing psychological variables and their ability to repatriate, the research showed that dispositional optimism was the strongest variable in determining resilience. The authors concluded that optimism was protective and discussed the need to train individuals to increase it — *which is possible.* Indeed, it's possible for you to learn ways to maintain a more positive outlook and stay optimistic.

Making a commitment

When a resilient person makes a commitment, they're setting goals and making promises to work toward achieving those goals, without wavering or being distracted. They are consistent with their actions and intentions, and they establish routines and habits that ensure success. Setbacks and failures don't stop them in their tracks. They may slow down to learn from their mistakes and reevaluate their processes, but then they bounce back and head back on the path toward achieving their goals.

You can be committed to your self-improvement, a relationship, a sport, or a purpose.

REFLECTION

Can you think of a commitment that you wavered from or lost interest in after a setback? Are you easily distracted or unable to prioritize your targets enough to be able to make the long haul and then wait to collect the final reward? How many times have you lost your commitment to start exercising or lose weight?

Being committed to making a change isn't easy. If it were, everyone would be successful at it all the time. You can better commit to change by developing these four elements:

>> **Connecting with purpose:** The more aligned you are with a strong sense of purpose, the more likely you will stay committed to your path. The purpose is the reason you want the change. Why do you want to lose weight, become a successful lawyer, or run a marathon? When you discover the purpose and don't lose sight of it, you're more likely to stay on the path, because you have a stronger emotional attachment to it.

» **Aligning with your heart:** Regularly align your purpose with your heart's desires. The more passionate you are, the more drive and commitment you will have to stay the course.

» **Delaying gratification:** You need to be willing to delay gratification, or reaping the benefits of the reward. If it's challenging, that means it takes time. Being patient and reminding yourself that a payoff will happen — but not overnight — helps you stay committed for the long haul.

» **Being willing to sacrifice:** When you're clear about your purpose, aligned with your passion and heart's desire, and ready to wait it out to collect the payoff, you're also willing to make the necessary sacrifices to get there. You may have to give up something or make an uncomfortable change, but the pros outweigh the cons, and you make the sacrifice anyway.

Embracing challenges

Resilient people are open to learning and growing, and they see challenges and change, including making mistakes or failing, as opportunities rather than threats. When faced with a challenge, they are excited and feel driven to work hard to achieve their personal best and are better able to adapt and be flexible. They perceive life as a journey, filled with new opportunities, and they believe that they're the co-creators of their life, so change and challenge are opportunities to be creative and innovative.

Many people, alternatively, fear change and prefer not to be challenged, or at least not in a way that will lead to failure or pain. They avoid taking risks and often lose out on having new experiences. How open are you to experiencing change? Do you welcome challenges, or do you prefer to keep life as it is?

You can become better at embracing challenges. Here are the four basic components:

» **Learn to be okay with uncertainty.** Whatever picture you have in your head of how life should be or a situation should turn out, erase it. Embracing challenges involves keeping on open mind about what the future may hold and enjoying the journey you're on now, in the present moment. This doesn't mean you don't make plans but rather that you realize that the best-laid plans often go awry, and that's okay.

» **Be curious.** Though they experience failures and setbacks like everyone else, resilient people don't let the negative experiences stop their drive to learn and create; they instead use these same experiences to stimulate them to discover, understand, create, and investigate. Resilient people don't stop being curious. This attribute supports them in feeling happier and maintaining a more positive outlook, motivating them to embrace change rather than resist it. Indeed, research shows that curiosity, whether in the young or old, is associated with less anxiety, higher life satisfaction, positive emotions, and psychological well-being.

REMEMBER

Continue to wonder about life, how things work, why things happen, where things go, or if something can be done in a different way. Enjoy asking questions.

>> **Look for creative solutions.** Rather than focus on the negative, or what you don't have, or ruminate on problems, focus instead on igniting your creativity and see the challenges as opportunities to find new solutions and problems to solve.

>> **Get support.** Remember, challenges aren't happening to you, but for you, with you and other people who can rally by you and support you. When you turn to other people and lean on them to help you through, challenges become more manageable.

Being confident

Resilient people have a strong sense of self-value and navigate their life with a lot of confidence. They believe in their ability to perform, adapt, and influence others to support them. They believe in achieving what others might think impossible, which drives them to forge ahead with determination and assuredness. They remain resolved despite failures, learning from their mistakes and not skipping a beat.

REFLECTION

How often have you felt total confidence in your ability to accomplish a hard task? How often do you find yourself riddled with self-doubt? You might feel confident in one area of your life and full of self-doubt in another. Low self-confidence unfortunately, undermines your ability to take risks, move forward, and be open to embracing and learning from challenges.

The more confident you are, the more committed and motivated you will be to stay on your path and bounce back from setbacks, and the more pleasure you will gain by simply living your life. Confidence comes from building your skills and competency, having a more positive outlook, improving your well-being, and accepting yourself. This list describes the basic elements you can develop to improve your sense of confidence:

>> **Don't compare yourself to others.** You're a unique individual and no one is like you, nor are you like anyone else. Your success isn't measured according to the success or failure of another person. Focus on yourself and how you can improve and grow. Comparing yourself to other people to determine your value is a reflection of low self-worth and lack of belief in your own journey and ability to achieve greatness on your own terms.

>> **Develop your competency.** Rather than put yourself down or compare yourself to others, work on developing skills, knowledge, and self-mastery. Practice and practice until you feel adept and competent. Hone your strengths and fix your weaknesses. The more you do, the more your confidence will grow.

>> **Set attainable goals.** If you set a goal that feels like a mountain you have to climb, you may become easily defeated and lose your confidence. Break the bigger goals into smaller, attainable goals. Each time you succeed, you inch closer to achieving the larger goal while also building your confidence in your ability to get there.

>> **Celebrate your wins.** Avoid dismissing your successes, especially when they're small. Every achievement deserves celebration. The more islands of success you create, the higher your confidence will climb.

Accessing Mental Clarity

A calm and open mind is a clear mind. A confident and competent person who knows their value is more likely to be decisive and clear when faced with challenges. Conversely, a person whose mind is filled with self-doubting thoughts and fears has a hard time seeing their way through hardships and making good decisions.

Anytime you believe you're not enough — whether it shows up as self-doubt and thoughts of being inadequate, feelings of overwhelm, worries about what others may think, angry feelings at someone or something else for taking away your power, or beliefs that you're not deserving of good or success — you sabotage your ability to think clearly, solve problems, think creatively, and make good decisions. Especially when you're negatively emotionally charged, the stress response is activated so that your brain actually shuts down, making complex and rational thinking difficult.

REFLECTION

Have you ever made a good decision when you were upset or anxious or angry? Was it hard to think clearly? Are you able to communicate your needs or be clear about what you want?

You can access better mental clarity in the very same ways you can build up your mental toughness, and this includes, first and foremost, quieting your thoughts and regulating your emotions so that you can become more detached and objective in your view of any given situation.

My client Melissa, for example, was extremely anxious about her upcoming performance review with her boss to see whether she qualified for a raise. Admittedly, Melissa was a hard worker, dedicated and passionate, and even putting in long hours at the expense of her personal life. She was worried, though, because she had never received any praise, was convinced she had done something wrong, and believed that her boss didn't like her, though she had no proof either way. Her anxiety was keeping her up at night, causing her to overeat and make mistakes and to be unable to think clearly, all of which made her more stressed and question all of her work.

Melissa and I talked a bit about how she viewed her own work and her abilities before knowing she had this meeting coming up. She told me she knew she was good at her job and spoke of all of her accomplishments. So I asked, "So why are you so anxious about this meeting? You're good at what you do. Why don't you believe in yourself right now?"

Melissa realized there was a disconnect between what she knew was true, or her own recognition of her competence and abilities, and the beliefs that her negative emotions and anxiety were leading her to think, which was that her competency and worth were predicated on being recognized by her boss.

The next step, therefore, was to guide Melissa to quiet the negative thoughts and emotions and see if her heart and mind could join together. I taught her a simple breathing technique aimed at lowering stress response activity and increasing relaxation, by turning down the sympathetic nervous system and turning on the parasympathetic nervous system. I also instructed her to be present with her emotions and the feelings in her body, to observe them, accept them, and allow them to come and go with the movement of her breath, and not to judge them or hold on tight, but simply to watch them move with her breath, like a curtain that moves with the breeze.

Within a couple of minutes, Melissa felt calmer and told me her mind was quiet, and her body felt relaxed and free of tension. When I had her reflect again on her upcoming meeting, she told me she no longer felt an emotion other than being ready for it and, come what may, knowing her value, no matter the outcome. She felt clear about how to present herself, and better yet, she felt focused.

If you read this book, you learn many skills and techniques like Melissa did to quiet your mind, regulate your emotions, and access your mental clarity. You, too, can develop the ability to have a resilient mindset, be mentally tough, remain mentally clear without confusion, and feel more in control of your life, even in the face of the unknown.

REMEMBER

You can't control the unknown — that's why it's the unknown! You can be in control of yourself, your emotions, and your responses, however, and choose to make peace with the unknown and embrace it as life unfolds. You can be confident in yourself, your abilities, and resources to handle uncertainty and commit to taking on challenges to enhance your growth, learning, and fulfilling your heart's desires.

As you continue on with this book, you can look forward to learning how to

>> Quiet your mind (Chapter 9)

>> Accept and let go of your fears and the need to control (Chapter 9)

>> Engage your senses and listen better so that you can fully experience and understand you inner and outer worlds (Chapters 9 and 10)

>> Allow yourself to be curious (Chapter 10)

>> Fill your heart with purpose and courage (Chapter 11)

>> Love and value yourself (Chapter 12)

>> Enhance your sense of commitment and competency (Chapters 13 and 14)

>> Open your mind so that you can stay clear, make critical decisions, and become adept at solving problems (Chapters 10, 11, and 15)

Chapter **5**

The Third Pillar: Achieving Emotional Equilibrium

motional equilibrium or balance occurs when you can objectively observe and accept your emotions without judging yourself, feeling the need to suppress them, or being overwhelmed by them, and instead use your emotions to heal, learn, and achieve growth. Emotionally resilient people are able to manage painful or difficult emotions, feel them without being consumed by them, and stay balanced despite the hardships they face.

This chapter will help you understand why emotions exist, how they influence your perception and behavior, and why achieving emotional equilibrium is necessary when working to achieve true resilience.

Emotions Exist for a Very Good Reason

Emotions are part of human nature. You have them for a reason. In the same way that the sensory fibers in your hand can tell you that the stove is hot or the bones in your ear tell you that the vibration of a sound is too loud, your emotions act as sensory signals, letting you know when you're safe and when you're being threatened. They serve the purpose of motivating you into action to warn others to back off or urge them to come close. Emotions inform your mind, letting it know it's okay to stop and smell the roses and see the big picture of life — or focus and get the heck out. As such, your emotions are intricately intertwined with your stress response, influencing stress hormones, and all bodily functions, including your heart rate, blood pressure, gastrointestinal system, muscles, and immune system — as well as the behaviors that ensue.

To summarize, emotions have the following roles:

>> **Signaling you:** They signal you to act when you need care or when you or someone you love is in danger or when you want to bond and connect with others.

>> **Signaling other people:** They signal other people to come closer or back off.

>> **Motivating behavior:** How you feel influences how you act.

>> **Influencing your body's physiology:** They influence your body and stress physiology, leading your pupils to dilate when you're scared and your muscles to tense, heart rate to increase, digestive system to shut down, or inflammation to increase.

>> **Motivating you to engage or disengage:** Positive emotions tend to encourage you to engage with your environment, including other people, and forge relationships; negative emotions encourage you to fight like mad, run like heck, freeze in place, and, sometimes, tend and befriend.

>> **Prompting your thought-to-action inventory:** Your emotions activate thinking patterns that are either broad (open-minded or rational, for example) or narrow (myopic or concrete).

This fact that your emotions are directly intertwined with your stress response and the ensuing behaviors is what can get you into trouble. When the negative emotional charge is high, your brain assumes that your life is being threatened and triggers the fight-or-flight response. It doesn't know the difference between being affected by your child's misbehavior, being late on a deadline, or being chased by a mugger. If you're emotional (negatively), it fires the stress response, which motivates the behavior that helps you feel better. You might scream, withdraw, stuff your face with food, or ruminate all night so that you don't sleep.

REMEMBER

The problem is, in short, that negative emotions can consume you and dictate your perceptions, behaviors, reactions, and decisions, and therefore your ability to stay clear-headed, communicative, mindful, and compassionate; enjoy balanced and loving relationships; and, ultimately, be resilient.

How Emotions Influence Perception and Coping

When you experience a particular emotion, your brain recalls any other time you felt the same way. It pulls forward the behaviors you used to feel better along with the assumptions or beliefs you came up with at the time. These assumptions and beliefs pertain to how you see yourself, as enough or not enough, and how you see your world, as safe or threatening or as happening to you or with you.

For example, perhaps, my client Clara repeatedly experienced rejection from her mother. Nothing was ever good enough for her mother, and if Clara didn't come home with good grades, she didn't get to have dessert with dinner. Without knowing it, Clara developed a belief that she wasn't worthy of being loved unless she did well in school. It showed up in her behaviors as she avoided intimate relationships and threw herself into her work, which never let her down, and eating sweets, which were always a comfort. At 46 years old, she was a successful businesswoman, and likely a workaholic, and she had a weight problem because she rewarded herself at the end of each day with a pint of ice cream. Anytime she went on a date, felt a semblance of rejection or feelings of failure, or had to deal with her mother, she would go to the bakery, buy a pie and eat it. The thing is, Clara knew rationally that she was a funny, loving, intelligent, smart, and worthy person. She also knew that her coping habits of overworking and eating too many desserts was unhealthy. The problem was that when she felt nervous, anxious, or any other negative emotion, she fell back into old patterns. Her emotions got the better of her.

Your emotions thus influence your perception of yourself and the world, both positively and negatively, and subsequent coping behaviors, which influence your ability to be resilient. Negative emotions tend to encourage you to feel victimized and negatively impact resilience, whereas positive emotions boost you to feel empowered, like a co-creator of your life, and to improve the following traits that reflect better resilience:

>> **Self-esteem or self-value:** Positive emotions are strongly linked to higher self-esteem.

>> **Flexibility and adaptability in the face of change:** People with positive emotions versus negative ones show less resistance and more openness to change.

>> **Clear judgment and broad thinking patterns:** Positive emotions prompt a more open and broad mindset, with better access to rational and creative thinking as well as better decision-making.

>> **Supportive relationships:** Positive emotions direct you to improve social bonds and to collaborate and communicate with others rather than fight with them or avoid them.

>> **Access to personal resources:** Positive emotions allow you access to physical, psychological, intellectual, and social resources.

>> **Coping under duress:** Positive emotions improve coping under stress.

Evaluating Your Feelings

Emotions are part of your human makeup, so you will experience them, often, and you may even experience multiple emotions at the same time. Can you recall a time when you felt angry, sad, elated, relieved, and guilty — all at the same time? It can be extremely unpleasant and distressing to feel this way, not to mention confusing. Being resilient doesn't mean you don't feel emotions, but rather that you're able to identify and evaluate them, which enables you to understand yourself better, heal negative beliefs, develop compassion and empathy, grow as a person, and improve mental clarity and decision-making abilities.

When you evaluate your emotions, you take the time to identify exactly what you're feeling, and why, so that you can gain a clear understanding of what it is you really need and want.

For instance, Julie was upset with her boyfriend because she felt he was ignoring her needs. Her boyfriend, meanwhile, claimed he was trying to understand Julie's needs, but she kept changing her mind, and he was ready to give up. I worked with Julie to evaluate her feelings and understand the source of her anxiety. When she was growing up, she told me, both her parents had to work evenings, and she recalled having to fend for herself most days and take care of her siblings. Julie realized that what she was craving was a sense of security.

Together, we figured out ways she could help herself feel more secure and then thought of some ways her boyfriend could support her to feel that way. Julie later communicated how she was feeling, and why, and told her boyfriend exactly what she needed, and he was easily able to comply. By taking care of herself, Julie was able to forge a stronger and more loving relationship.

The process of evaluating your emotions to gain better insight is covered in Chapters 10 and 11. For now, know that it entails following these action steps:

1. **Pause.** Take the time to pause and slow down your thoughts. Your best ideas and realizations come when you're relaxed or at peace (like in the shower or on a mindful walk).

2. **Validate.** It's important that you validate the way you feel. You aren't wrong, good, or bad for feeling the way you do. Validating prevents you from suppressing or numbing your emotions.

3. **Stay calm.** Use your breath or another relaxation technique to slow down the stress response to give you access to a calmer and more open mind. Your emotions are intertwined with your physiological responses such that there is a feedback loop. Your emotions influence physiology, and physiology influences emotions. By calming the stress response via relaxation techniques, you change physiology and improve access to positive motions and broader thinking.

4. **Reflect.** Ask yourself questions that will bring you some clarity around what you're actually feeling, why you're feeling a certain way, when you have experienced this feeling in the past, and whether there's an explanation for it all.

5. **Express.** Rather than keep inside the answers and reflections that arise, express them by writing them down or talking them out.

6. **Uncover.** Once you can better see what your emotions are and why you're experiencing them, you can then figure out the assumption, belief, and core need that's provoking them. Examples of core needs are safety, security, comfort, support, love, connection, recognition, respect, and growth.

Choosing to Manage Your Emotions

I personally have had times when I lost my cool (like getting frustrated when dealing with an automated phone tree when I have limited time) and other times when I felt angry or frustrated but chose instead to pause and mange my emotions so that I could be more balanced and effective in managing problems or setbacks. You too have the choice of deciding whether you want to experience emotional equilibrium. The trick is realizing that you have this option in the heat of the moment. That's what the "pause" is for.

Once you have paused, you have several options to manage your emotions. Whichever you choose, you will find that you feel calmer and gain better insight into yourself. These are some of your options:

>> **Identify.** Choose to be curious about your emotions, like being curious about a butterfly or a bee. Identify and label it. You might say, "Oh, look at that. I am feeling anger." Identifying and objectifying emotions diminishes their charge.

>> **Assess the pattern.** Reflect on the emotion and the impact it might have on you physically and psychologically, on your behaviors, and on other people (and therefore on how they affect your relationships or professionalism). You might notice that anger makes your face hot and that fear makes your heart race and muscles tighten in your neck. You might notice that fear makes you want to eat more or hide under the covers. Look for the patterns and the triggers associated with the emotion to give yourself insight into your behaviors and coping methods. Regularly assessing your emotions for patterns empowers you to be more in control of your emotions rather than let the emotions be in control of you.

>> **Nurture yourself.** Whether or not you have uncovered the core need in an evaluation process, you can safely assume that your negative emotions are telling you you're in need of nurturance, security, respect, value, or love. You don't have to know what it is to decide to nurture yourself with self-loving acts and thoughts of kindness.

>> **Accept what is.** Accept your feelings, your reactions, and the situation and feelings of others, without judgment. Avoid repressing, suppressing, shaming, or blaming. Allowing your emotions to be present without judging or pushing them away enables you to gain some distance from them, maintain positive detachment, and ultimately be able to let them go.

>> **Let it go.** Emotions have a charge. That charge normally needs to be released and expressed. You want to be able to release and express the energy in a way that isn't harmful to you or others. A variety of techniques enable you to release pent-up energy, whether it's some type of movement like karate or hitting a pillow, writing, exercising, screaming at the top of your lungs (in private), painting, laughing, crying, meditating, or engaging in creative activities.

>> **Redirect to the positive.** You can also choose to redirect your thoughts and attention to memories of positive experiences that remind you of times you felt the opposite, more positive feeling. If a situation causes you to experience feelings of being disrespected, for example, you can remind yourself of a time when you felt valued and honored. Positive memories enliven positive associations, emotions, and memories, expanding your point of view so that you align with more positive beliefs and expectations.

>> **Shift to gratitude.** When you feel grateful and lucky, you're more likely to feel more forgiving and able to stay open and positively detached. Another way to redirect your attention is by intentionally shifting your focus to gratitude. You can contemplate the reasons you feel fortunate in your life, find appreciation in the given situation, and find reasons to be thankful that you have been given this opportunity for growth and healing.

>> **Reappraise.** Ask yourself a series of questions that can provide you with answers and insights into a more logical, true, and less stress-provoking viewpoint, allowing you to restructure your thoughts and, ultimately, change how you feel.

Calming Your Emotions By Calming the Stress Response

When negative emotions run high, the stress response is activated, provoking more fear-related behaviors and more narrow-minded thinking. When you develop your self-awareness, you gain the ability to listen to your body's signals, aware of the stress response when it's activated and aware of techniques you have access to that will calm and regulate the stress response. It's so cool: You can calm the stress response by managing your emotions, and you can manage your emotions and calm the stress response.

Often, you don't need to do a deep dive and evaluate why you feel a certain way. You simply just need to know that you don't like the way you feel or the way you're behaving, which takes self-awareness. Once you have assessed that you're experiencing a negative emotion and you want to feel differently, you have at your fingertips some tools that can help you easily shift out of the negative state that involve paying attention to the body rather than to your thoughts or emotions and calming the stress response.

You can achieve this effect by employing relaxation techniques. These techniques help you control emotions by

>> Activating the parts of the brain that control the autonomic nervous system

>> Inhibiting the adrenalizing sympathetic nervous system

>> Stimulating the calming parasympathetic nervous system

>> Slowing down brain waves to create a state of relaxation

>> Reducing the production of stress hormones

>> Improving emotional processing

Examples of such techniques are progressive muscle relaxation, mindfulness, guided imagery, and movement meditations like yoga and tai chi. You can use these techniques to help you achieve relaxation while also improving your concentration and attention so that you're relaxed and alert, a state that is optimal for problem solving, self-awareness, and self-control.

There's no single right way to regulate the stress response, other than the one you actually do.

Shifting to Positive Detachment and Reappraisal

When you manage your emotions, you discover better ways of expressing yourself, gain insight into yourself and a given situation, communicate more effectively, and make better decisions. The key is to be able to detach from negative emotions so that you can experience them without being overwhelmed by them.

Also known as *positive detachment*, this state of mind enables you to loosen your grip on your thoughts and emotions and instead gives you space to breathe so that you can move toward accepting yourself as you are and the world as it is. Positive detachment does *not* involve suppressing or pushing anything away. It does *not* mean distancing yourself or creating a wall that separates you from something or someone because of your negative feelings and emotions. Rather, with positive detachment, you create some space between you and your emotions so that you're better able to perform cognitive reappraisal, a trait that emotionally resilient people possess.

Cognitive reappraisal represents the ability to change and reframe the way you think about a situation in order to better regulate emotions and lessen their impact. The opposite of this process is *suppression expression*, whereby you suppress, hide, or reduce your emotions by way of behavior (like changing your facial expressions or purposefully hiding your anger). People who are able to partake in cognitive reappraisal versus people who suppress their emotions

>> Experience and express more positive emotions

>> Have better interpersonal functioning

>> Enjoy a greater sense of well-being

WHAT DO YOU DO WHEN SOMETHING UPSETS YOU?

If and when something happens to you that upsets you, do you express your emotions or stifle them?

- Are you able to detach from the situation and see all points of view?
- How fixated on the story do you become?
- How long does it take for you to let go of the story and achieve some peace of mind?

With the process of positive detachment and reappraisal, you decide to focus on the present moment and disengage from habits of thinking and negative emotions that usually don't serve you. Instead, you focus on being in the now, on your thoughts or emotions as they come and go, and on being completely true to yourself and your true nature so that you become more peaceful and more self-aware and become liberated from your past and your limiting beliefs.

Enhancing Your Self-Awareness and Willingness to Grow

Self-awareness is a precursor to resilience. First defined in 1972 by Shelly Duval and Robert Wicklund, self-awareness involves being able to focus attention on yourself in order to objectively examine whether, and then how, your behavior is in coherence with your values and standards.

With better self-awareness, you're able to reflect and understand that your actions, words, and even energy impact your body, your life, and the lives of those around you. You're able to be honest and accountable with yourself, your strengths, and your weaknesses. By seeking to understand yourself better, through your own eyes and the eyes of others, you enhance your ability to achieve self-control, especially over your emotions. How self-aware you choose to become depends on how strong your willingness is to grow as a person.

Let's face it: Negative emotions can be extremely unpleasant to experience, and it's often easier to repress or suppress them than to go ahead and feel them. The result is that you lose your sense of self-awareness. To override this reaction, you need to be okay admitting that you may have been or done something "wrong" or made a mistake. You need to be wanting and willing to change and grow.

Always Choosing Love

The ability to bounce back from hardship and maintain emotional balance is predicated on the ultimate belief in a positive outcome and that, invariably, you're valued and loved. When negative emotions become all-consuming, people tend to shift away from feeling valued to feeling more victimized. A way to counteract this process is to enhance the feeling of being loved and connected.

The neurobiological changes that occur during the experience of love reflect in many ways the changes that occur during meditation. Levels of stress hormones fall, reward centers in the brain are activated, and feel-good neurotransmitters like dopamine, hormones, endorphins, and morphine-like substances course through your brain, helping you feel euphoric and full of positive expectation.

Interestingly, the experience of love seems to have an even more powerful effect, likely because love induces feelings of pleasure and security, leading to further feelings of trust and positive belief, resulting in motivation of positive behavior and further positive expectation. Love also stimulates *oxytocin,* a hormone that reduces stress response activity, lowers cortisol levels, protects dopamine neurons, and reduces anxiety. Less anxiety and less stress mean more access to your positive memories, positive emotions, higher cognition and thinking, healthier behaviors, and healthier memory.

Love comes in many forms — in your relationships, your self-care, and your spirituality. The more loving and balanced your relationships, the better your self-care; and the more spiritually connected you feel, the bigger your love reserves. The bigger your love reserves, the less likely you are to shift into a victim mindset, and if you do, the more likely you are to shift out of it.

REMEMBER

Negative emotions aren't bad, and you're better off not suppressing or repressing them. Rather, you should understand that they're signaling to you that you're in need of care and that you have a choice to learn from your emotions and manage them to find your calm — or to let them control you so that you lose control.

Chapter **6**

The Fourth Pillar: Cultivating Spirituality

Agrowing body of evidence is showing that spirituality is vital to human health. It has been found that a spiritual outlook makes humans more resilient and that people who have a stronger sense of purpose and meaning in their lives are more likely to have a higher quality of life, better health and functioning, and a greater ability to cope with adversity.

Though you can find many perspectives of what defines spirituality, most people agree that it translates to the sense of being profoundly connected to something larger, a sense of purpose, and a belief that there is meaning to life's experiences. Whether you believe in God or a higher power or you simply feel profoundly connected to nature, there's no right way to cultivate spirituality, other than to find the way that works for you.

This chapter focuses on the importance of having a spiritual outlook and practice and on how it affects resilience and what it entails to cultivate spirituality.

What Is Spirituality Beyond Religion?

I like to think of *spirituality* as the profound belief that you're connected to something larger than yourself, that there exists purpose and meaning in life, and, ultimately, that you're never alone.

The Latin origin of the word spiritual is *spiritualis*, "of or pertaining to breath, breathing, wind, or air, pertaining to spirit," and that of the word spirit is *spiritus*, "a breathing (respiration, and of the wind), breath; breath of a god," hence "inspiration; breath of life," hence "life;" also, "disposition, character; high spirit, vigor, courage; pride, arrogance." So, when I think about spirituality, I think of breath, vigor, breath of life, or inspiration, which essentially means that you can access spirituality anytime, anywhere.

Of course, you can connect with spirituality in a religious practice, though it isn't necessary. You don't have to be religious to be spiritual, though religious practices can enable you to be spiritual. The Latin root *religionem* (nominative *religio*) stands for "respect for what is sacred, reverence for the gods; conscientiousness, sense of right, moral obligation; fear of the gods; divine service, religious observance; a religion, a faith, a mode of worship, cult; sanctity, holiness."

Religion is simply one path to spirituality. You can also access spirituality by belonging to a spiritual community, communing with nature, being driven by a sense of purpose or responsibility, or by just breathing and knowing you're connecting with something greater, like the breath of life or the greater good.

This list describes the common themes that spiritual people share:

» **Connection:** Believing that you're connected to something greater and larger.

» **Trust and acceptance:** Trusting and accepting that life is a mystery and that your life is a journey of learning and discovery.

» **Purpose:** Living with a sense of purpose and responsibility, knowing your value, and believing that your contributions can have a positive impact in the world.

» **Humility:** Being egoless and aware of how small you are compared to the larger universe or big picture of life.

» **Loving kindness:** Opening your heart and allowing love to flow in and out. Everyone needs love, and your kindness goes a long way towards providing you with greater fulfillment while also helping others.

» **Meditation and prayer:** Knowing that it's in the silence that you truly hear and find peace, whether it's through meditation, prayer, or silent reflection.

» **Appreciation and awe:** Appreciating all that you are, have, and experience, including for others and the journeys they're on.

» **Compassion:** Knowing that each and every person is on their own journey, reminding you that everyone suffers in some way and so you should strive for compassion and forgiveness for yourself and for others.

Why Spirituality Supports Resilience

The sense of belonging and of being connected to something larger are qualities that support you to bounce back when you want to meet life's challenges, perform better under duress, hold a more positive expectation of the future, and foster positive emotions and better relationships.

Imagine that you're experiencing a sense of awe — perhaps you're gazing at the stars or the sunlight dancing on the water or you're watching your child walk for the first time, in awe of the miracle called life. You feel connected to something greater, and even though you aren't clear on the specifics of your purpose, you trust deep in your heart that you have a purpose and that it involves helping the world be a better place. You think to yourself, "Why was I worrying so much about that deadline? It seems so inconsequential."

When you experience life through this type of spiritual lens, you gain a better perspective on life, especially what you deem as stressful. You no longer sweat the small stuff, and you face the big stuff more adaptively. You are more *resilient*.

With a stronger sense of spirituality, you can

>> **Possess better coping skills:** A recent analysis by Harold G. Koenig of 454 studies found a strong correlation between improved coping with adversity and greater spirituality in people dealing with a variety of stressful situations, including medical illness ("Religion, Spirituality, and Health: The Research and Clinical Implications").

>> **Attract more social support:** Koenig's analysis also found that greater spirituality encourages community and a positive association with better social support.

>> **Feel more optimistic and have a higher sense of well-being:** Koenig found evidence in 256 studies of a positive association with spirituality and happiness and a sense of well-being.

>> **Employ healthier behaviors:** Most religious doctrines encourage taking care of the body and discourage behaviors that may cause harm. A review of the literature shows a positive correlation between spirituality or religiosity with habits such as smoking, exercise, diet, and sexual behavior.

>> **Experience better mental health:** With greater spirituality comes improved mental health and positive emotions, regardless of religion.

>> **Become more resilient:** Research examining the connection between spiritual fitness and resilience in army personnel found that different forms of spiritual intervention were linked with improved resilience and well-being.

Recognizing the Power of Awe

With spirituality comes the belief that every human is connected — somehow, some way — to one another, a higher power, or nature (or all three). It's a belief that makes use of the imagination and carries with it a great deal of awe.

Do you ever stargaze? I do, often. I gaze up at the stars, in awe, feeling a strong connection to a much larger universe, knowing that I am but a speck on the earth and that the earth is a small speck in the vast universe, which is itself a small part of a larger galaxy. When I was young, I would wonder whether I actually came from the stars, or maybe the moon. (I still do, sometimes!) It's all so mysterious and *awe*some. As Albert Einstein once said,

> The most beautiful thing we can experience is the mysterious. It is the source of all true art and science. He to whom this emotion is a stranger, who can no longer pause to wonder and stand rapt in awe, is as good as dead: his eyes are closed.

Feeling awe is incredibly powerful. It challenges your idea of "self" and your world view, engaging you to open your mind and realize that there exists a greater force around you. With this feeling, this awe, you're more likely to have a positive outlook and expectation, and a belief that you have what it takes to overcome adversity. In this way, feeling awe can promote many resilience characteristics, such as the ones described in this list:

>> **Being curious:** Drives you to want to learn and to be humble as you become increasingly aware of how much you don't know.

>> **Being creative:** Inspires a quest for knowledge and not taking anything at face value, leading to more critical and creative thinking.

>> **Being prosocial:** Motivates integrating into social groups and prosocial behaviors like sharing resources (including volunteering), generosity and sharing, kindness and compassion, ethical decision-making, and co-operation, and is in part, driven by a sense of belonging and feeling happier and more connected.

>> **Being more expansive:** Expands your perception of time and enables you to be more present in the now and more patient.

>> **Being purposeful:** Promotes your desire to make meaning and find purpose.

>> **Being positive:** Buffers the experience of loss and helps you stay positive in times of uncertainty.

>> **Being satisfied:** Improves your sense of well-being and life satisfaction.

Over 15 years ago, during a stressful period in my life, I remember sitting in my parent's garden with my eyes closed, ruminating and worrying about my job and finances rather than enjoying the beautiful day. And then I opened my eyes: In front of me sat my then 3-year-old niece, playing with a flower, as the sun's ray fell down and shined upon her. She looked like a little angel, and it occurred to me what an incredible miracle she was, bringing so much love into our family's lives. Just in the moment, she looked at me and asked, "Auntie, why do you have that funny look on your face?" I answered, "Because I am gazing at a miracle, honey." She then asked, "What's a miracle?" I answered, "It's when you're witnessing something extraordinary and magical." It took her a moment to think about what I had just said, and then her face registered comprehension and joy, and she began to run around and shout at the top of her lungs, "I'm a miracle! I'm a miracle!"

That scene made me realize that all people are miracles — that being human and everything that comes with it is nothing short of miraculous. I decided then and there never to forget that I too am a miracle and to make it my purpose to help others realize it, too. That little thought created a huge shift in my perception, enhanced my sense of purpose, and changed how I would forever view my life.

Searching for Purpose

Life has a tendency to throw curveballs, to challenge and confuse your way of thinking, and when it does, you have the choice to succumb to worry and confusion or decide that it's okay to be comfortable with not knowing because now you have the opportunity to seek truth, make meaning, and discover purpose. Resilient people do the latter —having a sense of purpose is one of their essential traits, because it keeps them motivated to overcome hardship.

When you have no sense of purpose, life can feel meaningless and can make getting out of bed in the morning challenging. It can lead you to shut down, disconnect, and become more negative in your thinking and less motivated to take care of yourself. In contrast, having purpose can drive you to feel more connected and want to do good in the world, for others and for yourself. It can help you recover emotional balance more quickly, ruminate less, and practice more positive coping methods. With a greater sense of purpose, you're more likely to believe that your life counts for something.

REFLECTION

Do you feel that your life has purpose or meaning? Have you asked yourself this question?

About 20 years ago, I sought advice from a mentor when I was feeling confused about my life and the direction I should take. I was unsure whether primary care medicine was my path and whether it was wise to jump ship and learn about other healing practices — something I had wanted to learn since childhood. I was deeply in debt from taking out loans to go to medical school, and leaving stable work was a risk I wasn't sure of. My advisor told me, "Follow your mission, follow your passion, and the rest will be gifted and given." I listened to her advice and left my practice to pursue my dreams, and her wise words are still with me today.

Finding a sense of purpose isn't something that happens overnight but happens over time and is part of your life's journey. You can enhance a sense of purpose in your life in a variety of ways, including these six:

>> **Explore a passion.** If you have a passion, follow it. Learn more about it. Immerse yourself in it because that passion will add meaning to your life and fill you with a sense of wonder and purpose.

>> **Find a mission.** A greater sense of mission improves psychological well-being, life satisfaction, self-esteem, and emotional balance. It can be an injustice you want to correct, a planet you want to save, a policy you hope to change, or a desire to bring love to the world. Finding a mission adds meaning and purpose to your life.

>> **Give to others.** Whether you volunteer your time, money, or expertise, the act of helping others benefits not only those you're helping but also your mental and physical health. Giving of yourself adds meaning and enhances self-value.

>> **Look for inspiration.** Inspiration enlivens your awareness of new possibilities and awakens your belief in the good. It transforms your way of thinking and drives you to learn, master something, and find value.

>> **Seek understanding.** When you believe that every situation in life is an opportunity to enhance your learning, understanding, and growth, your life becomes richer and more meaningful.

>> **Value your contribution.** Believing that you have made contributions that can have impact and can make the world a better place certainly enhances your sense of purpose in life.

Accepting the Mystery and Process of Life

Living a life of acceptance means letting go of your judgments and biases of how you think life or people *should* be. You see life for what it is, neither good nor bad, always aware that there's much that you don't fully know or understand. Acceptance leaves you open to learn, gather perspective, experience less emotional distress, garner more support, and build loving relationships.

The key to acceptance is remembering these five guidelines:

» **Accept everything.** Do you accept the day but not the night? Acceptance means that you do accept everything, light and shadow, up and down, right and left, and that you have undesirable and possibly ugly traits or habits, as does the world and humanity.

» **Accept without condoning.** Just because you have accepted yourself or another for having negative traits doesn't mean that the behavior stemming from that trait is okay. Acceptance enables accountability and understanding without diminishing the reality that a negative or hurtful outcome transpired.

» **Accept without internalizing.** When accepting reality, you accept both positive and negative aspects of yourself, others, or the situation while also accepting that behaviors can be hurtful or destructive without your casting blame or shame. For instance, you're able to accept that your tendency to get angry and express your anger by shouting is part of the reason you're having problems managing your employees. You're accountable for your behavior that is causing you to lead ineffectively, but you know that this doesn't make you completely ineffective as a person.

» **Accept equally.** Everyone handles stress differently, and no person has the same perception, even of the same situation. Every person has different genetics, a different upbringing, and different life experiences that affect their perception and spiritual maturity.

» **Accept the present moment.** There exists no right or wrong. Wherever people are, it is where they are. Ruminating on what happened in your past or judging based on an expectation of a future that hasn't happened takes you away from being present with reality. Focusing on the now allows you to see reality as it is in the present moment, allowing you to keep compassion, an open perception, and a clear mental state.

Becoming Peaceful through Humility

Like paddling on a river, sometimes you need to surrender to the current rather than try to paddle against it, especially when that current is bigger and stronger. It is in these times that you have to remember to yield. You might remember how small we humans are when it comes to Mother Nature, and that there are many things we can't control, though we can be guided and can listen and learn.

It's humbling to realize how little control you might have or that you don't know as much as you might have thought you did. Either your ego can feel threatened, or you can release your ego from the equation, surrender to the mystery, and find peace in your humility. When you do, you might find that your social bonds grow stronger, as will the commitment in your relationships and alliances. You might find that you develop better self-control, emotional regulation, and an enhanced ability to cooperate, and also find that other people trust you more.

What does it mean to let go of your ego and connect with humility? You uphold these beliefs:

>> **Learn.** You always have more to learn.

>> **Find joy.** You can find joy in life's simple pleasures.

>> **Be grateful.** You have reason to be grateful for even the smallest of blessings.

>> **Be human.** You're human — it's okay to make mistakes and not have it all together.

>> **Be vulnerable.** It's okay to ask for help, because it's a sign of authenticity, not weakness.

>> **Be humble.** Take time, every now and then, to remember that people are like grains of sand on a vast expanse of earth.

>> **Be accountable.** Take responsibility for your behaviors and actions without feeling shame.

>> **See value.** Be sure to see value in everything and everyone.

>> **Be kind.** Remember that everyone suffers in one way or another, and it's important to be kind and show love.

Expressing Loving Kindness

When spirituality is part of your makeup, you genuinely care — about the well-being of others, the earth, and yourself. You're aware that in your humanness, everyone suffers in some way, and everyone needs love and care.

When you express love and kindness, you do so knowing that some people are more fortunate than others and that it's in your power to care, to be generous, to be kind, and to give to others. And when you do, as research indicates, your generosity and kindness can forge resilience because volunteering, being kind, and helping others helps you live longer, have less depression, gain better functionality in later life, and experience greater happiness.

Expressing loving kindness doesn't mean enhancing intimacy or romantic love but rather choosing to care for everyone, even people you don't know. When you express loving kindness in your life:

>> You help when you can.

>> You listen with an open heart and without judgment.

>> You have empathy and can put yourself in someone else's shoes.

>> You're generous.

>> You're nurturing.

>> You're charitable.

>> You respect everyone.

>> You show fairness.

TIP

You can also do a daily loving-kindness meditation, or *metta,* a Buddhist meditation practice that dates back over 2,000 years and has been shown to reduce self-criticism and depression and to enhance self-compassion and positive emotions. The practice initially involves visualization and meditation phrases and then, after first extending love to yourself, extending it to people you care about and then, ultimately, to all living things. The purpose of this meditation is to melt down negativity you might have toward yourself or others and to melt down walls of separation, to open the mind and heart to deeper levels of feeling love and kindness. It's a practice that can not only instill in you a sense of connection and belonging but also bring you peace and stillness — qualities that support resilience.

Finding Stillness

When your mind is in constant chatter and you're under stress, then thinking clearly, being present, accepting pain or suffering, or feeling connected are hard to come by. Gaining access to your positive beliefs and deep insights often requires silence and finding stillness within yourself.

Finding stillness isn't just about relaxing or even just quieting the mind. It involves silencing the internal dialogue of the mind, separating from everyday stress and activities, and becoming aware of the existence of space, like the space between the leaves or the space between sounds, where boundaries disappear and your connection to all living things is a given.

You can arrive at stillness in many ways: Meditation and prayer are just two. Invariably, it's a personal experience. Whatever stillness practice you choose, whether it's for two minutes or two hours, you benefit, as the mind quiets, the body relaxes, negative thoughts dissipate, and a sense of peace and connection permeates. Finding stillness will support your resilience at multiple levels:

>> Physically, the mind and body regenerate and rest as stress hormones drop, sleep improves, blood pressure drops, and cholesterol and blood sugar levels are better controlled.

>> Psychologically, positive emotions like compassion are enhanced as well as prosocial behaviors while symptoms of depression and anxiety decrease.

>> Mentally, as the mind is given time for rest and regeneration, silence and stillness can allow for more clarity and decision-making. A regular practice of silence supports neuroplasticity in the hippocampus, or the growth of new brain cells in the part of the brain that is associated with memory, emotions, and learning.

>> Socially, a quieter mind and more positive emotions lead to improved social bonds and relationships. It can help you become a better partner, parent, sibling, colleague, or leader.

Feeling Lucky

Spiritually resilient people view themselves as lucky. They are able to appreciate every situation as an opportunity for growth; people for the value they bring; nature for the miracles it reminds them of; and the small things in life that can bring joy. Rather than focus on frustrations and disappointments, on what they aren't or don't have, or on the expectations that have not been met, they look at life as happening for them and with them rather than to them or against them, and they are truly thankful for the good in their lives.

As Ralph Waldo Emerson said,

> Cultivate the habit of being grateful for every good thing that comes to you, and to give thanks continuously. And because all things have contributed to your advancement, you should include all things in your gratitude.

Having and experiencing appreciation and gratitude are integrated into many religious and spiritual practices, whether it's giving thanks to God or a higher power, showing appreciation to Mother Earth and nature for her provisions and blessings, or gratitude to a person for helping you absolve karma. According to some research, effects of stress may be reduced for individuals who have gratitude to God. In general, though, appreciation and gratitude, whether involving a higher power or not, are associated with physical, psychological, and social benefits as well as improved resilience.

According to positive psychologists, appreciation and gratitude are not just actions but also represent positive emotional and cognitive states that have associated neurobiological effects that influence how you see yourself, others, and the world you live in — and thus how you behave and interact. Studies suggest that gratitude

>> Improves sleep

>> Provokes better self-improvement behaviors, when you stick to a health plan (exercise, diet, stress reduction, or emotional well-being)

>> Enables cardiac patients to sleep better and minimize inflammation and fatigue

>> Is associated with more life satisfaction and less burnout

>> Is associated with more resilience after trauma and is a buffer against depression

>> Inspires generosity and prosocial behavior

>> Promotes stronger social bonds and quality relationships

>> Improves job performance and feelings of self-efficacy

REFLECTION

Do you have a tendency to feel lucky or unlucky? Are you more likely to focus on all the "bad" things that may have transpired during the course of your day or week or the "good." For instance, when describing how they managed the holidays during the COVID-19 pandemic, some clients expressed how grateful they felt to be healthy even though they were alone on Thanksgiving while others complained that it was the worst day ever because they were alone. What is your tendency? Do you veer towards feeling grateful or miserable?

Showing Compassion

When you have a reservoir of energy and love to give and show other people, you give it because you can. You're able to move beyond your own problems to stay present, connected, aware, and mentally and physically healthy while showing concern, empathy, and generosity. This is the basis of compassion. Being able to be compassionate even in the toughest of times is a true mark of resilience and also of spiritual maturity.

My client David worked his way toward developing more compassion. He told me he was fed up with his domestic partner, who continually complained about his abusive boss, and wished that his partner would just quit his job or stop complaining. David complained, "He's driving me crazy. I don't understand why he doesn't just get over it or leave. I don't even think it's that bad."

I pointed out to David that whether his partner's boss was abusive was not for us to determine, but that we could figure out why this situation was causing David to be so upset. His reaction was presenting us with an opportunity to dig deeper into understanding him better. When I guided David to examine his anger and frustration, he discovered that beneath this emotion were his own memories of being criticized by his father, which he had blocked out by working harder and "toughing it out." When we dug a little deeper into these memories, David found himself crying, feeling the pain of his younger self who did not feel loved. I then led him through an exercise where he gave love and compassion to his younger self and then to himself as an adult. At the end of the exercise, I asked him how he felt about his partner. He said, "I get it now. I understand. I am going to support him better through this."

There may be times when you can be compassionate and other times where you find yourself annoyed, frustrated, or judgmental. The more spiritually aware and connected you are to loving kindness and to knowing that everyone is human and everyone suffers, the easier it is to shift into compassion for all, a trait that bodes well if you're aiming to be more resilient. Studies have shown that higher self-compassion is associated with better well-being. In addition, the more resilient you are, the easier it is to be compassionate, because you can reflect on the challenges you have overcome and be cognizant to the limitations and suffering that other people must be experiencing. You can stay calm, open, aware, loving, and compassionate to the human condition, no matter what you may be going through as well, because you also have compassion for yourself.

David found compassion for his partner's plight by first learning how to have self-compassion. Self-compassion is the key when it comes to resilience because if you give of your heart without taking care of yourself, you risk burning out or having compassion fatigue. Research demonstrates that self-compassion positively impacts emotional regulation and resilience and that the level of burnout in nurses is inversely proportional to the level of self-compassion.

REMEMBER

Everyone is human, and it's just as important to treat yourself with kindness and forgiveness, even if you have shortcomings or fail, as it is to love and forgive others. The more you take care of you, the more you can give to help others and the more you can remember that life is happening for you and with you rather than to or against you. With this attitude, you can find purpose and meaning, find the blessings in disguise, feel a sense of connection and belonging, and cultivate your resilience via enhancing your spirituality.

Chapter **7**

The Fifth Pillar: Striving for Quality Relationships

Humans are social creatures, never meant to survive on their own — they're biologically wired to bond with one another so that the species can survive, and it's hardly surprising that supportive relationships help them manage hardships and be resilient. The key word here is *supportive* — not all relationships will support your resilience and health. One study demonstrated, for example, that couples in troubled marriages produce more stress hormones during conflict, which continues throughout the day and night, than those couples whose marriages aren't troubled. Conversely, quality relationships buffer stress, help you live longer, help you heal faster, and improve behaviors.

Quality relationships involve mutual commitment and support, trust, genuine care, and the willingness to grow, collaborate, and compromise. They involve seeing value in yourself and others, good communication, acceptance, and reciprocity. This chapter covers what it takes to cultivate these quality relationships, and they can boost your resilience.

REMEMBER

The better your relationships, the more you can feel confident that you're cared for, that you can draw on people for support, and that resources are available to you that can help you overcome challenges and adversity.

Enjoying the Journey, Even When It Hurts

Creating quality relationships takes time, and it takes self-discovery. You will have moments of elation and moments of sorrow or discouragement. The key is to remember that you're on a journey: Your relationships help you learn more about yourself, and the quality ones provide you with people with whom to share your journey. Keep in mind that the journey has no endpoint and that there's no perfect person or perfect relationship.

This positive and open mindset allows you to be more open to people, to learning from them, and to seeing value in your interactions. It makes you more resilient because you

>> **Commit to learning and growth.** You stay committed to learning about yourself and about the person you're relating to and with. You commit to finding value in the relationship and in staying in for the long haul, even when times are tough, knowing that it's during the challenging times that you can best learn, grow, and love.

>> **Easily express gratitude.** Never take anything or anyone for granted. Remember to appreciate that you get to have the experience you call life and that whoever is with you is on the ride, too. Appreciate their presence — and the different aspects of your life that you feel grateful for.

>> **See value in everyone.** Value is everywhere. Assume that it's there, even when you're in a disagreement or an argument, or if you feel let down or hurt. Find the value. The value may be the opportunity you have been given to learn about yourself. The other person's argument may have value, even though it wasn't delivered in the best way. Seeing value allows you to also practice humility, understanding that you don't have all the answers and that no one is perfect.

>> **Show empathy and compassion.** Everyone suffers in one way or another and when they do, they can act unkindly, rudely, or inconsiderately. Understanding that you and other human beings suffer allows you to stay compassionate and show empathy.

>> **Receive as well as give.** A balanced relationship involves receiving and giving love, affection, respect, and other qualities. Mutual reciprocity helps build trust and strengthens social bonds, an asset when going through hardship.

>> **Enjoy joy.** Need I say more? Make time for play, laughter, and smelling the roses. Find the simple pleasures in life or laugh at the top of your lungs. Remember what it's like to be a child, and enjoy the ride.

Recognizing That It All Starts with a Relationship with Yourself

Everyone is human and will therefore make mistakes or act unkindly or selfishly at times. There will be arguments, disagreements, bumps in the road, and curveballs thrown by life. If you remember that you're here to be on a journey, that it's okay for you to be human and make mistakes, you will be better able to feel optimistic about life, be confident in yourself and not look to other people to make you happy. In the end, the relationship you have with yourself serves as the foundation for all your other relationships.

When you take care of yourself, your relationships have a better chance of success. Studies show that individuals who do take care of themselves, who show self-interest without selfishness, are happier. When you're happier, there's less chance you will look for happiness outside of yourself and more chance of being able to see people for who they are, not for who you want them to be.

My client Carol managed to be a successful executive but complained to me that "I'm terrible in love." She regularly dated men who were unfaithful or who didn't want to commit. She couldn't understand why she kept attracting the "wrong guys" and wondered if maybe she was the problem. I helped Carol better examine how she felt about herself, and her self-worth, and rather than admonish herself for her choice in men, to view this choice as a way of reflecting back to her something about herself. For instance, she could ask herself in what way she was avoiding commitment.

Through our work together, Carol came to understand that despite being professionally successful, she did not truly believe that she was worthy of being loved and that she chose men who she knew wouldn't commit, in order to avoid the pain of being with someone worthy who would eventually leave her. We made falling in love with herself a priority, and over time Carol truly blossomed. Her demeanor softened as she became more nurturing toward herself, more vulnerable, and better at discerning what sort of person she wanted to be in a relationship with. She also nurtured her friendships and strengthened those bonds, to enrich her life so that she no longer felt alone or desperate for romantic love. Over the course of a year, Carol did find love. She got married and had two children. The relationship still takes work and isn't always sunshine and roses, but she knows that when she takes care of herself, the bumps in the road that her marriage experiences are a lot more manageable.

Having a loving relationship with yourself means being on a continual path of self-discovery and one that's filled with love, respect, and commitment. You don't have to have yourself all figured out to have quality relationships, because your relationships also help you understand yourself better. If they're of high quality, they will support you to flourish and thrive. Having a loving relationship with yourself involves these practices:

>> **Embracing and accepting yourself:** Embrace and accept yourself as you are — faults, failures, weaknesses, and strengths.

>> **Practicing self-care:** Practice self-care and nurture your body, mind, and spirit by getting restful sleep, moving your body as it's meant to move, eating nutrient-rich food, and meditating regularly. Make self-discipline self-love, not denial or restriction.

>> **Respecting yourself:** Respect and find value in yourself. Self-respect and value show up in the way you treat and accept yourself and how you end up relating to other people.

>> **Knowing your core values:** Assess your core values, which are the set of beliefs that you live by that guide your behavior and moral views. Understanding yourself better allows you to find people who share your values.

>> **Taking time to reflect:** Take time for quiet and self-reflection, to understand yourself better or your connection with the larger universe that you exist within.

>> **Making a commitment:** Make a commitment to love yourself even at the times that you don't. Commit to staying true to your core values, beliefs, and path to self-discovery and resilience.

>> **Be your own best friend.** Treat yourself as if you are your best friend. Avoid negative self-talk, take care of your needs, and be kind to yourself.

>> **Being grateful:** Take time to appreciate the ways you're blessed or lucky. From the small things to the big, find gratitude in what you get to do and that you get to be.

>> **Asking for help:** Allow yourself to be vulnerable and ask for help when you need it. Allow yourself to receive love and kindness that reflects your willingness to admit that you're worthy of this love and support, not that you're weak.

Choosing to Commit

Whether they're personal or business, forming strong bonds requires loyalty and respect and a commitment to prioritize the relationship for the long term. When you commit, you give of yourself, honor your intentions, and follow through on your promises. As a result, you create trust and mutual value and give the relationship true integrity. With commitment, research demonstrates, relationships are more likely to last, and individuals are more likely to sacrifice for each other.

What does it take to commit? This list describes the requirements:

>> **Motivation:** Being committed to building strong social bonds, requires that you're motivated to achieve this result. It necessitates that you're willing to do what it takes to deepen the love and foundation of your relationships because the reward is high on your priorities list.

>> **Sacrifice:** Commitment requires sacrifice. A relationship involves more than just you, and sometimes you'll need to sacrifice your time or desires to make the relationship a priority.

>> **Self-love and belief:** Being committed to anyone or anything requires that you first be committed to yourself — to your growth and to loving yourself. You want to be the person you're looking for — trustworthy, loving, respectful, and accountable, for starters. You also want to be able to be confident and knowing of your worth, like Carol had to discover.

>> **Investment:** Relationships require investing time, love, and resources. When you commit, you take nothing for granted, and you put in the time and resources required to nurture the relationship so that it can flourish and last, seeing it through challenges and obstacles.

>> **Focus:** When you're committed, you show up fully and are present. You focus your energy on the relationship, choosing it above other projects or people and not spreading yourself thin.

>> **Discipline:** Commitment means that you're willing to go the distance and keep moving forward despite setbacks and hardship and feelings of being hurt or frustrated. It's your self-discipline that enables you to continuously take care of yourself and remember your goal and your commitment.

>> **Reward:** You commit because in the end lies great reward — deep love, admiration, cooperation, partnership, joy, belonging, or whatever else it is that you're seeking to have or to feel. When you remind yourself regularly of the reward, you're more likely to stay committed.

REFLECTION

Are you committed in your relationships? Take a moment to reflect on what being committed in a relationship means to you, and then ask yourself these questions:

>> How committed am I?

>> What and whom am I committed to?

>> What will commitment to this person bring me?

>> Am I committed to myself?

>> Am I willing and prepared to make sacrifices for my relationship?

>> What is the reward associated with my relationship?

Building Trust

Before the advent of homes, refrigerators, microwaves, mobile phones, and clothes, for that matter, your human ancestors had to rely on one another to survive. Trust was imperative, scientists believe, for sustaining social cohesion and cooperation, and thus resilience. Trust paved the way for people to stay together, collaborate, communicate authentically, support each other, feel safe especially when vulnerable, and feel like they belonged.

In the modern world, you can live alone, travel thousands of miles on your own, be connected with anyone, anywhere, by way of technology, and order take-out whenever you're hungry. Your survival isn't overtly predicated on necessarily relying on other people. As such, it might appear that you don't really need to trust anyone but yourself — though in reality you have to trust that other people are honest and thinking about what's in your best interest, like the farmers who grow the food you eat, the bus drivers who drive you to work, or the bankers who hold your money. But with so much uncertainty in the world, harmful pesticides in your food, politicians who constantly lie, and banks that raise their interest rates, trusting isn't easy to come by.

When you were born, you instinctively had to trust that your needs would be met by your parents. Then life got harder, you got knocked down or were witness to betrayal or corruption, and it became more difficult to trust, lest you get hurt again.

Fear of uncertainty and hardship can block trust, but it's that very uncertainty which necessitates that you build trust with people you care about and can therefore rely on. As a social being, you aren't wired to exist on your own, and it's important to learn to rebuild trust in order to cultivate quality relationships. So how do you build trust in relationships when it's so hard to do so? Try on these suggestions:

>> **Decide to just do it.** Being resilient requires you to take risks, and when you feel stronger within yourself, you make the decision to just do it. Get back in the ring, commit yourself to the relationship, and know that a reward is in

store for you. Know too that you may get knocked down, but if you do, you will grow and learn, and it's no reflection on you as a person.

» **Be consistent.** Being consistent and reliable enhances the feeling of safety for others. Stay true to your word. When a mom is consistent in providing comfort or milk for her infant, the baby develops trust that they will be taken care of in the future should the need arise. When you stick to your word, others know that you're reliable and a source of support.

» **Show up.** Being consistent involves being fully present in the good and the hard times. Showing up means being emotionally available, physically in attendance as situations permit, and doing things that reflect how much you care.

» **Listen openly.** Showing up and being fully present means you're listening. Listen without judgment and with empathy. When people feel heard, they feel safe and are more willing to be vulnerable.

» **Be vulnerable.** Be open to being wrong and to needing help. It's important that you can be trusted to admit mistakes. It's equally necessary for you to show that you trust the other person to help you. Trust involves giving *and* receiving.

» **Communicate effectively.** As important as it is to listen, it's important to speak. The problem arises when emotions run high and words that are spoken are hurtful or damaging to the relationship. Find your emotional balance, and remember the foundation of love that supports the relationship, which allows you to stay authentic, empathic, and sincere when you communicate. Mean what you say, think before you act, and speak from your heart.

» **Stay balanced.** People want to feel like they're important, a priority. Make the relationship a priority while balancing other priorities in your life. Don't overpromise, and be mindful of what you can and cannot do.

» **Be truthful.** Trust, after all, is built on being honest and being true to your word. Keeping your promises, showing up when you say you will, admitting when you're wrong — these are all aspects of honesty that serve as the foundation of trust in any relationship.

Can you recall a time when you were in a relationship with someone you did not trust? Here are a few questions to think about:

» Did you feel safe?

» Could you be vulnerable?

» Could you rely on that person?

» Did you feel stronger or weaker with that person?

Showing Respect

Quality relationships require that both or all people have mutual respect for one another. They honor, appreciate, love, admire, and believe in the other person for who they are, what they believe, and think. Such respect supports each person to feel worthy, valued, and recognized while also helping them feel like they belong. Experts have established that the giving and receiving of respect are essential for not only upholding group dynamics but also benefiting personal well-being. Some psychologists believe that respect may be even more important than love.

If you think about it and reflect on your personal experiences, this belief might make sense. Being told you're loved is a wonderful experience. But being told you're loved and then not being listened to, or having your thoughts dismissed or your beliefs ignored, can chip away at feelings of trust and reliance. When respect diminishes, contempt, disrespect, resentment, and turmoil can take over. Fear of rejection, disapproval, or not matching up abound, which can negatively influence a person's sense of self, worthiness, or belonging and, ultimately, influence how they behave in a relationship.

Showing respect in your relationship is something you want to do every day, all the time. It's reflected in how you speak to one another, listen, show up, argue, or compromise, because, at your core, you value one another and you respect yourself. Showing respect means that you do the following:

>> **Validate:** Honor the other person's feelings and needs, whether it's more attention or more space or the freedom to be openly angry. When you have mutual respect, you understand that feelings are just feelings that need to be expressed and that they don't reflect on you or anyone else being good or bad or right or wrong.

>> **Ask:** Be curious about the other person. Ask for their opinion. When you ask questions and show interest in someone else's thoughts and beliefs, it shows that you care and that you truly value their contributions.

>> **Listen:** It isn't enough just to ask. You have to *listen*. Being mindful, paying attention and listening to the other person creates a sense of safety where the other person can be vulnerable and open.

>> **Communicate:** Talk. Assume that the other person doesn't know what you're thinking, and openly communicate. Not taking the time to do so when life is busy causes the other person to feel less relevant and diminished in importance.

>> **Be honest:** Respect the other person enough to be honest, even if what you have to say may be hard to hear or scary for you.

>> **Remember:** Make an effort to remember information the other person has told you, such as what they like or don't like or prefer. From buying them their favorite shampoo to remembering that they mentioned being late for dinner, remembering shows that you're listening fully and honoring them.

>> **Encourage:** Celebrate successes, even when they're small, and encourage the other person to pursue their passions and goals.

>> **Maintain balance:** Each person has both strengths and weaknesses. Mutual respect means being able to respect each person for both aspects and then working together to balance out the other.

>> **Show self-respect:** Taking care of yourself shows that you're equally recognizing yourself as important, keeping the playing field equal. If you respect someone else more than you respect yourself, the imbalance can lead to resentment and self-doubt.

>> **Be accountable:** Taking responsibility for your role or the mistakes you may have made without casting blame or shame shows respect for yourself and the other person.

Establishing Healthy Boundaries

In any relationship, you must establish healthy boundaries so that you can be supportive and caring of another person's needs, without losing sight of your own. Such boundaries show respect for yourself and the other person — it isn't about putting up walls or a Keep Out sign. Rather, it entails creating respectful and sometimes flexible rules meant to keep you healthy, full of energy, confident, loving, and respectful so that you can best navigate your relationship. The healthy boundaries serve as fuel, in other words, to support your relationship so that you don't become overwhelmed or depleted by the demands of the relationship or by life itself.

Without such boundaries, you might find yourself giving without receiving; becoming depleted or being taken advantage of; or losing trust, self-esteem, confidence, and, ultimately, your relationships.

Here are some examples of unhealthy boundaries:

>> Being unable to say no, even when you're tired, overcommitted, or simply not interested in a particular activity.

>> Overcommitting and leaving little time for yourself.

>> Leaving your needs unexpressed either because you think they aren't important or you assume that the other person should know what they are.

>> Making everyone else a priority.

>> Believing that your value comes from helping other people, even when it's at your own expense.

>> Failing to protect your personal space, whether it's your body or the physical space you need in order to be alone, think, or take care of yourself.

I personally had to learn how to create boundaries with my family. We are a close family and, as a dutiful and loving daughter, I have made sure to visit my parents at least once or twice a week until this very day. (I'm in my 50s!) When I was younger, I used to feel torn between spending time with my family and being the dutiful daughter while also having my own life and managing my busy schedule. My concern for my father's health kept me from moving away from him to a different city because every year or two he was hospitalized for his heart condition. I found myself becoming resentful, which tainted my relationship with my parents. Rather than want to be with them, I felt obligated and often had a short temper and acted disrespectfully toward them. When I started carving out time for my self-care and improving my sense of worth and value (so that it wasn't predicated on being a dutiful daughter), I found that I enjoyed visiting with my family more and was able to feel more gratitude and love.

As such, taking time out for yourself to regroup, renew, and reflect serves as fuel that provides you with more energy and love to give other people. Here are some qualities that enable healthy boundaries:

>> **Space:** Allow yourself space to reflect, think, move, rest, and take care of yourself. Giving yourself space allows your energy to replenish and your self-confidence and self-respect to flourish.

>> **Acceptance:** Accept people for who they are, with their strengths and weaknesses. Acceptance prevents you from expecting someone to be something they're not or to provide you with things they cannot give.

>> **Self-care:** Take care of yourself so that you have more to offer others.

>> **Self-awareness:** Be mindful of your feelings, energy level, and thoughts. Knowing where you stand at any given time can enable you to decide when to give and when to receive or rest.

>> **Clarity:** Make sure your needs are stated clearly while also clarifying the other person's needs and reflecting on what it is that each of you can and cannot do. Work toward being specific and direct, to avoid misunderstandings.

>> **Wholeness:** Know that you're a whole and complete person with or without anyone else in your life. No one completes you. When you know that you're whole, you don't give up yourself to anyone in order to feel more valued or complete.

Improving Conscious Communication

Faulty communication is a major reason relationships break down. One person says one thing, and the other person hears something else. People think they're communicating clearly, but it turns out that their comments made no sense to the other person. Though people communicate all the time, they don't necessarily communicate *consciously:* They aren't making sure that they're being clear or that they're fully present and listening to the other person. The key is to consciously communicate with clarity, compassion, vulnerability, and empathy. Without conscious communication, misunderstandings and conflict can get the better of you and your relationships.

Given that there exists so many ways that misunderstandings can occur, to strengthen your relationships, you should engage in conscious communication, by following these seven guidelines:

» **Listen actively.** Experts confirm that positive relationships require being able to listen to one another. How often has someone been speaking and you were daydreaming, thinking of an answer or argument or judging what the person was saying? Everyone is guilty of such acts. Active, empathic listening means being nonjudgmental, open, mindful, curious, and engaged in the act of listening.

» **Ask for clarification.** Active, empathic listening alone isn't enough to enable clear communication. Engaging in confirming what you have heard and then asking questions and making sure you have heard the factual information correctly helps avoid misunderstandings, as does seeking clarification of the other person's intentions and reasoning. Don't assume anything, and if you aren't sure, you ask. Asking also shows that you care and are curious, which helps build trust.

» **Invite feedback.** Showing that you honor and respect someone's opinion improves the social bond and also shows you're open to learning. Invite the other person to share their thoughts and perceptions, and when you do, remember to actively listen.

» **Reflect back.** As you ask for clarification or invite feedback, you can also reflect back what you have heard and understood. Again, this emphasizes that you're listening, that you're invested, and that you care.

» **Encourage.** Encouraging the other person to speak is also a reflection of care and respect. Encourage them to talk when they're upset, by using language that invites them to speak without being judged, such as "I'm here to listen if you want to talk about it. No judgment." You can also encourage them to talk about their successes by showing interest and congratulating them and acknowledging what they did to have succeeded.

>> **Be accountable.** When people feel safe and mutual respect exists in a relationship, they feel more comfortable in being honest, and being honest then helps build trust and respect. Being accountable, therefore, and admitting when you're wrong or have made a mistake shows vulnerability, authenticity, and respect, which opens up the gateway for effective communication.

>> **Be comfortable with silence.** Often when someone is speaking, you think of what you want to say next and then, the second the person stops (or even before), you chime in with your thoughts or opinions. Good communication entails allowing silence to occur between statements. It allows for reflecting, fully listening, and giving the person space to finish their thought. Don't interrupt.

Expressing Empathy

As much as the foundation of quality relationships is built on commitment, trust, and respect, the ability for relationships to flourish and for bonds to deepen requires empathy. The ability to understand and be sensitive to the feelings of another person and to be driven to act on behalf of their welfare is important for cultivating high-quality relationships. In fact, evidence suggests that empathy is crucial for all mammals living in social groups who need to care for each other.

According to psychologists Daniel Goleman and Dan Eckman, three types of empathy exist, as explained in this list, followed by an example:

>> **Cognitive:** When you understand what another person might be thinking, such as "She seems to be having problems finding the right words to express herself"

>> **Emotional:** When you understand another person's emotions and have a physical reaction as well, such as "I can feel your pain in my heart"

>> **Compassionate:** When you understand a person's feelings and are moved to help, such as "I can see you're frustrated — how can I help?"

All forms of empathy help you better understand other people, how they're feeling, and what they're thinking, which helps you better respond to situations and be helpful. Feeling understood also has a myriad of benefits for you, because it improves your sense of safety, sense of belonging, and worth.

Like everything else, empathy can be hard to come by as you become entangled in your own problems and the intensity of your emotions. There are ways to cultivate empathy so that you can strengthen your relationship bonds, such as when you do the following:

>> **Listen actively.** Be fully present when engaged in conversation. Listen with all your senses, without judgment or interruption.

>> **Put yourself in the other person's shoes.** Imagine being in their shoes, and activate your mirror neurons, allowing you to feel what they might be feeling.

>> **Avoid assumptions.** Though you think you understand someone, avoid assuming that you understand completely. Stay open and ask questions.

>> **Acknowledge.** Without assuming that you understand everything, acknowledge that you can see or feel that a person is feeling a certain way and that you care.

>> **Be supportive.** Show support through words or touch if appropriate, or by offering to do something to help.

>> **Practice emotional regulation.** Distinguish between your and another person's emotions to avoid feeling overwhelmed or being burnt out. By being self-aware and mindful, you can regulate and calm your own emotions so that you can be present and unattached while also being empathic.

>> **Set healthy boundaries.** Having a great deal of empathy makes you concerned for the well-being and happiness of others, but it can lead you to spend more energy taking care of others than yourself. Create healthy boundaries so that you remain self-aware and clear about your needs, and *take care of yourself.*

>> **Practice self-care.** The better you take care of yourself, the more whole and balanced you feel, which helps you maintain boundaries and avoid confusing your suffering for someone else's.

Giving and Receiving

Reciprocity is another essential component of thriving relationships, involving an unspoken value system where there exists a shared, mutually beneficial give-and-take, whether it's empathy, love, gifts, or another form of support.

You discover reciprocity as a toddler, as you learn how to share and to take turns, and when you see how important it is to give back when you have received something. You learn about compromise and collaboration and then come to realize that sharing is caring and that when you care for someone else, the likelihood is that they care for you. You also learn that some people simply don't like to share — and it's those people who usually can't be trusted.

For many people, giving comes naturally. Receiving, on the other hand, isn't so easy, and asking for help — or for anything, for that matter — is even harder. Unfortunately, giving without receiving can lead to resentment and conflict and also burnout, fatigue, or depression. It can result in the loss of trust, respect, and empathy, chipping away at the foundation of the relationship.

REMEMBER

Of course, when you feel strongly about your own worthiness to receive and to maintain healthy boundaries, you're better able to choose people who are capable of giving while also feeling comfortable being vulnerable and asking when you're in need. The truth is that relationships that are one-sided and that lack reciprocity aren't relationships you want to cultivate.

Here's a list of abilities to strive for:

>> **To contribute equally:** Join forces with someone who's capable of providing meaningful contributions to the relationship that are equal to yours. If the other person isn't contributing effort, express your concern and see whether anything changes. If the person shows they aren't capable of contributing, you may want to give the relationship some space or walk away.

>> **To adequately communicate expectations:** Without asking for what you need, others may assume you're okay. Communicating your needs and expectations allows the other person to know what's happening and then give in a way that supports you.

>> **To accept reality:** I often tell my clients, "You can't squeeze juice out of a dried-up orange." For whatever reason, the person you're involved with may simply be incapable of balanced reciprocity. Accept what is, and then make a choice to stay or leave. Stay if you feel that the relationship has other rewards that make it worth sticking around, but let go of your expectations.

>> **To be accountable:** Do not cast blame or shame on other people. Instead, take responsibility for mistakes, and be accountable for your actions.

>> **To share the load:** Balanced reciprocity is reflected when all parties involved share the workload or burden in a given endeavor. If you're the one carrying most of the load, and if the other person refuses to step up to the plate, reconsider the relationship.

>> **To show gratitude and respect:** Ensure that recognition is awarded for efforts and contributions and that no one is taken for granted. If you're feeling like a doormat, communicate your needs and see what transpires. Providing only lip service and simply saying thanks isn't enough, as gratitude needs to be expressed through words and actions that reflect caring and respect.

Chapter **8**

The Sixth Pillar: Belonging to a Community or Team

All humans have an intrinsic need and motivation to belong, according to psychologists. Everyone desires acceptance, attention, support, and connection, and this desire influences your behavior, beliefs, and even your values. It affects what you might do to conform to gain acceptance, how you might see yourself in comparison to others, and how you might want to be seen. The stronger your sense of belonging, the stronger your chances are of being resilient.

Feeling like you belong stimulates dopamine reward systems in the brain, which is what propels intrinsic motivation, according to neuroscientists. These same reward centers are stimulated when you feel excitement from doing something you enjoy — or when you become addicted to a substance. Indeed, there are many rewards when it comes to feeling like you belong to a community or social group. The feeling of belonging supports self-esteem, self-efficacy (competency) in managing problems, and the belief that you matter — that you have something to offer and something to contribute. All these traits positively influence resilience.

Like many young adults who leave school to enter the working world, I found finishing my residency and joining the force of working primary-care doctors was *challenging*, not because of the job itself but because I lost my community of fellow residents, interns, students, and fellows — as well as nurses and other hospital staff. Because of the high stress level and workload in those days at Boston Medical Center, the staff had to work as a team, share values, and find ways to get along, because we had to spend a lot of time together. We understood one another, shared inside jokes, and bored other people with our conversations when we attended social functions that included nonhospital personnel. I didn't realize how important to me that sense of belonging was until it was gone, after most everyone — including me — finished their residencies and left Boston to pursue their careers. I remember feeling quite depressed and empty, as though I were going through withdrawal, and I had to make myself seek out opportunities to form one or more new communities. It took time, but it was necessary and worth it in the long run because I, like everyone else, needed the connection and support and sense of belonging.

This chapter discusses why belonging to a cohesive social support network is beneficial to your well-being. It can help you better recognize the ways in which being part of a community can boost your resilience, help you see what it takes to foster community resilience, and help you remember that being a leader is important for everyone.

Recognizing How Community Fosters Individual Resilience

The ability to manage adversity is a lot easier when you have the confidence that you're supported by someone, and when that someone is several people with a slew of resources that you can count on to help you. Studies show that, during disasters, individuals who are affiliated with communities that are equipped and prepared tend to manage the adversity better than those individuals who aren't connected to a community. A large population study in New Zealand of over 25,000 adults also found that when people's perception of social connectedness decreased, it was associated with worsened mental health a year later, and that being more socially connected was associated with improved mental health. If you need more proof that belonging to a community is good for you, another large study, of 4000 participants at Nottingham Trent University, showed a positive link between belonging to a group and happiness and life satisfaction.

Whether it's the sense of belonging that improves your mood or the knowledge that someone has your back, being part of a community does the following:

>> **Boosts motivation:** Whether you're motivated to do some good for others, eat healthy, or exercise, when the group you admire and respect is engaging in a given activity or behavior, you're more likely to do it, too. Your close-knit relationships motivate you to work harder, cooperate, and support one another.

>> **Improves sense of security:** When you know that several people have your back and that resources (emotional, financial, and material, for example) are available to you to access, your sense of security in your ability to handle adversity increases.

>> **Encourages reliance and cooperation:** Knowing that you can rely on others encourages you to offer the same in return. Having a shared goal that has benefits not only for you but also for the group encourages this mutual reliance as well as cooperation.

>> **Increases trust:** Feeling more secure and knowing that you can rely on others increases trust that your needs will be taken care of, and thus that you have resources to handle uncertainty. It also increases your need to be trusted, encouraging you to be supportive and more trustworthy.

>> **Fosters commitment and devotion:** Trust encourages stronger commitments — the more that people show up for one another, the more likely that they'll be committed and devoted to helping one another during difficult times.

>> **Provides new perspectives:** Having other people to turn to who can add new perspectives enables better problem-solving and creativity.

>> **Enhances learning:** Incorporating different perspectives and feeling secure to ask for help opens you up to learn and grow. You can also learn from the questions, mistakes, and successes of those in your group or community.

>> **Elevates performance:** You only have to look at athletic teams that work well together to note how a team leverages strengths and mines weaknesses, enabling an individual player to shine. On a team, each player has a valuable role. One person isn't relied on to do everything because the responsibilities are shared and success is accomplished by way of cooperation. Each individual is also inspired to work harder, better themselves, and make sure to take care of their fellow teammate!

Do you feel like you belong to a particular group, team, or community? What bonds you together? In what way do the people in this group inspire or encourage you?

REFLECTION

Becoming Stronger and Better Together

The extent to which a group or community can influence your resilience is dependent on how resilient the community is itself. Research has identified a variety of stressors that communities or teams face that can break their infrastructure and resilience during times of strife, such as poor communication or a lack of respect, organization, resources, or the desire to back up someone else. Putting a bunch of resilient people together, for example, doesn't necessarily create a resilient group, if each person behaves as though it's "every person for themselves." The stronger the community is as a whole, the better you can be.

In a 2006 study, researchers Robert Huckman and Gary Pisano from Harvard Business School analyzed more than 38,000 cardiac procedures and measured the success rates, reflected in patient survival rates, of more than 200 cardiac surgeons working in 43 different hospitals, to compare highly experienced freelancers to those surgeons who are part of surgical teams. They found that practice and experience improved the performance of heart surgeons only at the hospitals where they completed most of their procedures, and it decreased when they left to work at other locations. The study led them to conclude that heart surgeons were able to shine because of the support they received from a bonded team of colleagues.

The phrase *bonded team* refers to a cohesive group of people who share trust, respect, teamwork, and commitment toward a shared goal. As a result of this cohesion, the community is better able to adapt, maintain, or improve performance despite threatening or difficult challenges. Researchers demonstrate, for example, that unit cohesion in the military, described as "military-specific social support," is associated with better mental health functions after combat. This gives reason for the sayings "Stronger together" and "United we stand, divided we fall."

A myriad of positive practices promote group resilience and cohesion — and thus high performance and effectiveness. Scanning the scientific literature shows that the 20 characteristics described in this list are shared by resilient, cohesive communities:

>> **Shared values:** The group as a collective will bond because of shared core values that involve fairness, respect, value, and inclusiveness.

>> **Commitment to shared goals:** Resilience of a group is improved when the members have the same goal, making it more likely they will work together to meet the common end.

>> **Clear roles:** A team works best when members have a valued role that is more or less clearly defined. During times of need, they can then be trusted to follow through on their responsibilities without confusion.

» **Shared resources:** "What's mine is yours," is a motto that resilient communities live by (with healthy boundaries), whereby they pull together resources to meet a common goal, especially when met with trauma or adversity.

» **Contribution:** Every member contributes, and all contributions are valued.

» **Integration and inclusiveness:** Resilient groups celebrate differences, knowing that it's these differences that make them stronger.

» **Communication:** Effective communication between people is essential for a group to work together toward a common goal and be successful. It doesn't mean conflict doesn't happen, but that when it does, the group communicates and works together to find a fair-and-just solution.

» **Cooperation and reliance:** With effective communication comes cooperation and reliability. Members appreciate strengths and understand weaknesses, and they support and rely on one another.

» **Sensitivity and empathy:** Members within a resilient community care about one another and can display mutual empathy, warmth, and sensitivity to the needs and well-being of every member.

» **Encouragement:** Members who care about and believe in one another, encourage one another, and decide whether to keep moving during hard times or simply continue being who they are as unique individuals with value.

» **Celebration expression:** Success of a community occurs when members feel they have a voice that is heard.

» **Healthy boundaries and policies:** It's equally important for communities to have set policies and expectations for members, such that members understand what the community needs in order to thrive without having rules imposed.

» **Fairness and justice:** Resilient communities work toward treating everyone equally and are always looking toward ways to improve being more just and fair.

» **Forceful backup:** Speaking up about conflicting information, questioning decisions, and providing proof or backup information of why the arguments are valid allows for continual improvement, learning and growth.

» **Planning:** Coming up with an organized plan on how to manage crisis or problems, enables preparedness and confidence in solving problems should they arise.

» **Leadership:** Resilient communities often thrive by having a person (or people) at the helm who influences and guides the team to meet their goals.

» **Adaptability:** Success is more possible when the community as a group can change and adapt to challenging unforeseen events.

» **Compensatory behavior:** Members are adept at a variety of skill sets so that they are able to step in and act as backup for another member when needed.

>> **Performance monitoring:** To ensure processes, procedures, and skill sets are effective, it is important to regularly monitor the team's performance as well as the individuals within the group.

>> **Shared decision-making:** Cohesion is improved by giving value to opinions and making decisions jointly with leaders and other members.

Stepping into Leadership

Whether you're the captain of a sports team, CEO of a company, lead person on your team at work, a parent in a family unit, or a member of your neighborhood watch, you likely have a leadership role in some shape or form. Everyone is a leader to a certain extent because everyone influences others. As I see it, you can be a boulder or a pebble. Drop a boulder in a body of water and it creates large waves. Drop a pebble, and a small ripple of waves will follow. Both cause change, but one change is bigger than the other. All actions, in other words, have consequences — some big and some small, but still consequences nonetheless.

Whether you're the boulder or the pebble, you have influence. If you're a boulder, you have the ability to influence on the large scale. When you know that your actions influence other people, you want to decide whether you want this influence to have a positive or negative impact.

Zenger and Folkman, a leadership and organizational development firm, conducted a study that analyzed data on more than 500 leaders, to assess resilience along with nine other competencies. Gathering the information from peers, managers, and direct reports, they found that resilient leaders had a greater impact on effectiveness than nonresilient leaders (87 percent versus 12 percent, respectively).

REFLECTION

Who do you influence? Are you a pebble or a boulder?

What does it take to be a resilient leader and have a greater impact on effectiveness? It involves these characteristics:

>> **Humility:** Being humble and knowing that the community doesn't exist because of you and that you're honored to have the opportunity to help guide; being comfortable not knowing everything and being able to ask for help.

>> **Adaptability:** Being able to adapt quickly to change, and stay open to learning for growth and ways to improve.

>> **Inspiration:** Inspiring others to reach higher limits and work hard.

>> **Knowledge of the resources:** Knowing how to gather together the right people and resources.

>> **Collaboration:** Encouraging people to communicate and share differing opinions.

>> **Fairness:** Being fair and just when it comes to mediating between people.

>> **Curiosity:** Being open to ideas from others.

>> **Co-creation:** Challenging others to co-create a thriving community *with* you, not because of you.

>> **Commanding:** Being ready to take control and command with decisive action during hard times.

>> **Communicative:** Being able to communicate clearly and effectively, especially during times of need.

>> **Connectedness:** Knowing that you belong to the community and care about each member; believing that you are better together.

>> **Competence:** Being capable of assuming your duties as a leader, knowing how and when to prioritize and organize, and continuously learning to ensure that your skill set is one that supports the community to thrive.

>> **Self-awareness:** Being aware that you have influence on others and making sure you're in tune with your own energy so that you can stay balanced and optimistic and influence others in a positive, empathic, and decisive way.

>> **Strong core values and beliefs:** Being a positive influence, a good leader stays true and is unshakable when it comes to core values, such as respect, truth, and fairness.

>> **Optimism:** Maintaining a positive outlook helps relieve feelings of fear and doubt for the rest of the members.

>> **Emotional regulation:** Staying attuned to your emotions, regulating them when negative and staying balanced and positive.

>> **Open to learning:** Understanding that every situation is an opportunity for growth and that the members of a community have abilities and knowledge that you can learn from.

If you read this entire book, you will learn to develop these qualities and will find that you too can be a resilient leader, and perhaps you might be the one who leads your community to foster its resilience. (For details on becoming a resilient leader, see Chapter 15.) The first step you might take is ensuring that members of the community share the same values and core beliefs.

Sharing Values

Social cohesion happens when shared values are built together by the members of a community. These values reflect how they, as a whole, see themselves, others, the world around them, and their future. Their values shape their interactions, policies, and individual behaviors. A resilient community regularly reflects and challenges their values to ensure that people are on the same page with regard to ideas, beliefs, or objectives and that the values are positive and balanced, support the mission of the collective, enable a positive group identity, and are reflected in their actions and behaviors.

Shared values differ for each community. The commonality is that the values reflect the group's mission, strategies, goals, and objectives. They uphold

>> **A common purpose:** Members come together because they believe in a common purpose or goal, and this is reflected in the values of the community.

>> **The group identity:** Shared positive values bring people together and support a strong group identity.

>> **Confidence in competency:** Members have a strong belief in the possibility of achieving their mission and objectives, and this belief is reflected in their values. They share a collective confidence in the group's competency and potency.

>> **A positive culture:** When members share values and work toward upholding these values through action and policy, it encourages community spirit and a positive culture.

>> **Collaboration:** Members are more likely to join forces and come together when they share common ground and values.

>> **Engagement:** When members have a say in determining the community's values and mission, they are more likely to stay engaged and support one another.

>> **Respect:** Shared values can function as a community's moral compass, one that influences actions and behaviors, how they value one another, and how they show respect.

Showing Respect

For a team or community to work together and be adaptable in times of change and hardship, the members need to share mutual respect. When members respect one another as human beings — for who they are, their individual beliefs, and their contributions — effective collaboration, empathy, personal safety, support, and communication are possible, as well as the willingness to share resources.

Do you feel safe in expressing your opinions? If not, why?

Do people in your life support you to feel empowered and express yourself? Do you respect the opinions of others even though they may differ from yours? Are you open to feedback?

You might recall knowing someone who overcame adversity who is seemingly a role model for resilience, except that when it comes to working with other people, this person is condescending and closed off to the opinions of others and displays a lack of value for other's contributions or abilities, which destroys the cohesion of the group. My client Jake complained of such a person who joined his volleyball team. At first the team was excited for Louis to join: Because he was a star player, they were sure to win first place in their league that year. Louis wasn't a team player, however, and had little respect for strategy or ideas from other team members. Team morale was low, and Jake complained that one player had already left the team to join another league.

Members within a community that show mutual respect create an environment in which everyone is fairly treated, opinions are valued, inclusivity is practiced, and each person is supported to be able to perform at their best. Showing mutual respect is reflected when communities

>> Believe in the benefits of diversity

>> Recognize and celebrate individual differences

>> Respond with interest and care to differences and opposing opinions

>> Regularly ask others for input and feedback

>> Encourage everyone to express their opinions

>> Celebrate individual accomplishments and contributions

>> Express gratitude for and to one another

Building Trust

With respect comes trust.

Trust is crucial for a healthy relationship and thus for a resilient community. It's critical to have positive expectations when it comes to believing in yourself and your own abilities to overcome adversity — and even more so when it comes to believing that you can rely on others to do right by you.

When I was working as a medical resident at Boston Medical Center, we were regularly called to run a code blue, requiring us to try to resuscitate and revive an acutely dying patient. As the leader running the code, I only had to say a single word or phrase and the team would work together seamlessly. All supplies were ready to be utilized. Every person knew their position. In the face of chaos, they supplied organization and teamwork, which made the difference between life and death.

This code blue example is important not only because the team shared common goals, resources, values, and guidelines, but also because we had to respect and trust each other to contribute and to provide backup, which was critical every time we needed to perform under pressure. As a team, we were cognizant of how stretched to the limit other team members might be and were willing and ready to support one another. I for one can attest to how comforting it was to know that I had this type of backup. I also was witness to how this teamwork and respect created a positive morale and more efficiency when it came to working together.

Trusting that someone will back you up in times of need is trusting more than that person's skill sets — it's also trusting that person's values and that they will do the right thing. Such trust creates a feeling of safety and security. With security and trust, comes the confidence to be able to take risks when necessary and improvise.

REFLECTION

Can you recall a time that you had to work with a group of people whom you needed to trust? Were there certain people you trusted more or distrusted? How did it feel to be part of this group?

Being Able to Improvise

Working in city hospitals that were often short on supplies or staffing or time, our team of residents often had to improvise and think on our feet to literally save lives. Our success in any given situation was dependent on our ability to pull from our knowledge base from previous experiences, on the skillsets of each person, on the trust that each person was pulling their weight, and on the training that had prepared us for such events. The key here was that our ability to improvise was not random, but rather was based on countless hours of learning, planning, and rehearsing so that we could be prepared to do something new, if necessary.

Improvisation, in short, builds resilience. During difficult periods, it's often necessary to find creative solutions and responses when resources and time are limited. Engaging members in exercises that build creativity and innovative thinking and being able to think on their feet helps them develop their improvisation muscle. Such practice trains members to be better able to cope with uncertainty, focus on what they can contribute as events unfold, feel competent in the face of stress, and learn to trust and respect their team members and their competencies. As such, members of the community are able to improvise because they are

>> Diverse and adept in skill sets and perspectives

>> Knowledgeable about who-does-what and who-knows-what

>> Practiced and prepared for a variety of scenarios

>> Able to serve as backup for one another

>> Open and motivated to learning and creating new models for action

Finding Motivation

Resilient people have an inner drive and motivation to overcome difficult challenges. A group of people with a shared vision and mission who are motivated to meet adversity together form a resilient community that can get things done!

It's not enough to want change or to want to overcome hardship. You have to act, and act often, especially when the obstacles are large — and it takes a lot of motivation to do so. Scientist's Barbara Resnik has looked at the relationship between motivation and resilience and has asserted that motivation is different from resilience because it's based on an inner urge or drive and is not the actual response to a given challenge. The two are related though, she explains, since it takes motivation to be resilient.

Motivation is necessary to improve productivity and quality at work, and there are two main categories that influence motivation:

>> **Intrinsic factors:** You do something because it's internally rewarding. The rewards satisfy psychological needs that promote your sense of competence, connectedness, purpose, or autonomy, such as the possibility of growth and achievement, solid social bonding and relationships, finding purpose, and experiencing personal joy or interest.

An example is reading a romance novel for pure joy.

>> **Extrinsic factors:** You do something because you're seeking an external reward. The reward involves external gains that aren't directly related to your psychological needs, such as wealth, power, fame, or status.

An example is working hard to earn a bonus at work.

Resilient teams and communities require both intrinsic and extrinsic motivation to perform well under pressure, though, ideally, the members are largely driven by intrinsic factors, like their passion, core values, or sense of purpose. Sustaining this intrinsic motivation is challenging, especially when a given task is arduous and dull. This is when external motivation can come in handy in the form of genuine and authentic praise or recognition, and when a little bit of fun is thrown into the mix.

Having Fun

Resilient communities don't just focus on getting a job done — they also have some fun in the process. In my earlier example of working in medicine at Boston Medical Center, my team of residents was often faced with admitting and taking care of multiple sick (and sometimes dying) patients all at one time. I remember days and nights when it felt like we were in a battle together. We rolled up our sleeves, though, and did what we had to. Throughout that period, we also found time to laugh. Often, it was gallows humor, where we had to make our own fun in life-threatening situations because laughter literally kept us from crying. It not only boosted our mood and our energy reserves but also helped us bond to one another.

Indeed, science shows that laughter can elevate an individual's pain threshold and can buffer individuals from the negative effects of stress. Laughter also boosts social and nonverbal communication and encourages group bonding while protecting individuals from physical and psychological pain.

Fun doesn't need to be about laughter, but can be interwoven into meetings or how ideas are discussed and shared. Whether it's employing games, contests, team retreats, team-building exercises, or team meals eaten together, having fun helps group members bond, get to know one another better, relax, develop more trust, and maintain a more positive mood.

With positive mood comes positive expectation and belief, and motivation and psychological flexibility, which are key factors in adaptability during hardship.

If you want to build resilience, know that you're more likely to be successful when you have networks of support around you, and especially, when you feel like you truly belong to a supportive and cohesive community.

REMEMBER

Even if you're not a CEO or the appointed leader of your community, you have influence and the ability to take steps to strengthen your community bonds and enhance its resilience.

2

Laying the Foundation

Quiet your mind and learn to listen with your senses, using mindfulness and other meditation techniques.

Open your heart and mind and delve deeper to discover greater insight and intuition.

Get expert guidance on how to challenge your assumptions and beliefs and build a resilient mindset.

Chapter **9**

The Practice of Listening: Quieting and Sharpening Your Senses

Fully and actively listening involves turning off mind chatter and allowing yourself to be still so that you can be present and can truly listen with all of your senses — hearing, seeing, feeling, tasting, and touching. It's a practice that provides you with an abundance of information that you might normally miss out on while also giving you the benefit of quieting your mind so that you have access to objectivity, intelligence, and emotional regulation. Fully listening, therefore, allows you to be better able to be present, stay calm, learn, and make informed decisions.

Being resilient means being able to adapt to change and being able to make decisions during difficult situations. It requires that you stay level-headed, open, aware, emotionally balanced, and calm and have good listening and communication skills, which is more possible when your mind is calm and your stress response quiet. The key action steps to get there involve establishing a state of calm, practicing mindfulness, listening to your body, filling yourself up with love and compassion, and extending the love out to others. You might find that when you practice these steps, you not only feel better but also discover great insights.

In this chapter, you can see how to quiet the mind and how to sharpen your senses so that you can become an expert listener.

Deciding to Tune In to the Senses

What you see, hear, smell, taste, and feel influences your perception. Your senses inform your behaviors, motivations, and mindset. The color yellow, for example, may stimulate you to feel more alert; the smell of lavender, sleepy; the touch from a loved one, comforted; and the song that was playing in the restaurant when you broke up with your lover, weepy. Your senses enable you to process information, to learn, to be creative, and to assimilate memories.

It's challenging to engage your senses in today's world. On one hand, most people are too busy, stressed, emotional, and unaware to pay attention to their senses or to the present moment. They gobble down food, speed-walk down the street, and talk more than they listen as they rush to work, focus on problems, or mindlessly eat. On the other hand, while living in urban areas and spending excessive amounts of time on the screen (via devices such as phones, TVs, and computers), most people feel bombarded by information and have so much sensory overload that they have numbed themselves and tuned out.

Because your mind is constantly active in reviewing your to-do lists, ruminating over past situations, preparing for the future, thinking about yesterday or tomorrow, or wondering why, how, whether, or when something will happen, you are rarely present, and you miss out on the *now*. You likely often miss out on subtle nuances, nonverbal cues, or even what is actually being said, too. Imagine how many misunderstandings and conflicts could be avoided if only people were really listening!

REFLECTION

Do you remember the taste and texture of the food you ate this morning? Did you notice the color of the sky on your way to work? Were you aware of the tension in the room when you walked into the office? Did you actually listen to your spouse this morning? I don't mean just listen with your ears, but with your eyes and heart, too? Did you feel their emotions?

In reality, it isn't so hard to sharpen and tune in to your senses. You can do it every day, all day, if you choose. You can savor your meal. You can be present and empathize when your children speak. You can enjoy the breeze as it caresses your skin; notice the melody the birds are singing; and be aware of the aromas coming from the garden. Listening with your senses can enrich your world and enliven your everyday experiences, help you discover hidden treasures of information and meaning, find solutions to complex problems, or understand your colleagues or partner better.

Engaging in the Art of Listening

When you quiet the mind, you let go of thoughts, assumptions, or preconceived ideas regarding how something should be. You listen, hear, touch, taste, and smell everything as though you're experiencing it all for the first time. You allow yourself to be curious about other people, situations, and yourself. You ask questions, listen, and gather information that will help you communicate, respond, have insight, regulate your emotions, and strengthen your relationships.

Listening and engaging your senses is thus truly an art form, one that can free you from a lot of stress and probably heartache. It is an art form that requires that you:

» **Quiet your mind:** You let go of thinking and let mind chatter quiet down, allowing your mind to be like a blank canvas, ready to be painted by another person's words or the experiences you have.

» **Focus your attention:** You choose to focus your attention on a person, an object, or a situation completely. Direct your focus with intention.

» **Engage your senses:** When listening, use your eyes, ears, nose, and sense of feel. Observe nonverbal cues, the tone in someone's voice, or what you might be feeling in your body.

» **Loosen your grip on thoughts:** The mind wants to chatter and think. The key is to notice the chatter or thoughts and loosen your grip on them so that they can float away. Always bring yourself back to focusing your attention.

» **Repeat what you hear and understand:** To ensure that you have heard correctly, repeat or paraphrase the words you heard. Repeating also solidifies the information in your brain and memory. You aren't giving an opinion — you're simply repeating what you have heard.

» **Be empathic:** Put yourself in the other person's shoes. What must they feel like? Appreciate their point of view.

» **Pause before you respond:** By taking an intentional pause before you respond, you give your brain time to integrate what you have heard along with your own beliefs, feelings, and understandings, enabling you to respond in a thoughtful, intelligent, and empathic way.

How often do you find your mind wandering or thinking up an answer while someone is speaking to you? When you are speaking, do you notice if others are really listening to you? How often do you find that problems arise in your relationships because of miscommunication?

Being Aware of Stress Signals

High stress, studies show, impairs your ability to make decisions, especially when high risk is involved. With high stress and anxiety, the fight-or-flight response drives muscles to tense, the heart rate and blood pressure to increase, negative emotions to escalate, and the mind to narrow its focuses so that rational thinking is impaired. These changes aren't bad — they're simply the way your body is signaling you that you're feeling threatened and out of balance. (See Chapter 2 for more about stress.)

Many of the executives I coach have to deal with crisis situations regularly. John told me he had walked into his office one Monday morning and was instantly alerted to an emerging problem that required him to make a high-risk decision. The outcome was uncertain, and a wrong decision could have had a tremendously negative impact on the company. He had people to interrogate and information to gather, and at first he thought it best to cancel his session with me. Rather than cancel, he decided to use the session to help him achieve better calm because he was too angry to think clearly. Rather than go on a rampage of blame, he wanted to keep his cool and be better able to assess the situation accurately. After the session, he was able to not only achieve a state of calm so that he could gather information but turn the situation around to the company's benefit.

When your mind is narrowly focused, you miss out on the big picture. You tend not to listen, taste, smell, feel, or fully see. There's no space for it. In your mind, there is only space and time to fight like mad or run like heck. Of course, this is a truly effective strategy when you're being chased by a lion. It's not so effective when you need to have your wits about you and make rational decisions, communicate effectively, and gather pertinent information.

The problem is that in high anxiety and stress states your mind doesn't know the difference between a lion and a looming deadline. Both are deemed threats to your survival, even though, rationally, they are not. The key is to be attuned to your body's signals and your reactions. This list describes some of the stress signals you want to watch out for that tell you you're out of balance and not really listening:

>> **You overthink.** When stressed or nervous, you might tend to overthink everything — from what someone is saying, how they are saying it or why, or how a situation may turn out if you say one thing or another, for example.

>> **You get distracted.** It's hard to concentrate when you're anxious, and you find yourself thinking about other things, especially your worries.

>> **You interrupt.** Anxiety, anger, frustration, or fear tend to cause you to be more reactive and strong-willed, needing to prove your point or express yourself quickly.

>> **You miss cues.** When stressed, you tend to hyperfocus on certain things that seem to matter at the time, missing out on nonverbal cues and fully hearing what someone else is saying (including your own body when it's speaking to you, like being tired).

>> **You can be insensitive.** When you're caught up in stress, you lose awareness of and empathy for those around you. Speaking without focused attention and empathy can lead to making hurtful and insensitive comments.

>> **You jump to conclusions.** More stress leads to less patience as well as making quick assumptions without hearing all the information.

>> **You're impatient.** When stressed, most people become impatient. You want a result, to achieve a particular goal, or to simply feel better.

>> **You project.** Stressed or not, most people tend to project their own beliefs or images outward, viewing a person or situation through their own lens, which isn't the whole picture. In stress, this lens gets narrow and you tend to project even more.

>> **You hear selectively.** As the lens of awareness narrows, stress drives you to find solutions, feel better, or simply feel validated for feeling or thinking the way you do. Your listening shuts down so that you can hear only that which is validating your beliefs (positive or negative).

When you notice these stress signals, you have the choice then to calm your stress response, your emotions, and your mind so that you can listen better.

What are your stress signals? Do you tend to overthink, become impatient or jump to conclusions when you are anxious or upset?

REFLECTION

Establishing Calm

Has anyone everyone told you to calm down? How well did that work? Calming down is not so easy, especially when emotions run high and so is stress. Even without anxiety or stress, calming the mind is challenging because you're used to thinking and doing rather than being still and relaxing. Even though you're human, you aren't so comfortable with simply being, especially when stress takes over.

The good news is that you have tools available to you that can help you find this calm, and it's not so difficult after you get started. When you're calmer, the stress response is quieter, allowing your attention to broaden and your awareness to expand. In one study, participants took a 3-month meditation training. They were asked to watch images appear rapidly one after another to see how many target images they picked up before and after the training. The results showed that participants were able to pick up more of the target images after the training, reflecting that mindfulness improved attentiveness.

It's possible to calm the stress response. It just takes a little practice. You actually have access to a free tool that will slow the stress response effectively and help you get closer to feeling calm. It's called the breath.

The quieting breath

Your breathing changes with stress. When stress levels run high, the sympathetic nervous system is active, which stimulates your breathing rate to become more rapid and your breaths to become shallow. The physiological changes are meant to provide your muscles and brain with more oxygen so that you can "fight or fly." Your breathing also changes when you're relaxed, when the parasympathetic nervous system is active, allowing you to "rest and digest." Stress hormones drop, and neurotransmitters that help you feel happy and calm — like serotonin, dopamine, and Gaba — increase.

Researchers have discovered that there are particular respiratory patterns that emotions like anger, sadness, joy, or fear can elicit. They also found that by engaging in each specific respiratory pattern, the associated emotion can be provoked. In other words, you have the ability to affect your emotions with your breathing pattern. You can initiate a shift from the sympathetic nervous system (SNS) to the parasympathetic nervous system (PNS) by slowing down and deepening your breath, which can, in turn, improve your emotions and how you feel.

Experimenting with your breath

I truly believe that the best way to fully understand something is to try it out yourself. The following breathing exercises can guide you to pay attention to your emotions along with your breathing patterns. Try them out and note what transpires.

Breathing experiment 1

This first exercise involves simply paying attention to your breathing pattern and noticing if or how it changes with different thoughts or emotions, keeping in mind that there is no right or wrong.

1. **Notice your breathing pattern without trying to change it right now:**

   a. What is the rhythm?

   b. Are the breaths long, short, deep, or shallow?

2. **Think about a stressful situation or any issue that has been on your mind.**

   Perhaps it's a situation you can't seem to figure out or that you feel anxious or worried or even frustrated about.

3. **Label your emotion.**

   Identify what you're feeling.

4. **Pay attention and note the breathing pattern.**

Breathing experiment 2

This second exercise entails observing if and how changing the breathing pattern may influence how you feel emotionally and even physically.

1. **Direct your focus to your breath and note the breathing pattern.**

2. **Count 1-2-3 as you inhale, and then count 1-2-3-4-5-6 when you exhale.**

3. **Do ten cycles of breath, counting to 3 on the in breath and to 6 on the outbreath.**

4. **Notice how you feel. Label your emotion.**

Breathing experiment 3

This third exercise involves seeing if and how changing your thoughts might influence your breathing pattern and subsequently how you feel about a given stressful situation.

1. **Think about the stressful or worrisome situation again.**

2. **Examine your breathing pattern.**

3. **Label how you feel.**

4. **Redirect your thoughts to a positive experience.**

   Think about a time when you were laughing, having fun, watching a beautiful sunrise, or feeling gratitude. Allow yourself to imagine that you're there right now, enjoying the experience.

5. **Examine your breathing pattern.**

6. **Notice how you feel about the situation.**

As you may have noted, your breathing pattern changed with your thoughts and emotions, and your thoughts and emotions may have changed when you altered your breathing patterns.

This particular technique of elongating the exhalation activates the PNS, which can be effective in reducing stress response, heart rate, muscle tension, and emotional tension. As you become more relaxed, your mind also quiets and your ability to think more broadly, listen, and take in information improves.

REMEMBER

You can employ many different techniques to achieve calm. You can do a breath focus; shift your awareness to a more positive state like gratitude, awe or joy; or practice mindfulness. There is no right way. The key is to regulate the stress response and therefore quiet your mind so that you can be open to witness your daily experiences and fully engage your senses. An effective way of achieving this result is through the practice of mindfulness.

Practicing mindfulness as a calming tool

When you practice mindfulness, you witness the present moment without judgment. You don't attempt to understand, interpret, or conclude. You don't project your views or judgments. You instead allow yourself to witness the world and life as they unfold.

I personally found *mindfulness,* or the practice of witnessing the present moment without judgment, to be effective in calming my extremely active mind, and this tool is easily accessed in stressful moments. I could practice mindfulness anywhere, like when I ate, observing the food on my plate in awe as I noted the colors, aromas, textures, tastes, or even the effect of shadow and light as it fell on my plate. I could walk mindfully, noticing the breeze against my skin, the colors of the sky, or the sounds of car horns in the distance. I discovered that when I was in the moment, witnessing with wonder and awe and not thinking or worrying, my stress levels dropped, and I was able to cope more effectively with difficult situations.

I later found that I could use this practice to be witness to my emotions, behaviors, and thoughts and also to the behaviors, words, actions, and reactions of others. The element of wonder and awe engaged me to be more curious, to ask more questions, to be more empathic, and to feel more connected. In short, I was able to listen better and be a better doctor.

In the sections that follow, I give you examples of short mindfulness exercises. The first exercise uses a breath focus; the second involves engaging your senses; and the last is a mindful walk. Note with each exercise how you feel and what happens to your stress levels and your emotions, thoughts, and breathing pattern.

You can take as little or as much time to do each exercise. I recommend at least 5 minutes, but of course, do what you can. Eventually, try to work your way up to practicing mindfulness for 15 to 20 minutes at a time.

The mindful breath

You may want to sit or lie down. Whatever position you choose, ensure that you're comfortable and that you can stay alert yet relaxed. Follow these steps:

1. **Begin by breathing slowly, in and out.**

2. **Count 1-2-3-4 as you breathe in, and then count 4-3-2-1 as you breathe out.**

3. **Breathe in through your nose, and breathe out through your mouth.**

4. **Let the breath simply flow without trying.**

5. **Observe your experience of breathing.**

   Notice the temperature of your breath as it moves in and out, the rising and falling of your chest, the expansion and contraction of your belly, and the way your lungs fill and the way they let go.

6. **Allow your thoughts to rise and fall with your breath.**

7. **Allow yourself to be aware of how the breath fills your body with life.**

8. **Notice your connection with the breath of life.**

9. **Notice how you aren't holding on to anything, letting go with your breath.**

10. **Simply observe your experience.**

    Witness the breath of life filling your body and then being shared with the world.

Listening with all your senses

I recommend doing this exercise outdoors, though you can do it anywhere. The goal is to ignite all your senses, and usually there are more stimuli outside than inside. Follow these steps:

1. **Wherever you are, begin by breathing slowly in and out and noticing your breath.**

   Be aware of how your breath moves in and out, how the chest rises and falls, and how your thoughts come and go with the breath. Bring your awareness to noticing how everything comes and goes like your breath. Feelings, sounds, smells, sights, and tastes all come and go like your breath.

2. **Ask yourself how your body feels.** How do your feet feel resting on the floor or the earth? What do you feel underneath your feet? What do you feel touching your body? A breeze? Sun? Do you feel warm or cold? Where do you feel?

3. **Notice what you hear.**

   What do you hear? Passing cars? Birds singing? The wind? Rain? Leaves rustling? Babies crying? Sounds are coming and going.

4. **Sights are coming and going. Name what you see as the sights come and go.**

   What do you see? Colors? Clouds? Shapes? Wrinkles? Spots?

5. **Smells are coming and going. Name the scents and odors you detect.**

   Do you smell flowers? The air after it rains? Garbage? Baked goods?

6. **Tastes are coming and going.**

   What do you taste? Is there a taste in your mouth?

The mindful walk

One of my favorite mindfulness practices involves walking in nature. You can practice mindful walking anywhere, but I prefer being in nature, where I can engage all of my senses in the experience. Like the other mindfulness exercises, this practice is a great way to clear your head and restore your sense of balance and ability to fully focus and listen.

The key to taking a mindful walk is to focus your attention on the experience and to take your time. There is no rush. Follow these steps:

1. **Begin by walking at a natural pace, placing your hands wherever it feels comfortable.**

2. **Count each step up to the number 10 and continue to start over every time you reach the number 10.**

3. **As you walk, concentrate on the sensations you're experiencing in your feet as they touch the ground.**

   What do you feel as the foot rises and falls? How do your feet feel as the weight shifts?

4. **How do your legs feel? How about the rest of your body as each step leads to a shift of weight or movement?**

5. **How do your arms feel? What do you feel?**

6. **How does the rest of your body feel as you move into the next step?**

7. **If thoughts come up, simply notice that you're thinking, and gently bring your focus back to being aware of your body as you walk.**

   It's okay. The mind will wander.

8. **Are you noticing any sounds? Smells? Sights?**

9. **Notice what you see, hear, smell, or taste with curiosity and openness.**

   There is no judgment. Nothing is good or bad. You're simply noticing. You're open and aware. You're not judging or looking to fix or change anything. You're simply aware of the present moment.

10. **Shift your awareness back to noticing the physical sensations, especially how your feet feel touching the ground.**

11. **Come to a gentle stop and stand still. Notice what you feel standing still.**

Each of these exercises helps you quiet the mind and bring your awareness into the present moment. You can incorporate mindfulness into every aspect of your life. When you do, you may find that you're better able to achieve emotional equilibrium and pick up on information and nuances you hadn't been aware of before, including messages your body may be sending you.

What might be the different ways your body talks to you or sends you messages, and when do you listen or not listen?

REFLECTION

Listening to Your Body

When you aren't present and fully listening, you can miss out on important cues, subtle nuances, and how your body is speaking to you. How many times have you experienced a gut feeling that someone was lying, but you didn't listen? Or perhaps you ignored a tingling in your foot and kept exercising, only to later experience severe pain from sciatica because a disc slipped in your spine. Or maybe you ignored the slightly heavy feeling in your chest when you heard your friend's message on your voicemail, telling yourself you would call the friend later because you had too much work to do, only to find out later that your friend's parent had passed away, and the friend was calling for support.

Your body is a sensory organ. Your senses inform your brain so that it can make decisions and instruct you in how to act. Over time, your brain develops a database of sorts on how to act or behave in a variety of situations, so you don't have to think about it much or pay much attention. You don't think about how to walk up the stairs, for example, or the sensations that your feet experience as you shift your weight. The problem is that there are times when paying attention and being attuned would save you from reacting automatically and making a poor decision. You can become a master of understanding your body by doing the practice of scanning your body.

Scanning the body

Learning the language of your body requires just a little mindfulness practice that involves scanning your body and noticing how it responds and the sensations that arise. The following body scan exercise guides you in how to notice sensations that arise in your body to a variety of signals or images.

Body scan exercise 1

To prepare, on several pieces of paper, in large and bold handwriting, write down the following words or phrases, making sure that each word or phrase has its own, separate space, with plenty of space between it and the other words:

Sunrise	Laughter
Grief	I made a mistake!
Great job!	Filthy garbage dump
My feelings are hurt.	I'm worried.
Poverty	Joy and gratitude
Withdrawn	I'm excited.

Bring your awareness to your chest and take note of sensations you're experiencing. Just observe whether your chest feels open, closed, relaxed, tight, heavy, or light, and notice the rhythm and flow of your breath.

State the first word or phrase several times, and notice any changes that occur in your chest and your breath. Do the same for the next word, and the next, and so on. You may want to record yourself stating the words or phrases and then listening to the recording as you pay attention to how your body reacts.

Body scan exercise 2

Pick the top two or three words or phrases that your body reacted to most intensely in the preceding section, and choose at least one word or phrase that led to a more contracted or tense feeling and one that elicited a more relaxed and open feeling:

1. **Find a comfortable sitting position.**

You may want to close your eyes or keep them open.

2. **Focus on your breath. Notice your breath move in and out.**

Without effort, allow your breath to slow down, inhaling deeply and exhaling completely.

3. **Let your thoughts flow in and out with your breath, allowing the mind to empty.**

4. **Bring your awareness to the top of your head, and slowly start moving your awareness down the entire body.**

Take your time in each location to notice any sensations you may be experiencing. Notice whether you feel tingling, tension, ease, lightness, or heaviness, for example.

5. **Label what you feel, and avoid focusing on it or judging it.**

Nothing is good or bad. Gently move your attention to the next area or observation.

6. **When you have completed a body scan from the top of your head to the bottom of your feet, noticing any sensations or what you feel, think about the first word or phrase.**

7. **Notice how your entire body reacts.**

Do you feel an opening or a closing, or a tightness or relaxation, somewhere other than in your chest? Observe without judgment.

8. **When you're ready, think about the next word. Notice how your body reacts. Where do you feel the tension or relaxation?**

9. **Bring your awareness to your breath, and observe the breath as it flows in as you inhale and flows out as you exhale.**

As you breathe in and out, observe the energy in your body moving with your breath, like a curtain that moves in the breeze.

You aren't holding onto anything — you're just allowing thoughts and energy to move with your breath, in and out, back and forth.

Words, emotions, feelings, thoughts, tension, and relaxation all move with your breath like a curtain that's moving in the breeze.

10. **Do this for at least ten cycles of breath.**

11. **When you're ready, observe how you feel.**

You may have noticed how differently your body responded to each written word, and eventually how your body responded to the flow of your breath. The words elicited an emotional response, which affected the stress response, up or down, while the breath focus lowered the stress response and created a sense of calm and relaxation.

Your body is reacting all the time to your environment and your inner thoughts. When you take the time to listen to your body, you have a better ability to regulate your emotions and also to tune into your intuition. You're also better able to tune into empathy and understand other people.

Mindfully tuning into empathy

The more attuned you are with your own body's signals and sensations, the better you can recognize and notice nuances or nonverbal cues that reflect how other people may be feeling.

You can be better at observing another person's energy — that they're sitting with their legs or arms crossed or that their facial expression reflects worry. You can be better aware of your own reactions to this body language, create balance within yourself, and respond more empathically.

For example, when I was a resident, I noticed that most of us doctors, when speaking to patients, had our arms crossed over our chests. I found it curious, and when I examined my own motivation to cross my arms, I realized it was a way of protecting myself, of not getting too close, which we sometimes had to do so as not to cry all the time. I realized that if I were a patient and the one being approached with crossed arms, I would feel more vulnerable and less cared for. With this insight, I made a concerted effort to uncross my arms and found that it did make a difference in how the patients responded to me.

REFLECTION

How do you feel when someone talks to you and their arms are crossed? Do you feel less connected? Does this person come off as being more aggressive, cold, or disconnected? What is their body language conveying to you? How do you respond?

When you tune into your body, you can pay attention to body language, your own and other peoples'. You can hone in on nonverbal cues, your emotions, and how other people are feeling, and when you do, you can mindfully shift your awareness to be more present, open, and empathic.

Here's how to practice the mindful empathic shift:

1. Take note of the sensations you're experiencing in your body.

2. Allow your breath to deepen and lengthen, inhaling slowly and fully and exhaling slowly and completely.

3. Take note of the sensations and without giving them direction or letting them affect your judgment, allow them to come and go, like your breath.

4. Breathe in the breath of life.

5. **Allow the breath of life to flow into every cell of your body until it overflows with your breath.**

6. **Observe your connection with all of life through the breath of life.**

7. **Observe the other person with a gentle gaze.**

8. **Allow feelings or sensations to arise with regard to how this person may be feeling.**

   Notice what transpires in your body. What do you feel and where?

9. **Breathe in loving kindness until it fills every cell of your body, and let it flow out as you exhale.**

This process allows you to calm your stress response and be more present and empathic to another person. As it did for me, this process can help you recognize better what messages you may be conveying with your body language and that you might want to bridge a better connection and act with more compassion.

Listening with Compassion

Listening fully and being compassionate toward others are challenging feats to accomplish when your mind is full of your to-do lists, worries, or frustrations, or when you're emotionally charged. That's why it's important to take the time to be mindful and to pay attention to your body's signals. Honoring your body and creating a sense of calm is a way of taking care of yourself and showing yourself compassion. When you're overflowing with compassion for yourself, it gets a lot easier to offer that compassion to someone else.

Developing self-compassion

Self-compassion involves understanding that you, like everyone else, are human and that you make mistakes, you hurt, and you have emotions that need calming. Practicing self-compassion can lower stress levels and stress hormones, quiet the stress response, and help you feel calmer while also broadening your perception and awareness. The key is allowing yourself to receive love and kindness, which in turn allows you to feel safe, connected, and relaxed. After you're centered, you're better able to show compassion for another person.

Showing another person compassion is to understand their plight and to know that they have their own path to follow and their own imperfections to deal with, just as you do. It doesn't mean that you condone negative behaviors, but rather that you appreciate that they may be suffering.

You can't "try" to be compassionate and also be authentically compassionate. True compassion is a virtue that occurs without effort because it comes from the state of quiet and peace. A wonderful way to enhance self-compassion so that it can overflow freely to others is to do a compassion meditation, as I describe next.

Practicing compassion meditation

You can practice compassion meditations in many different ways. In general, the meditation involves allowing yourself to receive love and compassion until the point that it can extend outward. It's a wonderful way to find your quiet and your center while also helping you feel more connected, compassionate, and forgiving toward others.

1. **Find a comfortable position, either sitting or lying down.**

2. **Bring your awareness to your breath and count 1-2-3 as you breathe in and 1-2-3-4-5-6 as you breathe out, allowing the exhalation to be longer than the inhalation.**

3. **Witness your breath as it moves in and out, as it comes and goes, for several cycles of breath.**

4. **Observe your chest rise and fall, expand and contract, let in and let go with every breath that you breathe in and out.**

5. **If thoughts come into your mind, simply take note and allow the thoughts to move with your breath.**

6. **Notice any sensations you may be experiencing in your chest.**

   What are you feeling? Does it feel open, closed, relaxed, or tight? There is no right or wrong. You're simply witnessing and noticing sensations.

7. **As you breathe in, say silently to yourself, "I breathe in and I breathe in love and compassion."**

8. **As you breathe out, say silently to yourself, "and I let go of everything else."**

9. **Repeat these phrases with every breath you breathe in and out.**

   Do this for at least a minute, if not more, observing and witnessing your experience and sensations.

10. **As your chest fills with love and compassion, begin to say silently, "I am filled with love and compassion" as you inhale, and say, "I let go of everything else" as you exhale.**

    Do this for at least a minute or more, observing and witnessing your experience and sensations without judgment.

11. Begin to notice that the love and compassion within you is overflowing without effort, along with your breath.

It's moving with your breath like a curtain moves in the breeze. Compassion and love flow in and out with ease, like your breath.

12. Silently observe compassion and love flow in and out, observing how you feel.

13. Say silently, "Love and compassion flow through me."

Notice how and what you feel, repeating this phrase for at least one minute or more.

14. You can direct this love and compassion to anyone or anywhere.

15. When you're ready, bring your awareness back to your chest, taking note of how it feels.

Does it feel open, closed, relaxed, tight, heavy, light? Simply notice without judgment.

Chapter **10**

The Practice of Gaining Deeper Insight

Studies show that self-reflection and self-insight predict resilience. People who self-reflect also examine their emotions, thoughts, and experiences. They are self-aware and more likely to work toward regulating their emotions and achieving calm. With their greater tendency to challenge their own limiting beliefs and assumptions and to stay open to learning from challenges and change, they have a greater propensity to have access to insight — and this insight, in turn, provides them better outsight.

This chapter explains how to practice self-reflection, quiet your mind, overcome limiting beliefs and narrowed thinking, and broaden your perception so that you can develop the ability to have insight, especially during difficult times.

What Is Insight?

Have you ever had an aha moment? It's quite fascinating to think about what actually has transpired to bring you to that moment of insight, when a deep or even gut feeling resonates with you, and you recognize you better understand something. That little "Aha!" moment changes you and your perspective forever.

The little moment is actually not so little. It's borne from a lifetime of observation, experience, and knowledge and reflects a merging of your conscious and unconscious minds. It results from a coalescing of information you have gathered over time, observations and self-reflections you have had, and your intuitive input.

What is known about insights? We know that insights

>> **Occur in an instant in time:** Ideas or realizations can appear spontaneously, or they can appear after a period of analysis. But when they occur, it's as though a melding of all the experiences and information you have ever had or learned then culminate in a realization that becomes clear to you in an instant.

>> **Capture the true nature of something:** You don't just merely understand something superficially; rather, you fully grasp and capture a profound understanding of what is true.

>> **Involve your intuition:** You don't arrive at this truth simply by acquiring knowledge or by observation — your intuition is also involved.

>> **Penetrate through superficial assumptions:** Like a laser, your vision and mental acuity become focused, and you're able to see what lies beyond superficial appearances, judgments, and limiting beliefs.

>> **Shed light so that you can solve problems:** What you understand in an instant "sheds light," allowing you to see and understand something clearly and to better solve problems.

>> **Enhance self-knowledge:** Better light and vision enhance your self-knowledge and your ability to better understand yourself — and therefore help you discover wisdom.

Seeking Truth: The Journey to Insight

The journey to gaining the kind of insight that will enhance your resilience takes courage because it involves having the desire to seek truth. The truth isn't always easier to hear or face. If it were, people wouldn't spend so much time avoiding it.

Your current perception of yourself and your world is based on your past and what you have learned, including how to cope and what brings you value, causes you pain, or gives you joy. Facing the past or your current beliefs and assumptions to question what may be false is hard and often too painful or scary, so most people avoid doing so. A truly resilient person isn't afraid to face adversity, which means they have the courage to confront their misconceptions and fears because their journey is to seek truth.

If you think about it, you have been taught from day one of your existence how to perceive the world and yourself by someone else. Culture, society, religion, schools, and parents have programmed you how to be and how to behave, what is good or bad, and so on. Some of these teachings are narrow-minded in scope; others are broader. But what is true? Do you truly know yourself and who you are? Do you see the world as it is or how you think it should be or through the myopic lens of what you have been taught?

REMEMBER

To see truth and gain insight, be open to believing that some or all of what you currently know might be false, which means staying open to changing yourself and your worldview and being willing to turn off your preconceived ideas and thoughts. It takes being adept at quieting your mind, broadening your perception, connecting with your intuition, and tuning in to your wisdom, especially when you're stressed and facing uncertainty.

The journey to seeking truth and thus gaining insight involves following these six steps:

1. **Pause and quiet the mind.** The first step is to put the situation on Pause. Whether you take a few minutes, days, or weeks, you need to step back, quiet the static in your mind, and take in a bigger view of the situation.

2. **Listen and tune in.** The quieter you are, the more you can listen — to subtle nuances that you may not have noticed; to your body, your body language, or your intuition; or to other signs and signals that may appear that will give you direction.

3. **Be curious.** Ask questions. Be curious about the process. Look for patterns and connections as events unfold. Ask questions using the words *why, how, what, when,* and *what-if.* See what unfolds. There are no correct answers — only good questions.

4. **Dig in.** Examine your feelings, thoughts, beliefs, and emotions more deeply. Look into yourself and your own assumptions and preconceived ideas. Try to understand the origin of your beliefs and why your emotions exist. Research the details and invoke critical thinking. Digging in ultimately enables you to better regulate your emotions in times of stress and to have more clarity around a given situation or subject.

5. **Write.** Journal your observations and thoughts. When meditating or taking part in a mindfulness practice, take time afterward to do some stream-of-consciousness writing and see what comes out on paper. Write down your observations or signals you may have noted.

6. **Suspend time.** For now, let go of the need to know, and allow yourself to be comfortable with not knowing. Have patience and trust that the process needs time to unfold and that you're too close to the situation to see it clearly. Time is often all you need to gain more perspective. Meditate, take a walk, do something creative, or spend time in nature to quiet and open your mind and relax your body. It's when you're most relaxed that everything becomes integrated, insights arise, and wisdom forms.

Throughout this chapter, I discuss how to use these steps to improve your insight.

Quieting the Mind

Your first goal on the path toward resilience is to quiet your mind. When your mind is quiet, you create space for new ideas to flow and your senses to be awakened. A variety of meditation practices can help you quiet your mind. I personally prefer *mindfulness meditation*, a practice of focusing attention fully in the present moment, without judgment and without holding on to any thoughts.

Handed down from teacher to teacher over thousands of years since the time of Buddha, mindfulness meditation has its origins in early Buddhist practices. Known as *vipassana* meditation, the practice involves seeing things as they are. (Also see Chapter 9 for using mindfulness to calm yourself.)

The following mindfulness meditation exercise can help quiet your mind and teach you how to practice seeing things as they are. For this exercise, choose an object to focus on — perhaps a piece of fruit, a book, a lamp, or another inanimate object. Then follow these steps:

1. **Find a comfortable position to sit.**

   Choose a quiet place where you won't be interrupted.

2. **Breathe normally, and gradually start slowing and deepening your breath, allowing the body to relax.**

3. **Bring your awareness to the object of focus.**

4. **Notice the object of focus.**

   What do you see? What do you feel or sense?

5. **While focusing on the object, observe the wanderings of your mind or the physical sensations you might be experiencing, all the while bringing your attention back to the focus.**

6. **You can name or label what you experience or notice.**

For instance, you may focus on an orange and say to yourself, "Seeing orange" or "Smelling tanginess" or "Feeling softness" or "Feeling relaxed breathing" or "Feeling peace."

7. **Move from sensation to sensation, without stopping anywhere for too long.**

Always keep your focus on the object, allowing everything to be part of the whole experience. Name sights, sounds, tastes, smells, or sensations you might be experiencing in the body or images, thoughts, or emotions that come up.

REFLECTION

When you're ready, take a moment to notice how you feel. Are you more relaxed? Does your mind feel clear? What is your perspective now, especially of this object or a problem you may have been thinking about before this practice? Has it changed?

Tapping into Intuition

Information from your conscious mind is often limited and analytical. In contrast, the information that arises from your unconscious mind is usually more imaginative and creative and can often appear radical and illogical. With stress and negative emotions, the conscious mind can become so rigid and loud that it blocks your ability to tune in to the unconscious mind and your imagination and intuition. When you silence the banter in your mind and calm the stress response, you allow the two minds to merge, letting your intuition awaken as well as your ability to understand something without the need for conscious reasoning.

I started giving credence to my intuition when I was a resident in medicine. I remember one instance when I was called down to the emergency room to evaluate a patient for the intensive care unit. It was 6 o'clock in the morning and we had only one bed. "This patient had better be really sick," I thought. The patient I was asked to evaluate was not that sick, and we agreed he could move to another floor.

As I was examining this patient, though, an indescribable heavy feeling came over me, as though something terrible were about to happen. I slowly turned around to face the patient in the nearby bed, an elderly man being evaluated for constipation. I said, "Sir, are you all right?" He responded, "I feel like doom." I still get chills when I think about it now, 25 years later. Whatever possessed me I am not sure, but I simply could not ignore the horrible feeling I was experiencing. I quickly listened to his heart and noted that the sounds were far away and a bit weak. I didn't hesitate. I went to the ER physician and told him I would not be taking the first patient, but would be taking the person next to him. The ER doc was dismayed, but was used to my bossy and determined manner, and so he was happy to unload a patient from the busy emergency room.

The attending physician in the ICU was not so happy that we had a full 24 hours ahead with no open beds, and I had made no diagnosis. As he berated me for my decision in front of the students and interns outside the patient's room, the patient suddenly went into cardiac arrest and, fortunately, we were right there and were able to resuscitate him. My attending physician said, "I will never doubt you again," while I thought to myself, "Neither will I. Neither will I."

I like to think of my brain as a radio with different frequencies: When my mind is quiet and I tune in just right, I can get clear access to insight. At other times, when my mind is busy with thoughts, it's like my brain is full of static, inhibiting my ability to gain clarity. Static is especially common for most people when they're bogged down by fears or worries or dealing with high-risk or challenging situations.

Clear the static. The quieter and more open you are, the easier it is to tune in directly to your intuition and your insight.

Clearing the static

Akin to playing with the dial on the radio to clear out the static, you might need to patiently take your time until you find clear reception. Once the static is cleared, you can tune in to your feelings and listen to your intuition.

My client Tim complained of being under a tremendous amount of pressure at work. He needed to make a big decision about whether to sign a contract for moving to a new building. He and his lawyer had reviewed the contract with a fine-tooth comb. Nothing seemed to be wrong with the contract, but Tim still hesitated — it was a big move that would cost a lot of money. He told me he felt a sinking feeling in the pit of his stomach but wasn't sure whether his gut instinct was telling him something was wrong or he was nervous about taking such a big risk. He had been ruminating and losing sleep over the decision for days.

I guided Tim through a meditation exercise that enabled him to clear the thoughts in his mind and calm his fears so that he could discern what his body, or his gut, was trying to tell him. In his quieted state, he asked his gut, "What are you trying to tell me?" The answer was this: "Don't sign the papers. Not now. Wait." The feeling was so strong that Tim decided to literally listen to his gut and postpone signing the papers. Three weeks later it was announced that COVID-19 was indeed a pandemic, and recommendations were being made for offices to close and employees to work remotely. That settled it.

I realize that this story sounds like a tall tale, but Tim isn't the only person who has had such experiences. Remember that he also had done his homework and had already completed an analysis of the situation. He wasn't acting solely on his gut — he was also aware of what was happening in the world. The missing piece was that he wasn't also taking his intuition or his gut instinct into account. After clearing the static and connecting with his gut instinct, he was able to make a sound decision that stemmed from the merging of his conscious and unconscious minds.

If you want to learn how to clear the static in your mind, try the following exercise, in which you use a mindfulness technique to focus on the present moment, but in this case using your body as the focus, or object:

1. **Find a comfortable position in which to sit for the next five minutes or so.**

   Choose a place that is quiet and where you won't be interrupted.

2. **Start by breathing normally.**

3. **Bring your awareness to noticing your body as it sits wherever you are.**

   For example, notice that your body rests on a chair, a bed, or the floor and that it's in this present moment, in this particular place.

4. **Notice any sensations, feelings, or thoughts that might arise.**

   You're not trying to analyze or figure anything out. You're just noticing. It's as though your awareness is radar and it's picking up blips on the different wavelengths before it moves on with its scan.

5. **Bring your awareness to the space between the blips — between your thoughts and your breath and what you notice or experience.**

6. **Notice the silence.**

7. **Notice how you feel and gently bring yourself back so that you can write about your experience.**

REFLECTION

How does your body feel? Do you feel differently? Write down your observations if you like and see what flows out.

Mindfully tuning in

With your mind quiet, you can tune in to feelings and thoughts and take note of other subtle nuances around you and within you. You can then gain a deeper understanding of yourself and how your body talks to you through physical sensations.

The mindfulness exercise in this section guides you to tune in to your body. You may want to practice for five minutes or more.

First focus on a situation that elicits a negative emotional response, such as a situation at work, at home, or out in the world. Follow these steps:

1. **Sit quietly and allow the situation to come to mind.**

2. **As you do so, bring your awareness to sensations you're experiencing in your body and mind.**

Scan your body like radar, noticing feelings, emotions, or thoughts and without holding on to them or analyzing.

3. **Label the physical sensations.**

You might say, "Feeling chest tightness," or "Stomach contracting," or "Head feels tight."

4. **Label the label.**

For instance, when you notice that your chest feels tight, you might say to yourself, "This is joy" or "This is frustration."

5. **Continue scanning with your radar.**

Don't stay in one thought or experience; rather, observe your experience, labeling along the way. You're not analyzing why, but rather simply stating. Trust in the connection between the sensation and the label.

REFLECTION

Do you feel differently? Can you recognize ways your body speaks to you? Do you have a gut instinct that's clearer to you now with regard to the situation? Write down your observations and see what flows.

Enlivening Curiosity

Becoming more adept at having clear insight requires that you actually want that insight. It means having a deep desire to gain more knowledge. It means that you're curious, and you ask a lot of questions because you know that the answers will inform better decision-making — and also more questions, which means more learning. You don't take anything at face value, and you don't live your life like a robot, only doing what you're told, because that's boring!

Scientists confirm that curiosity motivates learning and influences decision-making, and "is crucial for healthy development." As a baby, you want to touch, feel, and taste everything in sight. You use your senses to engage with the world, which helps you form new understandings and knowledge. The more you learn, the more you start understanding how things work and the relationships between things, and then you begin to recognize patterns. The more knowledge you acquire, the more your questions become refined as you seek new explanations and specific understandings. The downside of growing older, for many, is that as you acquire specific knowledge, you let go of your imagination and your need to be curious.

I remember as a child I would gaze up at the moon, believing that I came from there. I had quite an expansive worldview, believing anything was possible. As I grew older and developed intellect and reasoning, this belief was ousted by a more scientific understanding of the moon, the earth, and the galaxy. What did not die down for me was my insatiable curiosity. Wanting to understand, experience, grow, learn, and experiment led me to break down the perceived barriers of Western medicine and forge new paths of practice and understanding. My curiosity motivated me challenge my preconceived assumptions and beliefs and be more open to esoteric and spiritual practices.

The problem for most people isn't that they aren't inherently curious — it's that their curiosity and intuition shut down when they're anxious or experiencing great conflict. When distressed, you tend to become inattentive and unattuned, and your thoughts and behaviors tend to be judgmental and rash. When you enliven your curiosity muscle, along with your intuition, you become empowered to stay open and connected and more insightful, even during periods of conflict and stress.

The following sections discuss the steps you can take to enliven curiosity and connect it with your intuition.

Ask questions

Many people are scared to ask questions and think there has to be a right answer. I truly believe there is no dumb question and there is no right answer, yet there *is* a way to ask questions that breeds more information and answers you seek.

First practice asking. Take any given situation or problem and ask questions using the words *what, when, why, how, who,* and *where.* Here are some examples:

>> **What** is the problem? Underlying issues? My perception or perspective?

>> **When** did it start? When does it happen?

>> **Who** cares? Causes it? Can solve it?

>> **How** does it happen? Can I change my perspective?

>> **Where** does it happen? Do I need to look?

>> **Why** is it important? Does it persist?

Switch up the questions and give them direction

Once you have had some practice, see whether you can start asking questions differently, to give them direction and purpose. As Michael Gelb, author of *How to Think Like Leonardo De Vinci*, writes, "Some people like to muse on the philosophical conundrum 'What is the meaning of life?' But more practical philosophers ask, 'How can I make my life meaningful?'" Here are a few examples:

>> "What am I supposed to do?" becomes "How is this an opportunity to learn?"

>> "Why do these situations always happen?" becomes "What are the patterns that are consistent in the many situations I experience?"

>> "How could you do this to me?" becomes "What motivated you to behave in such a way?"

Relax into not knowing

It's in your human nature to seek answers because it helps you feel more secure and in control. Let go of your need to know the exact answer. Trust the journey you're on and that the right information will come your way at the right time. Perceive yourself and your world with openness and awe, as limiting beliefs and preconceived ideas vanish and your mind is open to new possibilities. Here are some examples:

>> **Imagine that you have landed on the moon. Everything is new.** You awaken your sight and hearing and taste buds and feeling centers to fully experience this newness. What is everything? You know absolutely nothing. It's all new! What draws your attention? Colors, sounds, textures?

>> **Visit a theme park, supermarket, or shopping mall.** Wander aimlessly, as if you were on the moon.

>> **Walk in nature and observe.** Engage your senses and roam around without a destination or clear objective in mind.

Improve reception by being more receptive

The best ideas and insights form when you're relaxed and your mind is quiet, when you're more fully receptive, as in these examples:

>> Practice mindfulness or other meditation techniques.

>> Spend time in nature, bathing your senses in the experience.

>> Gaze at the clouds and observe the shapes, the sky, and the space between clouds.

>> Take a nap and keep a notebook near your bed, in case ideas come.

TIP

Keep a notebook in which you do stream-of-consciousness writing, not holding back or judging what you write. Here are some ideas for what you can write:

>> **Take time to write at the beginning of your day, asking questions that may guide your observations during the day.**

When writing this book, for example, I often found myself stuck on a certain subject. Whenever this happened, I jotted down some questions related to the subject, like "What am I missing?" or "How can I see this situation differently?" or "Are there patterns in nature that can teach me?" I would then start out my day with my mind and my senses wide open and keep notes about my observations.

>> **Throughout the day, write down your observations, ideas, or thoughts that come up.**

>> **Get in the habit of journaling at the end of the day.**

Note or add to your observations, and look for patterns or connections as you allow your intuition to guide you.

Digging In to Emotions

A quality often associated with great leaders and other resilient people is the ability to identify emotions and control them to enable better decision-making and navigation of complex situations. This *emotional intelligence* is defined as "the capacity to be aware of, control, and express one's emotions, and to handle interpersonal relationships judiciously and empathetically." Interestingly, researchers believe that curiosity is a predictor of emotional intelligence, which makes sense: You would have to be curious about your behaviors and reactions to take the time to examine your emotions.

When you possess emotional intelligence, you know that your emotions reflect your brain's way of letting you know that you're out of balance or feeling threatened and that your stress response switch is on. You're aware that you have a choice: to let your emotions guide your behavior or to regulate your emotions and view them as guides that help you gain deeper insight into yourself.

The practice of regulating your emotions involves being self-aware, in tune with your body's signals, and willing to dig deep. The following exercise will guide you in how to dig deep and examine your emotions:

1. **Find a comfortable position to sit or lie down.**

   Choose a quiet spot where you won't be disturbed.

2. **Choose a stressful situation to focus on.**

   Pick one that causes you to feel angry, anxious, worried, or sad or to experience other negative emotion.

3. **Allow yourself to feel the emotion.**

   Acknowledge to yourself that you're feeling badly. Intentionally do not try to suppress or repress your feelings or thoughts.

4. **Give your feelings credit for being your guides to deeper awareness and insight.**

5. **Redirect your focus away from the emotions for a moment.**

   You're calming the stress response and therefore lowering the electrical charge of the emotion. In this case, redirect your focus to your breath.

6. **Focus on the breath as in moves in and then out.**

   - Count 1-2-3 on the inbreath and 1-2-3-4-5-6 on the outbreath.

   - Allow thoughts to come and go with your breath.

   - Continue this focus for a minute or more.

7. **Allow the situation to come to mind again and bring your awareness to your body.**

   Scan your body as you observe any sensations you experience, noticing in particular where tension, heaviness, or sensation is the strongest or most intense.

8. **Label the sensation and label the feeling, making the connection.**

   For instance, you might say to yourself, "Feeling chest tightness" and "Feeling betrayed" or "Feeling stomach contraction" and "Feeling insecure."

9. **Ask questions to the area of the body.**

   The answers to these questions bring you closer to understanding why you're being triggered to feel this particular way or ways and to seeing what your underlying limiting belief might be. You can ask yourself these questions:

   - Feeling, why are you here?

   - Have I experienced you before?

- When did I first feel this way?

- What circumstances in the past have led to the same reaction?

- Why do I feel this feeling?

- Where does this feeling come from?

- What am I learning about myself from this feeling?

- How is this feeling reflecting what I believe about myself and my value?

- Is there another way I can feel that promotes self-value?

- What happens when I connect to this positive feeling?

10. **Spend time listening to the answers that arise within your mind.**

Reflect on images, words, phrases, or insights that come forward. You may want to write now, letting the words flow without holding back or thinking too much.

11. **When you're ready, bring your awareness back to your breath.**

Continue with the mindful breath practice for at least a minute or more, and follow these guidelines:

- Become aware of the inbreath and that when you breathe in, you're breathing in the breath of life that connects you to all living beings.

- When you breathe out, you're aware that you aren't holding on to anything, that you can't hold on to your breath even if you try, nor can you hold on to anything else.

- Give yourself as much time as you want with this breath focusing practice.

Analyzing Insights to Make Decisions

New insights can inform better decision-making as Tim's insight did for him. (Refer to the earlier section "Clearing the static.") The process involves making a disciplined analysis of the conscious observations, your life experiences, your expertise, your intuition, and your understandings. It involves organizing your thoughts, systematically testing theories, and looking for connections, patterns, and possibilities that will inform your decisions.

Some insights are simply aha moments that change your perspective on things, but don't necessarily require you to make an impactful decision. At other times, a decision you need to make can have lasting consequences, and you should ensure that you have rigorously organized information into familiar patterns that can be judged and analyzed, which will serve as stepping points for new actions and strategies to take place. The following sections walk you through the steps to take to get there.

Articulate the problem

When defining the problem, try to focus on asking questions that give you a 360-degree view of a situation and help you identify goals, large and small, that you can focus on. Be creative in your inquiry so that questions are open-ended and can lead to more questions. This process helps you develop clarity on goals and objectives that will get you closer to finding a solution.

For example, my sister was worried about my niece, Maia, who was staying up late doing her homework. The problem she felt was that

>> Maia has too much homework.

>> There isn't enough time in the day.

>> No activities can be cut out of the day.

Focusing on only what was wrong was not helping Maia complete her homework, nor was it alleviating anybody's stress, which is usually the case in most situations when you focus on what's wrong as opposed to focusing on clear goals and objectives.

As we did in Maia's situation, ask yourself what you want your decisions to accomplish and what your goals and needs are. This form of inquiry will guide you to seek information that presents new alternatives and solutions.

In Maia's case, because she has a lot of homework and only limited time during the day, we asked these kinds of questions:

>> What are the objectives? What do we want Maia to accomplish?

>> What approaches is Maia using to study?

>> Are the approaches efficient?

>> What does Maia need in order to be more efficient?

>> What does Maia need to do to help her level of understanding to improve efficiency?

>> Is there a way to prioritize Maia's day more effectively?

Clarify objectives

Dig deeper and ask more questions by asking why, where, when, how, what, and especially what-if. By asking such questions, you will be able to draw out the picture and be able to narrow in on the most important concerns and objectives and be able to express them succinctly.

Back to Maia, we asked her these questions:

>> How do you feel when it comes to doing your homework?

>> Why do you think you feel this way?

>> When does it happen most? Is it a particular subject?

>> What do you feel happens with your ability to focus?

>> What if you weren't anxious? Would you be able to focus better?

>> How do you want to feel?

We dug deeper into evaluating Maia's homework assignments and also into how she felt about each of her teachers, her own expectations, and her anxieties. After we asked what she wanted to feel, she said she wanted to feel more confident and focused. The objective thus changed from getting homework done to several more specific objectives that included helping her lessen her stress and feel more focused.

Do some research

It may be that you have to consult literature, law, or books to better understand appropriate protocol or understand how other people may have dealt with similar situations. You may need to seek advice or clarify the information you have gathered with respect to the new objectives you have established. Ask for the opinion from someone you trust. Ask with openness and receptivity, without fear of judgment or of being somehow wrong. There is no such thing — there is only gaining knowledge. Note any factual information that addresses your concerns and provides you with more specifics.

Activate your whole brain

You now have the opportunity to use your *whole brain*, which means that you can merge logic with your imagination, by taking the facts and objectives you have in front of you and using your imagination to be creative about possible solutions. An effective way to use your whole brain to assess situations and find insight is by *mind mapping*, a technique that taps into your visual, contextual, and special brain centers that enable better problem-solving. (For the full details on mind mapping, see Chapter 17.) You just need a topic and a blank sheet of paper and some pens, markers, or pencils. First you draw a symbol or picture that represents your objective, and then you draw lines that radiate out from this symbol, like branches that stem from a tree, with associated words that come to mind. The goal of this technique is to let your ideas flow without thinking too hard.

Take a break

You can better see patterns and connections and stay open to new thoughts and ideas when you take the time to step away and relax your body to clear your mind. Spend time in nature, gaze up at the stars, ask open-ended questions into the air, and stay receptive as you proceed through your day. When you come back to looking at the situation after taking some time off, you will have a more expansive view.

Make connections

All along the way, continue to ask questions of yourself. Examine how you feel, evaluate your role in the co-creation of the situation, determine what it is that you can learn, and see how the situation presents an opportunity for growth. Spend time being mindful and reflective, and stay open to seeing connections and patterns. As you gather information and work with your own intuition, you will be able to draw out a detailed and clear picture of the situation and the problems and possible solutions.

Gaining Wisdom to Ask More Questions

Deepening your insight is the path to a more resilient life, because you're better able to navigate through life and relationships, find meaning and purpose, and openly and curiously work toward finding solutions for even the most challenging of problems. Ultimately, all the insight you gain will bring you more wisdom, which will spur you to search for more wisdom and start asking more open-ended questions that may not lead to decisions, but perhaps to a new direction.

My favorite question to pose to people, which I will pose to you now, is to ask what they think of the question "What is the meaning of life?" It's a wonderful question to ponder, because it can influence you to go deeper into the recesses of your mind and soul to find an answer and discover deeper wisdom.

Of course, there is no single answer, nor is there a correct answer. What you will find, when you let your mind wander and wonder, is that you get more questions.

Is the meaning about making meaning — about having all sorts of experiences, positive and negative, so that you can reach the deeper truth of who you are? Is it about learning that no matter how many curveballs life may throw at you, you're loved and your journey is to discover the ultimate expression of that love amid the chaos? And what is that expression of love? Is it altruistic activities or your relationships with others, with the earth or universe, and with yourself and the gifts bestowed upon you? Or is what you know of life just a grand illusion — all the things you deem important and worthy are all but illusions that have little meaning other than to offer you experience so that you learn that you're loved?

So many questions! The more you know, the more you realize you don't know, and there lies the key to the resilient mind. You're comfortable with not knowing, and you look forward to your life's journey in your pursuit of truth and great insight. As you ponder the meaning of life, you might also ask yourself, "How can I make my life have more meaning?" This question leads you to all sorts of new trajectories and experiences — and to more questions.

Chapter **11**

The Practice of Shifting Your Mindset

Resilience is put to the test when life throws you curveballs, and the situation unexpectedly seems to change for the worse. Some people are able to adapt and bounce back, and others find it harder, often succumbing to feelings of helplessness or hopelessness. The adaptive ones are able to respond effectively in the midst of this stress and to navigate through the challenges, rise above the problems, and come out of the rubble even stronger, wiser, and more confident than before. They are *mentally resilient.*

You may recall from Chapter 4 that the *resilient mindset* is one where you possess mental toughness and can access mental clarity, especially in times of duress. A *resilient mindset* entails having a strong sense of control of your life, control over your emotions, a commitment to persevere until you succeed and achieve your goals, confidence in your abilities and your self-value, an openness to change, and a positive outlook that helps you see failures and challenges as opportunities rather than threats.

Your journey begins with some self-examination. You won't know what to fix unless you take a look, will you?

The good news is that even if you aren't one of the resilient ones now, you can join the ranks in time, because there are many strategies you can learn and skills you can develop that will enable you to build resilience.

This chapter walks you through the evaluation of your beliefs and teaches you strategies that will help you shift your way of thinking and build a more resilient mindset.

Co-Creating Your Life

Life happens with you, not to you. *You* are the co-creator of your life. When you realize this as your truth, you're on the path to having a resilient mindset as you begin to see every situation in your life as an opportunity to have a human experience — to grow and learn and become the best version of yourself. Your life becomes richer, fuller, more meaningful, and more gratifying as a result.

REFLECTION

Let's take a look at some questions to help evaluate how you rate: Does life happen to you or with you?

>> Do you tend to feel victimized when life knocks you down?

>> When stress accumulates in your life, how do you feel about your life? Do you get overwhelmed, anxious, dispirited, or easily annoyed? Do you take a deep breath, take better care of yourself, and get at it?

>> Do you tend to get angry easily and yell at people? Why? What did they do? Did they do something *to* you?

>> Do you tend to inwardly withdraw or shut down when you feel upset or overwhelmed? Why? What is really going through your mind?

>> Do you tend to blame others for your misfortune? Or do you blame yourself when something goes wrong?

>> Do you try to find meaning from difficult situations?

>> When something goes wrong, do you try to learn from your mistakes or do you beat yourself up?

>> Would you describe yourself as a worrier? Or do you see yourself as a calm problem-solver?

>> Do obstacles cause you to want to give up or motivate you to want to work harder?

>> Do you focus on problems and what is wrong or on building solutions?

How you perceive yourself influences how you experience your life and, more so, how you handle uncertainty and adversity. If you perceive yourself as a victim or as broken or sick or unworthy or lacking value, you're less likely to handle adversity and trauma effectively or adaptively. You're more likely to cast blame, complain, or withdraw, hindering your ability to solve problems, ultimately succeed, and be your best self. If you perceive yourself as whole, valued, and capable, on the other hand, the reverse happens: You experience life as a journey. It's one that will have ups and downs, and no matter the circumstance, you have the ability to influence the outcome and therefore your reality.

Becoming Aware of Limiting Beliefs

Within the crevices of your mind, many stories exist, and they fall into one of two categories: the story of why you essentially suck and the story of why you're nothing short of amazing. The negative stories tell the tale of why you may not be good enough, why you don't have enough and why you're limited in your ability to be happy or succeed, and why life is unfair, that if only life would be kinder, you could be greater. The positive stories tell the tale of your greatness, of your triumphs over hardship, your accomplishments and the truth about your value and worth. Unfortunately, the negative stories usually win out during hard times, and when they do, the limiting beliefs associated with them prevent you from growing and expanding your potential, from enjoying healthy relationships or succeeding in achieving your goals, especially when dealing with challenges.

Limiting beliefs are convictions that restrain you in some way. They're essentially fallacies that you believe based on past experiences that keep you stuck and unable to move forward.

For instance, you may have had your heart broken in a relationship and since then have decided, "I can't trust anyone." So you throw yourself into work and avoid relationships because you can't risk having your heart broken again. Your boss might be happy, but at what expense?

REFLECTION

Let's examine this example and break it down to better understand the negative consequences of a limiting belief. The statement is, "I have been hurt too many times. I can't trust anyone."

>> **What is the underlying belief?** Does it support seeing growth, taking risks, or seeking opportunity — or the opposite? Does the statement encourage you to feel empowered and confident or insecure and stressed?

>> **Is it logical or true?** Is it true that you can't trust everyone? Your close friends? Family? Everyone? Is no one trustworthy? Is this a logical statement?

>> **What does holding on to this belief accomplish?** Does this belief keep you safe and prevent you from being hurt? Does this belief prevent you from feeling rejected, unwanted, undervalued, or unloved?

If the thought or assumption isn't true or logical and is based in fear, it's likely a false or limiting belief. Mind you, if the thought is true and logical, it's usually a valid belief that is meant to limit you from action to keep you safe, like knowing that it's a bad idea to go swimming in freezing-cold water — because you could freeze and die. The difference between the limiting belief and the latter example is that the former is a distortion of what is true and the latter is actually true.

The bottom line is that limiting beliefs *limit*. You hold on to them because they keep you safe. The problem is that they also keep you from experiencing life and believing in your ability to bounce back from adversity stronger and better.

Watching Your Words

You can examine your assumptions and beliefs by paying attention to your word choices as you speak throughout your day. Notice whether you're making sweeping generalizations, predicting a future that hasn't happened with your assumptions, being overly negative, labeling yourself a person or situation, or experiencing negative emotions. Pay attention to the words or phrases you use and ask yourself whether the statement is true or logical. Then see if you can reframe the statement.

The following sections present five examples of statements people often make that reflect limiting beliefs. Notice how often you might make similar statements during the course of your day.

"I can't"

Notice how many times you might say, "I can't," and then ask yourself whether the statement is factually true or logical. Making this statement sets limits on your abilities and your belief in yourself.

Example:

Statement: I can't take one more day of this.

Is it true or logical? Is it true or logical that I can't take one more day?

Is it limiting me in some way? Yes, it makes me sound weak, like I don't have the ability to weather the storm.

The belief: I am weak.

The truth: The truth is that I can because I am showing up every day. It's just hard, and I'm tired.

Reframe: This situation is challenging, and I am amazed at my grit, which pushes me to show up every day.

"Always" and "never"

Always, *never*, and *no one ever* are words you use when you're making all-or-nothing statements that rarely are true or logical. It's highly unlikely that you're "always late" or that you "never get recognized." Making this statement generalizes your past into one lump of a belief that isn't all true and also predicts a negative future, which has yet to happen.

Example:

Statement: No one ever listens me.

Is it true or logical? Is this true? *No one?* Was there at least one time and one person who has listened to me at some point in my life?

Is it limiting me in some way? Yes, it makes me sound like a victim, all alone on an island.

The belief: I am invisible.

The truth: The truth is that a lot of people do listen. I just feel like I am not being listened to in this moment.

Reframe: It feels like I am not being heard in this situation. Is there a reason I need for them to listen to me?

"Should"

I often tell my clients to avoid "shoulding" on themselves. Saying *should* casts blame and shame on yourself, implying that what you're doing is wrong and somehow bad. It dismisses your experience in the moment and its value, and you discredit yourself.

Example:

Statement: "I should have exercised today."

Is it true or logical? There is no truth or logic in this statement because who knows what I should be doing? I don't have a microscopic lens on my body's cells.

Is it limiting me in some way? Yes, it causes me to feel badly about myself, and it reduces my motivation. It's a downer, because it disqualifies the positive aspects I see.

The belief: I suck.

The truth: The truth is that I know that exercising would help me become healthier and that I have options in my life to exercise or not. I don't *have* to do anything. It's my choice.

Reframe: I could have exercised today, and I still have opportunities later to move my body.

"I can do that, but___"

Often people qualify their accomplishments or ideas with the word *but*. When you add *but* to a statement, you diminish the value of the accomplishment or attributes or even your own contributions. Changing the *but* to *and* adds value to the statement and enhances a more positive attitude and mindset.

Example:

Statement: I cleared half my closet, but it's not enough.

Is it true or logical? This statement may not fall clearly into the True or Logical category, though I can ask myself what I mean by *enough*. Enough for what? Could I have done more, given the amount of time I had?

Is it limiting me in some way? Yes, it makes me feel like I didn't accomplish much, when I actually did.

The belief: I'm a failure.

The truth: I worked hard today and got a lot done in the amount of time I had. I can always pick up tomorrow where I left off today. There's only so much anyone can do in any given time. I did well, actually.

Reframe: I accomplished a lot today.

"This is who I am"

When you make this statement, you limit yourself by applying to yourself a label that isn't open for change. Changing your attitude so that you believe in your self-value and view your life as a continuous journey of self-discovery would help you avoid making such statements.

Example:

> **Statement:** I am the strong one.
>
> **Is it true or logical?** What does it even mean, to be "the strong one"? I may be strong, but it sounds like I'm the only one who is strong. That is neither true nor logical. Nor is it true that I am strong all the time.
>
> **Is it limiting me in some way?** Yes, it makes me feel like I have to be strong all the time and that I can't be weak. This may be why I don't feel comfortable asking for help.
>
> **The belief:** I am only valued if I am strong.
>
> **The truth:** The truth is that I am strong-willed, energetic, resourceful, and quite resilient. And sometimes I have less energy, feel vulnerable, and need support.
>
> **Reframe:** I am a human being who is physically and mentally strong, and people often seek my help and support.

TIP

Keep a journal as you make your way through the day or week so that you can record every instance of making a statement that reflects and perpetuates self-limiting beliefs, attitudes, and behaviors. Also take note of how differently you feel after you reframe your belief.

Introducing Stories

My client Jessica signed on for her virtual visit, complaining that, on her way home, several people were running on a crowded walking path and not wearing pandemic masks. She said to me, "You can't even enjoy a walk outside in nature! People are so selfish and rude."

I reflected back to her, "That is certainly upsetting. Maybe we can explore this situation further and see whether your anger can reveal more about you." She agreed to humor me, so I asked her to reflect on her feelings and tell me what emotion she felt most strongly. When she told me it was anger, I asked her to scan her body and tell me where she felt the most tension. She answered, "My chest is tight." I then I asked her to imagine that *she* was the anger in her heart and to answer, by freely letting the words flow out, the questions I would put forth.

Me: "Why are you angry?"

Jessica: "Because those people are threatening other people's lives. It's wrong."

Me: "I understand why you feel this way. There's a pandemic happening currently. Is it true or logical that all people are selfish and rude?"

Jessica: "No, it's not true. Some people who are running by now are wearing masks. How nice of them!"

Me: "Ah! So there are nice people in the world?"

Jessica: "Yeah. I guess there are."

Me: "So, why are you so angry? Did it make you feel something about yourself?"

Jessica: "I guess so. If I think about it, their lack of awareness made me feel invisible, like I don't matter."

Me: "I understand that. That makes sense. You don't know what is going on in their minds, and perhaps if you asked them directly, you might matter to them, but you will never know. What you can do is understand why this is triggering you to feel like you don't matter. Nobody can make you feel something you don't feel about yourself as well. In other words, somewhere in your heart, you fear that you don't matter, and this situation is bringing up that fear. So, let's see whether what you believe is true. Is it true that you don't matter?"

Jessica: "No, it's not true. I matter. I matter a lot."

Throughout this exercise, she admitted, she could feel the tension in her body ease, especially with her last statement. I then had her focus her attention on her breath and take long, deep breaths into her chest, allowing herself to be present with the experience, honoring and thanking those runners for giving her an opportunity to learn, grow, and heal.

Situations that arise today can trigger positive or negative emotions and a subsequent belief, statement, or behavior. Your emotional memory is loaded with stories of your successes (positive emotions) and failures (negative emotions) along with the associated positive and negative beliefs, respectively. In other words, emotions come with stories, so when you experience a negative emotion today, it brings with it every other time you have felt the same way in the past. For this reason, you can find yourself having extremely strong negative reactions to relatively innocuous events.

Let's play out a couple of scenarios for a better understanding of this concept. As you read them, reflect on how you might feel and react.

Scenario 1: Feeling insulted vs. eager to learn

Your colleague isn't taking your advice. You're convinced that the person is wrong and that they'll sabotage the entire project. An argument ensues.

>> How do you feel?

>> Do you get upset or angry? Do you feel threatened, and why? Or do you feel nothing at all?

>> Do you complain to HR, to your spouse, or to anyone who will listen?

>> How do you interact now with your boss? Do you stop speaking to that person? Is your behavior more adversarial?

>> How is this situation affecting your motivation and desire to provide input?

>> How is the situation making you feel about yourself?

>> Have you felt this way before?

>> Is there a limiting belief or story that you can draw out?

>> Is it possible for you to respect that your boss has a right to disagree and ask them to share with you their point of view and reasoning because you're interested and eager to learn?

Scenario 2: Feeling shame vs. accountable

A friend or an intimate partner is criticizing you for never listening or never doing something you've been asked to do repeatedly, like take out the garbage. An argument ensues.

>> How do you feel?

>> Do you feel ashamed or angry, both, or nothing at all?

>> How do you react? Do you withdraw, criticize in return, or become defensive or offensive?

>> How is this situation affecting your motivation and desire to contribute to the relationship?

>> How is the situation making you feel about yourself?

>> Have you felt this way before?

>> Is there a limiting belief or story that you can draw out?

>> Is it possible for you to respect your friend's or partner's feelings and have compassion for them, and also be accountable for your actions without shaming yourself? Is there a reason you haven't complied with the request? Perhaps some compassion can go your way as well?

REFLECTION

No one has had a perfect past. Everyone has had experiences when they were criticized, ignored, disregarded, or disrespected. For some people, the negative experiences accumulated to form a negative self-belief that they weren't worthy of respect or love or being recognized so that when events transpire in their life today that challenge or threaten their sense of value, they can become emotionally triggered. If you inherently know your value, for instance, the issue of feeling respected or valued by someone else is moot. You're able to recognize, for instance, that your colleague's actions certainly can be interpreted as disrespectful, and it's likely that the person is acting from a place of fear and stress, and for this you can have compassion, without condoning the behavior. If you possessed an inner trust in yourself, in your self-value, and in knowing that you could influence a positive outcome, you would be more prone to staying open and compassionate and handling the situation with calmness and professionalism.

Awareness exercise: Using emotions to tell a story

You're more likely to succumb to an overactive stress response and therefore to negative emotional, psychological, and physical complaints and thoughts when you feel like a victim or that you are not valued. You're also less likely to be accountable and to be able to bounce back after life throws you a curveball.

TIP

I find it helpful to take the time to evaluate the different stories you might be holding onto that lead you to have a fixed mindset or limiting beliefs. Because your emotional memories are storing these stories for you, you can use your emotions to guide you to them.

In the following awareness exercise, you use your emotions to guide yourself to a belief. The goal is to notice patterns of how you react both emotionally and physically to different situations and the beliefs associated with them. Notice how you feel and what you think, and then journal your response without thinking too hard. There is no right or wrong answer. Allow your thoughts and descriptions to flow freely.

Story 1: Examining the victim story

1. Think about a situation that ignites anger, anxiety, resentment, grief, or another negative emotion.

2. Notice the sensations that you experience in your body — particularly, changes that occur in your chest, jaw, stomach, head, or back as well as your breath. Do you feel tension, constriction, heaviness, restriction, or another sensation? What do you feel and where?

3. Label the feeling in your body and label the emotion. You might say, for instance, "Feeling chest contraction" and "Feeling angry."

4. Notice how strong the emotion is and whether it escalates the more you think about the situation.

5. Rate the experience on a scale from 0 to 10 in its level of intensity, where 10 is quite intense and 0 reflects no experience of the emotion.

6. Take note of what you want to do right now. What type of response, reaction, or behavior do you feel compelled to provide?

7. Focus on the area of your body where the feeling is most intense.

8. Ask the area of your body, "How does this situation cause me to feel unsafe, less secure, or less valued?"

9. Ask, "Is it true that I am unsafe, less secure, or less valued?"

10. Ask, "Have I felt the same way at other times? When is one of the earlier times? What happened?"

11. When you're ready, begin to write. Journal your observations, answers, and thoughts as they arise in your stream of consciousness. Write about it, the emotions, the feelings, as if you're writing a story about how it's making you feel you are not enough — usually related to safety, security, or sense of value. Write freely and allow any associated memories or thoughts to come forward.

12. Review and label. Review what you have written and see whether you can answer the following questions:

- What is the most prominent emotion and feeling? (See the following list of adjective choices.)

- What is the most prominent bodily reaction?

- What is the story of not having enough or not being enough that is associated with these feelings?

- How does this victim story recur in your life? What are some examples?

13. When you finish reviewing and labeling, move on to Story 2.

Adjective Choices

Aggressive	Alienated	Amazed	Awed	Acceptable
Anxious	Ashamed	Astonished	Awful	Brave
Beaten	Blissful	Belligerent	Bold	Brilliant
Calm	Careless	Cancerous	Compassionate	Confident
Confused	Courageous	Critical	Despair	Detestable
Devastated	Disappointed	Embarrassed	Empty	Energized
Frightened	Fulfilled	Guilty	Hateful	Hopeful
Hostile	Humiliated	Hurt	Important	Inadequate
Indifferent	Infuriated	Insignificant	Inspired	Isolated
Intelligent	idealistic	Impotent	Jaded	Jinxed
Joyful	Liberated	Loathing	Lonely	Loving
Obnoxious	Optimistic	Overwhelmed	Painful	Peaceful
Powerful	Powerless	Proud	Radiant	Rational
Rejected	Remorseful	Respected	Relieved	Shocked
Scared	Satisfied	Terrified	Victimized	Vulnerable
Worthy	Wonderful	Withdrawn	Worried	Worthless

Story 2: Examining the victor story

1. Bring your awareness to your body. Scan your body and notice sensations you might be feeling, and then rate the intensity of the feeling elicited by the negative situation in Story 1, using the scale from 0 to 10.

2. Allow yourself to think about a situation that elicits feelings of confidence, appreciation, love, success, invincibility, power, or another positive feeling.

3. Briefly notice the sensations you experience in your body and how they may be different from ones you experienced in Story 1. Allow the observations to come and go.

4. What emotions are you feeling? Label your feelings, emotions, and physical experiences (for example, "Feeling confident," "Feeling happy," and "Heart open.")

5. How are you feeling about yourself right now? Do you feel safe, secure, and valued?

6. Focus on the area of your body where you feel the experience most intensely and ask, "When have I felt this way? Were there other events in my life when I felt the same way?

7. When you're ready, write down your observations and thoughts as you did in Story 1, this time letting the story flow about being valued and being enough.

8. Review and label and then answer these questions:

   - What is the most prominent emotion and feeling? (See the earlier list of adjective choices in this chapter.)

   - What is the most prominent bodily reaction?

   - What is the story of having enough or being enough that's associated with these feelings?

   - Why did the situation make you feel successful or confident?

   - Did you overcome some great hardship or a physical challenge?

   - How does this victory story recur in your life? What are some examples?

Do you have a tendency to identify with one story more than the other? Are there certain situations when you feel more victor than victim or vice versa?

Challenging Assumptions

You always have a choice about how you want to perceive yourself, even when "bad" things happen. You have a choice to either fall victim to your misfortune or forge ahead and learn to see any situation as an opportunity for growth — which means that you redefine your greatness, not your weaknesses. You have a choice to stick to your limited beliefs and assumptions or challenge them and empower better decisions and actions and a resilient mindset.

You can practice these actions daily to challenge your assumptions:

>> **Watch your words.** Pay attention to your word choices and your reactions. Pause when you find yourself making generalizations or using other limiting words.

>> **Look for patterns.** Look for patterns of a fixed mindset. See if you can make connections with stories or limiting beliefs you have labeled previously and your behavior or reactions in the past. Examine knee-jerk reactions.

>> **Ask yourself tough questions:** Ask yourself to dig deeper into the validity of your assumptions or statements. Is it true? Logical? Where does it come from? How does this serve you? It is helpful in this situation?

>> **Keep an open mind.** See value everywhere and stay open to learning something new, related to either the situation or yourself.

>> **Choose growth.** Choose not to connect with your story of victimization, and instead choose to seek learning and growth.

>> **Nurture a positive self-view.** Remember your story of victory, and take time to nurture this positive self-view.

>> **Take a time out.** Give yourself time and space to work through the assumptions that are associated with intense emotional responses or pain. Good decisions and effective communication are rare when a negative emotional charge is in place.

>> **Write about it.** Write freely without holding back so that you can untangle your thoughts and your beliefs. Write without filtering yourself.

Toughening Up Mentally

I never quite understood the concept of mental toughness until I started taking part in CrossFit, an exercise program meant to challenge participants physically and mentally. When I first started, I remember being scared out of my mind that I would suck at it and that I might get injured. My attempts at being an athlete were squashed when I was in a car accident at the age of 15, which led to chronic back pain and frequent visits to physical therapy. In the past, I had attempted to take part in other exercise regimens, but would end up back at the physical therapist's office in tears and in pain. I had made myself believe that this would be my life. I would never be in shape and would always be in pain. At the age of 43, though, I knew I *had* to get my physical health in order or else I would be prone to obesity and heart disease, like others in my family. So I made myself join CrossFit because my boyfriend at the time was active in the sport.

The first week there, one movement I made caused my back to give out. I cried. I felt like a failure — like my back would always limit me. I felt humiliated and weak. After letting myself have a brief pity party, I decided I wouldn't let my fear of being hurt and not being good at something hold me back. I went to the coach and asked him to work with me to figure out ways I could strengthen my back and slowly build myself up to be able to complete the other movements. And that's what I did. Rather than cry if I started to feel back discomfort, I stretched, took time off, and then went back at it. The stronger I became physically, the more I started having the same attitude in other areas of my life. I started looking at hardships as challenges to be reckoned with, not as obstacles that shut me down. I developed mental toughness.

Can you recall a time you toughened up mentally? You may recall the many times you gave up, lost interest, or felt too discouraged to meet a given goal. I know I have. The question is, which of these attitudes do you want to uphold when faced with adversity or hard challenges? Do you want to give up or keep moving?

Toughening up mentally requires that you follow these steps to get there:

1. **Align with your core values.** The first step in developing mental toughness is to assert your *core values* — or guiding principles or positive beliefs that inform your behaviors and actions. Whatever goal you focus on, you want that goal to align with your values. Examples of core values are respect, freedom, integrity, honesty, trust, service, responsibility, and leadership.

   Make a list of as many core values as you can think of. When you decide on a goal, align the goal with the appropriate core values.

2. **Remember your purpose.** Once you have aligned the goal with your core values, use this as a basis to now drive your further action so that when you're in doubt, you can remember your bigger purpose. Being driven by purpose is an internal motivation, which is more likely to keep you engaged and focused than an external motivation (like money or a pat on the back).

   State your purpose and write it down.

3. **Break it down.** You know your goal and your purpose, so you have the drive. Now you want to break this down into smaller goals that you can address one-by-one. In essence, you're cutting down a mountain into smaller hills that are easier to climb.

   Break down your goal into smaller tasks that move you toward the right direction.

4. **Embrace the pain.** Keep putting one foot in front of the other. It may seem like it will take a lifetime to achieve your goal. Whether you're seeing a mountain or multiple hills, you know it will take lots of time and even more effort. It won't be easy, and it might be painful. Embrace the discomfort and learn from it. Remember the statement "This too shall pass," and you will come out stronger, wiser, and better.

5. **Practice mindfulness.** Without judging or negating anything you feel, witness, and observe, practice being in the present moment — fully aware and fully embracing your human experience.

6. **Reframe your brain.** When you find yourself becoming more negative or your limiting beliefs are rearing their heads, take a break and realign with your purpose and values so that you can reframe how you approach the obstacles and challenges you're facing.

   Use the skills you have learned to shift into your story of success and see setbacks as opportunities for growth rather than failures.

7. **Take care of yourself.** If you're tired, strung out, or sick, you can't have the mental capacity to keep moving.

   Nourish your body with restful sleep, a nutrient-rich diet, regular exercise, meditation, and time off to relax and play.

Milking Meaning from Hardship

Shifting your mindset involves changing the way you approach difficult challenges, not only understanding that you aren't a victim of circumstance but also choosing to milk the situation for meaning so that it builds you up rather than destroys you. Studies suggest that negative experiences can boost *comprehension*, or your ability to understand how events fit into your broader self-narrative and world narrative, which helps you get through it. Evidence also suggests that this ability to find meaning from life's experiences, especially the challenging ones, may be a mechanism that supports resilience.

REFLECTION

Do you tend to extrapolate a broader understanding of yourself, your relationships, or the world from events that transpire in your life? Do you seek understanding and ways to gives hardships purpose?

As always, you can choose to take life as if it's happening to you or look deeper and find ways to learn and grow, for life to be richer and more purposeful and to take life as if it's happening with you. You can discover ways to enrich your life that help you find meaning. The following sections discuss seven steps to milking life for meaning.

Step 1: Find lessons and inspiration

One way to search for meaning from a difficult experience is to look for a lesson or a new understanding about yourself, another person, a situation, or perhaps even a new skill you didn't realize you had. These lessons inspire you to forever see yourself and the world differently and inform future behavior and actions. These are examples of questions you can ask:

>> What have I learned about myself?

>> Have I changed as a result of this situation?

>> What feelings have been brought up as a result of this situation?

>> How can I use this as an opportunity to heal a hurtful memory or belief?

Step 2: Reappraise your story

Milking a situation for meaning can involve examining the stories that emerge from you in an effort to explain and understand the situation while also working toward a better understanding of yourself. Reflect on the chain of events, what preceded or led to an event, who was involved, why or how you think it may have happened, and so on. As you examine this story, also note your own assumptions, beliefs, or participation. For example, you can

» Create a timeline of the event.

» Write a story, naming all the characters.

» Observe any assumptions or beliefs and see what is true or not true.

» Query about your own participation in the event — to you or with you.

Step 3: Count your blessings

It's not uncommon to look back in time and be grateful that you made a decision or made a statement like this one: "Thank goodness I left when I did. If I had left five minutes later, it could have been me in that accident." Whether you're using hindsight or you're actively experiencing hardship, being able to find blessings in disguise can help you find meaning. Doing so helps you broaden your view of the situation while also helping you count your blessings. Take these actions:

1. Think about how a situation might have played out differently or worse and then ask, "What if?"

2. Compare the new scenario to the current one.

3. Examine your role.

4. Look at the patterns.

   For example, the movie *Sliding Doors* examines parallel timelines to explore the different paths a woman's life takes. One scenario explores the trajectories and consequences that transpire after she boards a train just before its doors slide closed and then arrives at home to find her lover in bed with another woman. In the second scenario, she misses the train as the doors slam in her face, and different consequences follow. Throughout the movie, you're able to see patterns related to individual behavior, timing that is not in one's control, and personal (the main character's) self-awareness or involvement in the co-creation of the outcome.

Step 4: Ask for help

Especially if you consider yourself strong in some way, you may tend to want to solve or manage problems on your own. During difficult times, turning to other people for help and support can enable you to face your own fears about being vulnerable, help you gain new perspectives from people who aren't standing so close to the situation, and also forge stronger bonds. Take these actions:

1. **Make a list of people you can turn to during difficult times.**

2. **Set the intention to nurture these relationships.**

3. **Practice communicating with these people, learning how to clearly express needs and the sort of support you might need.**

Step 5: Remember victories

In difficult times, rather than feel victimized and defeated, reflect back to a time when you felt the opposite. When negative emotions run high, you have a greater tendency to fall prey to limiting beliefs and feelings of overwhelm. Recalling times when you were victorious, happy, or confident or you believed in a better world can broaden your view so that you can reappraise your story. Take these actions:

1. **Think about a situation when you felt positively.**

2. **Write out your story of greatness.**

3. **Look back at diaries, photos, or other aspects of social media where you can be reminded of better times.**

4. **Reflect on the positive experiences and connect with your positive story so that it's fully embodied.**

Step 6: Take care

When the going gets rough, many people get rough on themselves as self-care habits fall by the wayside. The result is that these folks are not only getting beaten up by life but are beating themselves up as well. By enhancing self-care, you shift this dynamic to one of self-love, self-worth, and the belief that life is happening with you, not to you, because *you* are the co-creator. The better you take care of yourself, the bigger your bandwidth to handle, and make meaning from, a difficult situation. For more on taking care of your physical health, check out Chapter 16.

Step 7: Connect with love and awe

When you connect with love and awe, neurochemicals like oxytocin, dopamine, and endorphins fly through your brain, lowering the stress response and broadening perspective. When you experience a sense of awe, you're more drawn to wanting to find meaning and learn. Follow these suggestions:

>> Think of a situation that elicits the feeling of awe or love, like a beautiful sunrise, watching your child walk for the first time, or gazing into the eyes of someone you absolutely adore.

>> Spend time in nature, finding a scene of beauty to admire with awe.

>> Reflect on miracles. Realize miracles all around you — your own existence, how larvae turn into butterflies, how someone invented the toilet, and so on.

Changing Attitude to Optimism

Studies suggest that optimism confers better health, both mentally and physically. It enables the positive expectation that bad situations may motivate positive and constructive action, broader thinking, seeking of support, and improved immunity. Supported by the psychologist Barbara Fredrickson's research, this positive attitude and mood make people more resilient because they're able to transform negative feelings into positive ones.

The good news is that it's possible for you to train yourself to be more optimistic. You can follow these six steps to get there, involving doing much of what you have already learned about and adding a few more positive twists.

Step 1: Practice mindfulness

Rather than ruminate on the past or worry about the future, stay present, in the moment, without judgment. Practicing mindfulness or nonjudgmental awareness of the present moment helps you get into the habit of being present in every aspect of your life. The practice teaches you to let go of intrusive thoughts and, as a meditation, turns down the stress response, relaxes the body, opens the mind, and connects you with more positive emotions. Take these actions:

>> **Be in nature.** Walk in nature and immerse your senses in the experience. Also known as *shinrin-yoku,* or forest bathing, this practice can lower stress levels, improve cognitive functioning, and increase immunity.

» **Bathe luxuriously.** Take a bath and enable your body to relax while you observe the sensations you experience while being in the water and the aromas of the bath soap.

» **Breathe.** Do a breath focus, observing your breath and the sensations you experience in your body.

» **Meditate in motion.** Stretch and do yoga or another form of slow movement, focusing your attention on the different feelings, sensations, and experiences.

» **Be with the negative.** Sit with your negative thoughts or assumptions and simply observe them without judging.

Step 2: Change your words

Words and thoughts affect your stress response, emotions, perception, and the subsequent behaviors and actions that follow. As discussed earlier in this chapter, limiting beliefs can be reflected in your word choices, and these beliefs inform your behavior and attitude. What can you do?

» **Be mindful.** Practice nonjudgmental awareness and observation of your thoughts, statements, and assumptions.

» **Watch your words.** Notice your use of negative words or phrases related to yourself or your situation.

» **Observe feelings.** Notice what kind of feelings the negative words or phrases elicit and how this affects your attitude.

» **Replace with positive wording.** Replace the negative word or words with a statement or phrase that is more constructive and positive. For example, you might change "I can't" to "I can learn"; "I should have" to "I could have"; or "It will never" to "It might." Make sure the positive aspect is not too far-reaching to be possible or true.

» **Observe feelings.** Notice the feelings that arise with the more positive statement, and observe your attitude.

Step 3: Deepen your connection with a force larger than yourself

Having a narrow view of yourself and your world, which happens with a fixed mindset, can exacerbate feelings of helplessness and hopelessness, especially during difficult times. In contrast, when you feel connected to something larger, foster a broader view of yourself and the world, and choose to milk meaning from experiences, you're more likely to have faith in a positive outcome. Indeed, studies show that spiritual intelligence is positively associated with optimism. Because spirituality is essentially the profound belief that you belong to something larger, you have many ways to tap in:

>> **Pray to a higher power with gratitude.** It doesn't matter what you believe in, just that you believe in a higher power or an entity bigger than you that is helping you. When praying, avoid phrases that align you with feeling victimized. Instead, use words of gratitude and appreciation. For example, I encouraged a client to change her prayer from "God, help me make it through the day" to "God, thank you for giving me life today." If you repeat these two phrases, you might notice the different feelings and attitudes each one elicits.

>> **Meditate on love and the connection.** You can bring your focus to your heart and imagine that love and gratitude are filling your heart and then flowing out from your heart and connecting you to the oneness of all living beings.

>> **Experience awe while spending time in nature.** Observe the miracles all around you. Observe that rivers flow and seasons come and go, and that the sun rises and falls, allowing yourself to connect with the impermanence of nature and therefore life.

>> **Connect with others.** Meet up with a religious, spiritual, or meditation group and pray or meditate together.

>> **Volunteer.** Choose to give to others who are less fortunate, reminding you that there's more out there than just you. Volunteering also enables you to feel better about yourself.

Step 4: Shift your attitude to gratitude

Optimists always find something to be grateful for, and evidence suggests that giving thanks can make you happier. Dr. Martin E.P. Seligman, a leader in positive psychology, found in one of his studies, for example, that students showed a huge increase in happiness scores after they wrote and personally delivered letters expressing gratitude to people for acts of kindness that they were never thanked for. Follow these suggestions:

>> **Keep a gratitude journal.** When going to bed at night, jot down at least three or four events that have transpired or occurred during the day that you're grateful for. Read them aloud every morning.

>> **Practice giving thanks for everything.** You might be thankful that you have food on your plate, you found a parking spot, or that you have two feet or a mailbox. The object of your gratitude can be something big or small. You can

even be thankful for the negative in your life. Even though a situation is hurtful or scary, appreciate somewhere in your mind that there's a silver lining somewhere or an opportunity for growth. You don't have to figure it out in the moment, but give thanks, knowing that it's there and that you're open to discovering what it may be. You can journal in your gratitude notebook and see what transpires.

>> **Count your blessings.** Several times a day, reflect aloud on reasons that you're lucky, and then write them down in your notebook. Begin by stating, "I am so lucky because . . ." or "I feel so blessed because. . . ."

>> **Write a thank-you note and deliver it.** Write a thank-you note to a person who has been kind, perhaps someone you know well or the customer service agent who helped you solve your computer problem. You can also thank that person in person, though adding a thank-you card or note may add to your happiness as well as the other person's.

>> **Write a thank-you note to yourself.** Write a thank-you note and put it in the mail, addressed to yourself.

Step 5: Be your own coach

Sometimes all it takes to shift out of a negative state of mind is a bit of positive self-talk, such as "You can do it!" or "Hang on — you've got this!" Making such positive statements can counteract statements that are self-defeating and negative and instead encourage you to push through and believe in your ability to persevere. Follow these suggestions:

>> **Set your main goal.** Contemplate the big goal you want to achieve. Make sure this goal is aligned with your core values to provide you with an internal drive to succeed.

>> **Give yourself a plan.** A coach usually programs a training plan. Devise a plan and set small goals that will incrementally bring you toward where you want to be.

>> **Pat yourself on the back.** Often, no one other than you will recognize your efforts. Pat yourself on the back and congratulate yourself for accomplishing each goal, as small as it may be.

>> **Visualize success.** Once you have drawn out the plan, spend a minute or so visualizing the process and see yourself succeeding.

>> **Believe in solutions.** If you experience a setback, be your own coach and believe in your ability to find solutions.

>> **Encourage.** Use encouraging phrases and words regularly that motivate you to keep going and pushing on.

Step 6: Enjoy the adventure

It's sometimes difficult to find silver linings or the blessings in the chaos. To help support a more positive mindset, engage in activities that remind you of the joys that life can also bring. You want to be reminded that life is an adventure, full of highs and lows, and that it's all part of the human experience. While you're here, you might as well enjoy the ride! Here are some suggestions:

>> **Relax with friends.** Spend time with people who lift you up and are also positive.

>> **Have a hearty belly laugh.** Laughing turns off the stress response and stimulates feel-good chemicals to fly through your brain. Do laughter yoga, watch a funny show, or tell yourself some great jokes.

>> **Engage in play.** Go have fun. Follow a hobby or passion and fully immerse yourself in the activity.

>> **Laugh at yourself.** Practice seeing the humor in your life and your own actions. Taking yourself less seriously helps you broaden your perspective and lighten up a bit. I laugh at myself all of the time. It's great fun!

>> **Embark on daily adventures.** Create a daily practice that involves perceiving a daily chore or an activity as an adventure. For example, pretend that you're on an adventure or scavenger hunt when you go grocery shopping.

REMEMBER

Indeed, life is an adventure and you are here to have experiences — positive and negative. Life is happening with you, not to you.

3
Evaluating and Strengthening Relationships

Improve your relationship with yourself and enhance your self-worth.

Build strong and healthy relationships and uncover the relationships that may no longer serve you.

Evaluate the resilience of your community and explore ways to build and create a positive culture of care.

Embrace your place as a leader and challenge yourself to lead with vision.

Chapter **12**

Improving Your Relationship with Yourself

Resilient people take responsibility for their actions and attitudes and are constantly working toward self-improvement. They have a positive self-image that enables them to hit their stride and keep moving to achieve their goals, despite setbacks or failures. Their positive self-belief allows them to forge healthy relationships and maintain a strong sense of self-mastery. Studies show that high self-esteem is associated with psychological resilience and that low self-esteem is associated with psychological maladjustment.

This chapter spells out how self-worth and a positive self-image support resilience and gives you tools to help strengthen self-belief by improving the relationship you have with yourself.

Connecting Resilience with Self-Worth

Truly resilient people have a positive self-belief and self-image no matter what is happening in their lives — whether life is moving along smoothly or throwing them curveballs, whether they succeed or whether they fail. These folks are able to celebrate their successes and still remain positive when they falter, viewing setbacks as opportunities to learn and grow. In other words, resilient people don't look outside of themselves to feel valued — they already know their value at their core.

REFLECTION

What do you believe? Do you believe, at your core, that you are a valued and unique individual? Can you hold that belief without comparing yourself to the successes or failures of others? Is your worth dependent on your marital status, your weight, your looks, your income, or whether you win or lose?

Most resilient people share several traits that reflect a positive self-image, which invariably enables them to get through hardship. These include:

>> **Avoid being affected by others' opinions:** You don't let others' opinions affect their own self-image or value.

>> **Recognize their uniqueness:** You recognize what you have to offer that makes you special.

>> **Take pride in achievements:** You feel proud about all your accomplishments, big and small.

>> **Risk rejection:** You will risk rejection in order to show your true self.

>> **Desire to grow:** You aspire to become better as a person.

>> **Show self-compassion:** You are more kind, rather than critical, to yourself when you make a mistake or fail.

>> **Learn from mistakes:** You see mistakes as opportunities to learn.

>> **Self-reflect:** You take time to reflect on your emotions and try to understand your feelings.

>> **Practice gratitude:** You feel a strong sense of gratitude and regularly count your blessings.

Everyone has situations or times in their lives when they feel confident and worthy and others when they feel the opposite. The question is, are you confident of your worth at your core?

Believing in Your Worth

When you believe in your worth, you don't look outside of yourself to feel worthy or validated. You feel empowered and confident in the face of challenges and problems. You don't take things personally, you don't compare yourself to others or seek external approval, and you aren't defined by life's events. When you believe in your worth, you can then

>> **Feel free to make mistakes.** You won't judge yourself or negate your efforts when you make mistakes. Instead, you welcome mistakes as opportunities to learn and grow and then accept them as a part of being human.

>> **See everything as fodder.** Along with your mistakes, you perceive everything that occurs around you as holding opportunity for learning, growing, and deepening your awareness and sense of self.

>> **Persevere.** Because you avoid viewing mistakes as failures and because opportunities abound, you persevere and push through setbacks. Your self-belief gives you the courage and drive to persist and keep going.

>> **Stay open.** You lack any fear of being judged or of making mistakes, so you're curious, open, and receptive to learning — to advice and seeing how life unfolds.

>> **Believe in the possible.** You don't take things personally, and you believe in yourself and your ability to find solutions and achieve a positive outcome.

>> **Remain true.** You never lose sight of yourself, your values, and your goals by comparing yourself to other people and worrying what other people might think. You stay true to yourself.

>> **Attract support.** You believe in yourself, and your conviction influences other people to believe in you as well so that they're willing and wanting to help and support you.

>> **Take care.** You value yourself and believe that your body is a temple. No matter the challenges in your life, you take time for self-care, nurturing yourself so that you're more fit to handle anything that pops up.

>> **Maintain healthy boundaries.** You feel whole within yourself, so you know when to give to others and when to take care of yourself. You're clear about your values and priorities and you can express your needs clearly.

Cultivating resilience means developing most if not all of these traits. The more positively you view yourself, the more capable you will feel about overcoming challenges, believing in your ability to succeed despite setbacks, and the likelihood that you will choose the right people to be part of your close network of support. As you read on, you will be asked to evaluate your relationship with yourself and use this information to guide you toward what needs strengthening.

Noting Self-Criticism

Most people, myself included, can be their own harshest critics.

Think about it for yourself. When you're wracked with self-doubt, how do you respond to your boss criticizing your work? When you don't believe in your abilities to be alone, how likely are you to leave an unhealthy relationship? Do you forgive yourself when you make a mistake, congratulate yourself when you succeed, or accept yourself with your imperfections? Do you take good care of yourself?

I have lost count of the number of times I have heard people make these statements:

"I can't believe I did that. I'm such an idiot."

"I'm so stupid."

"I'm never going to understand this."

"I'm a failure."

"Why can't I ever learn?"

These statements may seem innocuous, but in reality they convey a lack of confidence in oneself and in one's abilities, strengths, resources, and support. They reflect negative self-talk and self-criticism. In many ways, self-criticism can motivate you to learn more and grow, and to enhance self-awareness. On the other hand, it can also block growth and negatively affect your self-esteem. You can use self-criticism to learn from your mistakes as a way to develop better behavior, for example, or use it to shame yourself and feel less valued.

My friend Jocelyn called me once in a panic. She had clicked Reply All to a work email meant to be private and to be sent only to the sender, who happened to be a friend. Jocelyn was worried because the language she used was personal and a bit inflammatory. As she spoke, she kept beating herself up and saying, "I can't believe I did that! I am such an idiot, and I am so embarrassed. I am going to need to avoid everyone for a while."

After letting her vent for a bit, I asked her whether she wanted to keep venting or get some help, and she chose the latter. We did some deep breathing together to calm her emotions and help her find her center. Then I said, "You made a mistake. You weren't paying attention. You're human and you make mistakes, and you especially make them when you're stressed. What is in this situation for you to learn?"

Jocelyn self-reflected and said, "I need to take a timeout for myself and be more mindful. I am going to practice being more mindful. I may need to apologize to the others and will do so as I am accountable for my actions. It will work out in the end."

In this situation, Jocelyn was able to shift out of her negative self-talk by calming her emotions and using self-reflection. She was able to see that, in a negative state, her self-criticism was leading her down a path of low self-worth. When she was able to shift into a more positive state, she was better able to be accountable for her actions without denying her value.

Self-criticism can thus be a reflection of how you relate to yourself.

REFLECTION

Do you accept yourself as you are, as a valuable human being who makes mistakes while acknowledging a desire for growth and further development, or do you admonish yourself for failures or not being good enough? Read on and evaluate your self-value.

Evaluating Your Self-Value

How you relate to yourself — especially with regard to your imperfections, failures, or mistakes — reflects your self-value. Your self-value, in turn, informs your behaviors, decisions, and self-confidence, and the stronger it is, the better you're capable of forging ahead and believing in yourself during hard times.

The following is a self-value inventory checklist that will help you evaluate your relationship with yourself and your self-value:

Self-Value Inventory Checklist

Pick the answer that best applies.

1. I know I am valuable.

Never true	Rarely true	Not sure	Sometimes true	Always true

2. I think positively about myself.

Never true	Rarely true	Not sure	Sometimes true	Always true

3. I don't need validation from other people to feel good about myself.

Never true	Rarely true	Not sure	Sometimes true	Always true

4. I am not afraid to ask for what I want or need.

Never true	Rarely true	Not sure	Sometimes true	Always true

5. I don't worry about rejection. I accept myself anyway.

Never true	Rarely true	Not sure	Sometimes true	Always true

6. I do not think I am inferior to other people.

Never true	Rarely true	Not sure	Sometimes true	Always true

7. I don't feel like a failure.

Never true	Rarely true	Not sure	Sometimes true	Always true

8. I am confident that if I can't do something, I will figure it out.

Never true	Rarely true	Not sure	Sometimes true	Always true

9. I can accept criticism without getting upset.

Never true	Rarely true	Not sure	Sometimes true	Always true

10. I don't berate myself when I make mistakes.

Never true	Rarely true	Not sure	Sometimes true	Always true

11. I am able to say no to people when I know I need to take care of myself.

Never true	Rarely true	Not sure	Sometimes true	Always true

12. I treat my body as a temple, no matter what happens in my life.

Never true	Rarely true	Not sure	Sometimes true	Always true

13. I eat food that is healthy and nutrient-rich.

Never true	Rarely true	Not sure	Sometimes true	Always true

14. I exercise frequently throughout the week.

Never true	Rarely true	Not sure	Sometimes true	Always true

15. I make sure I get restful sleep.

Never true	Rarely true	Not sure	Sometimes true	Always true

16. I take time to relax and take care of myself.

Never true	Rarely true	Not sure	Sometimes true	Always true

Take your time evaluating each question and your answers. Sometimes people think they have a better relationship with themselves than they actually do. Do you know of any areas that need strengthening?

Building up your self-value means learning to think about yourself more positively and taking good care of yourself physically, emotionally, and spiritually.

Starting to Take Action

At times you may feel good about yourself, and at other times you may feel more self-critical and less confident. The goal is for you to know, on the deepest level, that you're valued no matter what you do or what happens, and that it's normal for you to sometimes feel badly or negatively.

The first step is to simply be *self-aware* — aware of what you're feeling at any particular moment. Once you know, you can consciously choose in which direction you want to go: toward beating yourself up or toward lifting yourself up.

Practicing self-awareness

When you start paying attention to your behavior, thoughts, feelings, or beliefs, you begin to notice how often you put yourself down, look for validation, compare yourself to others, or engage in other self-defeating or self-deprecating ways.

Self-examination is an ongoing process. The way you react and behave is never wrong. It's not right, either. Whatever you notice is fodder, enabling you to learn more about yourself and why you have negative beliefs in the first place.

You can begin the process by posing these questions to yourself:

>> When do I put myself down?

>> When do I compare myself to others? What is it usually related to? What are my insecurities? When do they show up?

>> How often do I doubt my decisions? Is it about certain subjects or most of the time?

>> When do I believe in myself? What are the situations? How does it feel when I do?

>> How well do I take care of myself?

>> When I am stressed, what are my habits? What do I choose to do?

>> When did I start behaving this way?

>> Where did I learn this self-doubt? What is the limiting belief?

Making a conscious choice

The observations you accumulate for self-examination should also reveal to you the times you feel confident or successful. Being more self-aware alerts you to how both positive and negative mindsets can coexist. The goal is for you to make a conscious choice to feel positively about yourself more often than not. You choose not to empower and give credence to the negative self-talk and choose instead to focus on your value.

You can take action by following these steps:

1. **Think about a situation when you felt confident, powerful, worthy, or another positive feeling.**

2. **Describe the feeling and how you felt about yourself, as if you're writing your story of victory.**

   Write down as many positive adjectives as you can think of.

3. **Close your eyes and contemplate each adjective, allowing the feelings associated with each word to fill your body.**

Allow yourself to relive your story of victory. Tell yourself to remember this feeling for other times.

4. **Examine your notebook containing observations of your negative statements, actions, or beliefs.**

    See how you might reframe the situation from the standpoint of feeling positively about yourself.

5. **Watch your step in the future.**

    If you catch yourself putting yourself down, ask yourself how you can restructure this thought, statement, or action to one that is constructive and representative of who you truly are at your best.

Celebrating yourself

When you move into self-doubt and limiting beliefs, you tend to forget the good stuff. You forget your wins, all the times you did feel confident or valued, and the belief that you are indeed capable of success or feeling good. It happens to the best of us. In my past, I have personally berated myself for "never" or "always" doing something wrong, and this went on until I started correcting myself and remembering my victories as well. When the stress response is highly activated, the tendency is to focus on the negative and only the negative. When you make a conscious effort to remember your wins, you're less likely to fall into the trap of self-deprecation while also better regulating the stress response. Celebrate yourself every day for big or small accomplishments, recognizing your worth, strengths, abilities, and value.

These are some actions you can take now:

» **Keep a separate notebook.** Mark down the times when you feel good, victorious, and valued.

» **Note during these times the sources of this feeling.** Did the sense of value come from you or from someone or something recognizing you or validating you?

» **Remember the positive.** If you notice that your sense of accomplishment or values is ignited because someone else recognized you, focus on the positive feeling and see if you can reframe the situation to feeling valued first and then being happy about the accomplishment.

» **Celebrate with self-loving actions as well as words.** Perhaps you buy yourself some flowers or take yourself out to a fine dinner or write yourself a thank-you note or love letter and then mail it to yourself.

Keeping an inventory

As you recognize and validate yourself, start identifying your strengths, abilities, and qualities, especially ones that are unique to you. Look for qualities that you bring to every situation in your life, whether it's work, home, or friendships, for example.

For instance, one of my clients was asked by his boss to create a succession plan, or how he envisioned himself succeeding and what his goals for the future might be. My client felt overwhelmed by the task as he stated, "I don't like to promote myself. I just do my job and hope that I will be recognized and then promoted to whatever is next. I worry about pointing out my weaknesses because then I might be viewed as inadequate."

Can you see how his self-doubt or insecurities were limiting him from looking forward and planning and taking responsibility for his own learning and growth?

I instructed him to approach the task as an exercise that could help him learn more about himself. I told him to list and review his abilities and accomplishments and to also look at his weaknesses to figure out what he might need to learn to move forward. His team, for example, trusted him, and he was extremely adept at listening and helping them feel at ease in speaking to him. He was able to realize that his ability to forge strong relationships with trust and communication is an amazing quality. He also came to understand that one of his weaknesses was understanding some of the technical issues that often arise in the company. So he made a list of ways that would help him gain more technical knowledge.

REMEMBER

Keeping an *inventory* of your strengths and weaknesses is not an exercise where you judge yourself for being good or bad — it is instead a list that's meant to support you to know your value because you're confident in your abilities and you're motivated to learn and grow.

You can start to keep an inventory by taking these actions:

>> **Take an inventory.** Throughout the day, create an ongoing inventory of your qualities, competencies, and accomplishments.

>> **Pause to reflect.** When you feel good about something you have done, take a moment to reflect and elucidate your qualities or abilities that enabled you to accomplish this feat.

>> **Count everything!** Whether you have managed to always get to work on time (quality of being punctual), managed to pull off a surprise party (resourceful and discrete), or able to resolve a conflict between employees at the office (effective communicator, empathic, and so on), everything counts.

>> **Review your positive qualities.** Regularly read over your list, and remind yourself of your positive qualities and ways you're valued.

>> **Note areas of your life where you want to grow and improve.** Look for weaknesses, note setbacks or situations where your efforts were not successful.

>> **Do your research.** Research ways to learn the skills you need to improve on your weaknesses.

Accepting and being your unique self

Knowing your value means understanding that you're human and therefore imperfect. You are, however, perfectly imperfect and one-of-a-kind. Your imperfections aren't cause for putting yourself down, but are rather manifestations of ways you can lift yourself up. They can be road signs that urge you to grow and learn something new or reflections of your own individual uniqueness.

Your goal is to learn to fully accept yourself as the unique individual that you are — imperfections and all. Here are some guidelines to help you get there:

>> **Avoid comparing yourself to others when noticing a perceived imperfection.** Someone else will always perform better or worse than you, and neither makes you more or less valuable.

>> **Get the right focus.** Rather than focus on what is wrong, focus on what is right.

>> **Give your imperfection a new job description: a representation of your perfection as a unique individual.** Always remember that your imperfections add to your uniqueness, of you being you.

>> **Use your mistakes as opportunities for growth.** Learn and develop new skills and knowledge. Use the situation as an opportunity to become stronger and smarter.

>> **Live and act with integrity.** No one can make you feel badly about yourself — only you can do that. When you live your life with integrity, you start believing in your own integrity. Be authentic, truthful, and ethical. If you find yourself wanting to lie or hide or pretend to be someone you're not, examine the reasons you're feeling compelled to act this way, and then align with your worth and integrity. Act from this place.

REMEMBER

You're perfectly imperfect! There is no one like you anywhere.

Holding on to your vision

Wherever and however you find yourself at any particular moment, accept yourself and your behaviors, thoughts, or actions while holding in your heart the vision of your true value. You are human. You will make mistakes. Your limiting beliefs will show up in your life. On some days you'll feel positively, and on other days, negatively. There is no right or wrong. What exists is a vision of who you are from a lens of value. Hold on to it.

This list describes some actions you can take today to hold on to the vision of your value:

>> **Take time to contemplate and meditate on your story of victory.** Allow yourself to see yourself as confident, strong, loving, and compassionate, for example.

>> **Create a vision board.** Write down positive statements, add photos and magazine cutouts, and use markers and crayons to create the picture of your vision. Refer to this "story" anytime you need reminding, by either reading the story or closing your eyes and remembering the vision.

>> **Have a few of your loved ones evaluate your strengths and positive qualities.** Sit opposite at least one person who absolutely adores you — or as many as five or six. Each person takes a minute or more to look into your eyes and speak from their heart, listing your positive qualities and what they admire about you. You listen, receive, and write down what you hear. Keep this list in your purse or wallet to refer back to any time you need.

>> **Find opportunities to accentuate your competencies and abilities.** Then you can continue affirming this vision.

Being loving toward yourself

If you love and believe in yourself, you can forgive yourself for being human and making mistakes. Be kind toward yourself, treating yourself as if you were your own best friend, and find gratitude even in the smallest actions or deeds. When you feel special, you forgive and accept yourself for other imperfections. The key is to love yourself and treat yourself with loving kindness.

Here are some actions you can take now to love yourself more:

>> **Avoid self-critical or derogatory statements.** Especially avoid using words like *should* or *can't*.

- **Speak lovingly.** Ask yourself what you might say to someone you love, and use those words instead.

- **Give thanks.** Focus on what you have rather than on what you don't have. Keep a gratitude journal and reflect on ways you're lucky and grateful.

- **Accept compliments.** Rather than deflect or rebuff, simply say "Thank you." Receive the compliment even if you feel uncomfortable.

- **Honor your body.** Believe that your body is the temple that houses your magnificence. Without a healthy body, you cannot let your light shine in this world.

- **Pamper yourself.** There's nothing wrong with a little love-me gift every now and then, which may be a physical object or simply giving yourself some Me Time to relax and take care of yourself.

Taking Care of YOU

Between exercise, healthy nutrition, meditation, and a good sleep regimen, you can nurture your body to stay strong and vibrant. When you feel strong physically, you have energy, and this energy supports your mental attitude and bandwidth to handle challenges. The problem is that many people let go of positive self-care habits when they're under stress or when they feel that their care is needed elsewhere. The truth is that everyone has value, but no one and nothing has more value than you or your well-being.

When you take care of yourself, you have the energy and bandwidth to care for others or do great work. According to researchers, individuals who make conscious healthy-lifestyle choices feel more masterful about themselves and their accomplishments, feel confident spending time among people who are younger, and uphold a positive mental attitude while tending to live longer and happier lives.

What does this mean for you? It means choose *you*. If you don't take care of you, who will?

Rather than look outward for people, places, or things to complete you, focus on people, places, or things that can support you to be at your best. You want to ask yourself whether it fuels you to really feel good about yourself and within yourself. Ultimately, you want to learn to have a deep connection with yourself, your desires, and your passions, and to do what you can to support yourself to thrive.

The next eight sections are a guide for taking care of you.

Nourish yourself with nutrient-rich food

Eat foods that fuel your mind and body to be healthy and strong. Foods high in fat and sugar content may comfort your anxiety initially, but they also cause inflammation, fatigue, and more depression or anxiety. (See Chapter 16 for more details on healthy nutrition.)

REMEMBER

Food is neither reward or punishment. It's *fuel*. It provides your brain and body with energy, energy that comes from fiber, proteins, fats, vitamins, and minerals.

Exercise and stay active

Find ways to keep your body fit and strong. If it's an activity you enjoy, you're more likely to stick with it. You can jog, dance, or do yoga or weight training and build movement into your everyday routine. (See Chapter 16 for details on improving your physical hardiness.) Here are some different types of exercise to help you stay active:

>> **Metabolic conditioning:** In this type of conditioning, you get your heart rate up at least three times a week.

>> **Resistance training:** Use weights or your own body weight at least two times a week.

>> **Walking:** Walk as often as you can instead of driving.

>> **Nature:** Being in nature will help you feel more energized and less focused on discomfort.

>> **Exercise buddy:** Working out with a friend can help you stay accountable and also ensures that you enjoy the activity.

Connect with support

Turn to other people to support you to feel good about you. In other words, surround yourself with other individuals who can help you reflect and stick to training, a healthy diet, and positive emotions and outlooks. (See Chapters 13 and 14 for details on improving social bonds and relationships.)

>> Choose the right people from your friends and family who you know can support you to be at your best.

>> Let go of, or spend as little time as possible with, people who criticize you and bring you down.

>> Seek counseling or support from a coach, therapist, or healer.

>> Join a support group for extra care of reciprocity.

>> Join a spiritual community where you share positive beliefs and meditation practices and display acts of compassion and gratitude.

Quiet your mind

The mind is a wonderful tool, but negative thinking hinders your ability to connect with your value. Take time to quiet the mind and find peace to enable relaxation and reflection. (See Chapter 9 for more details on quieting the mind.) Here are a few tips to help you quiet your mind:

>> Choose from a variety of meditation practices.

>> Take a mindful walk in nature, focusing on the beauty and wonder around you.

>> Regularly take time to do a mindful breath focus, shifting your awareness away from your thoughts and simply focusing on the movement of the breath and the sensations you experience in your body.

>> Practice visual imagery. For example, you can imagine that when you exhale, your thoughts dissolve into the sunlight and that when you inhale, the sunlight enters your mind. As you continue this process, the light eventually moves throughout your entire body, filling you with a sense of peace and joy.

Heal through your negative emotions

Quieting the mind and building self-awareness enhances your ability to catch your negative emotions before they gain momentum, and then you can use the opportunity to take better care of yourself. (See Chapters 9 and 10 for more on working through negative emotions and beliefs). Here are some suggestions for healing:

>> Pay attention to how you feel from moment to moment.

>> If and when you feel negatively, don't judge yourself — simply be aware and honor your feelings, knowing that your emotions are signals telling you you're in need of care.

>> Notice how your body reacts to these emotions. Where do you feel the energy show up in your body? What does it feel like?

>> Breathe into the area in your body where you feel the emotion. Gently breathe love and compassion into your body.

>> Reflect as you want with regard to why the emotion is there, in what way it's serving you, and how it's a reflection of your feeling hurt, ineffective, or undervalued.

>> Reflect on your value and your positive story.

Have fun!

Wake up in the morning and choose to have a luxurious and adventurous day. According to science, you live a longer and healthier life when you're happy. Here are some suggestions for having fun:

>> Find ways to be more playful. For clues, observe a child at play.

>> Go out with friends and enjoy yourself. (I wrote this book during the 2020 pandemic. If it's still happening when you read this, make sure you practice social distancing and wear masks if required.)

>> Sign up for a dance class, even if you have two left feet, so that you can laugh at yourself, or watch a funny movie.

>> Discover new ways of being that put a smile on your face and a laugh in your heart.

Appreciate all that you have and all that you are

When you're filled with gratitude, you're more likely to see any situation as an opportunity for growth and meaning rather than as bad, or even as a curse. You're more likely to feel happy.

Here is an exercise I have named I Am a Miracle, which you might find helpful, especially in those times that you cannot seem to find anything to be grateful for:

I Am a Miracle

1. Think about the definition of a miracle: "a surprising and welcome event that is not explicable by natural or scientific laws and is therefore considered to be the work of a divine agency."

2. Close your eyes and repeat, "I am a miracle."

3. Smile.

4. Say it again.

5. Smile even wider.

6. Say it again.

7. Open your eyes.

It's okay to rest

Resting and recovery are just as important for your well-being and reaching your goals as being active. Here are some suggestions:

» **Take the time.** Give yourself time and space to meditate, relax, and take some Me Time.

» **Say no when you need to.** It's okay to say no and choose to take care of yourself. You aren't being selfish; rather, you're taking care of yourself so that you can give later.

» **Set boundaries.** Set them in your relationships and with yourself to allow time for you to take care of yourself so that you can be fully present in your life.

» **Get restful sleep.** Turn off electronics in the bedroom, relax a couple of hours before sleep, and make sure your bed and bedroom are comfortable and quiet.

Whatever you choose to do, set the intention to be on the path to loving yourself. Believe in your own ability to create and have joy, ease, comfort, and love. Do what you need to do to feel alive, vibrant, and healthy. When you feel good, you radiate goodness and you attract more of the same.

Allowing Love In

At the core of low self-value is the belief that you aren't worthy of being loved. For most people, over the course of their lifetime, they have experienced hurt, betrayal, neglect, or abandonment that has led them to believe that they aren't important or worthy of love. As a result, people have closed their hearts so as to avoid getting hurt, which has led to a disconnection from themselves and the ability to let the right people in.

I had this realization after a relationship ended in my 20s. I felt betrayed, hurt, and taken advantage of by my former boyfriend. I kept asking myself, "Why?" and "Why doesn't he love me?" and "Why am I not good enough?" and "What did I do wrong?" When I realized that I was berating myself for someone else's actions, I took the time to sit with my emotions, my negative beliefs, and the pain in my heart to try to answer those questions truthfully and with compassion. The truth was, I realized, that my value was not predicated on whether he loved me; that I did nothing wrong other than trust someone I knew wasn't trustworthy (the signs were there before), which happens to the best of us; that I was guilty of loving and nothing else and was therefore forgiven; and that just because someone doesn't love me doesn't mean that I am not loveable. I understood that I was looking outside of myself to feel loveable when I had the ability to provide that love to myself. It was then that I started embarking on my journey to understanding love better, to love myself better and let love in.

REFLECTION

Do you let love in? Do you accept compliments, allow people to help you or make sure you take care of yourself?

You don't have to wait for other people to give you love to have it. You can do it yourself by opening your heart to love itself and by taking the myriad action steps and techniques I describe that involve taking care of you. You can start now to allow love in by

>> Being vulnerable and asking for help from your support people

>> Practicing gratitude and appreciation

>> Allowing yourself to feel, even negatively, and seeing all of yourself as valuable

>> Intentionally nurturing yourself through your self-care practices (nutrition, exercise, and sleep, for example)

>> Spending time in nature and feeling a sense of connection and awe

>> Engaging in meditation practices that build self-compassion, love, and forgiveness, like the following meditation for opening the heart.

Meditations to open the heart have been done by many a healer and meditation practitioner in a myriad of variations. There is no right way — just the way of opening your heart to receiving some form of love, whether it's gratitude, compassion, or awe, for example.

The following is a meditation exercise that will guide you to open your heart so that you can fully receive love:

1. **Find a comfortable position.**

Make it somewhere quiet where no one will disturb you.

2. **Close your eyes and bring your awareness to the center of your chest.**

This area is known as the *heart center*.

3. **Gently breathe into and out of the heart center, counting 1-2-3 as you breathe in and 1-2-3-4-5-6 as you breathe out.**

4. **As you breathe in and out, observe any sensations or feelings that you're experiencing in your chest.**

Does it feel open, closed, relaxed, tight, heavy, or light? What emotions do you notice? Observe without judgment. There's no right or wrong. You're just observing energy.

5. **Be aware that you're observing energy in your heart and noticing what it feels like.**

6. **Allow your breath to start moving the energy in your chest, like a curtain that moves with the breeze.**

It's effortless. Just let it move in and out with your breath.

The energy in your chest is gently moving with your breath like a curtain that moves in the breeze.

7. **As you breathe in, imagine that you're breathing in unlimited love and infinite intelligence from the universe into your heart, and that when you exhale, you're simply letting go of everything else.**

Breathe in unlimited love and infinite intelligence, exhaling and letting go of everything else.

With every breath, your heart fills with unlimited love and infinite intelligence until it's so full that this love and intelligence begin to overflow.

8. **Observe that there is no separation between your heart and the heart of the entire universe, because you're connected by unlimited love and infinite intelligence.**

You may want to say to yourself, "Our hearts are one heart."

You may want to see other hearts as your heart connects with other hearts, unlimited love, and infinite intelligence flowing freely.

"Our hearts are one heart."

9. **Stay in this state as long as you want.**

10. **When you're ready, give thanks for the fullness of your heart and the fullness of your being.**

Chapter **13**

Creating Quality Relationships

Studies show that positive social relationships are linked to greater psychological and physical well-being. Close relationships — among family, friends, neighbors, or colleagues — offer you emotional and material support, help you feel accepted and more connected, and give you a sense of belonging — all qualities that can give you a boost when times are tough. Different people might serve different purposes in your life, such as one friend you turn to for practical advice and another who provides emotional support. The healthier the relationship and the higher its quality, the stronger the bond and the more that relationship will support you to be resilient.

This chapter helps you examine your relationships and offers ways to create quality relationships that are meaningful and secure and that boost your resilience. (For more information on quality relationships, see Chapter 7.)

What Constitutes a Quality Relationship?

Quality relationships are those in which you feel happy, safe, connected, and understood. These relationships thrive on mutual respect, commitment, trust, and empathy. Rather than succumb to misunderstandings and dissolution during conflict and stress, these relationships instead grow stronger, and the bonds deeper. Whether they are platonic, familial, romantic, or collegial, quality relationships share these seven foundational characteristics:

>> **Commitment:** Strong social bonds happen when the individuals are committed and invested in the relationship for the long run. They make the relationship a priority and are committed to its growth and success. They commit to one another and are loyal, honest, and respectful. They support one another to feel secure enough to feel vulnerable and to ask for help.

>> **Respect and interest:** Building deeper bonds means getting to know another person more intimately. The desire to get to know someone better — their past and current ideas, beliefs, or thoughts — invariably shows that you value them and respect their journey while they in turn feel the same with regard to you.

>> **Healthy boundaries:** Committing, giving, and loving are most effective in strengthening social bonds when healthy boundaries are established, where each person makes sure they have time and space to take care of themselves. Creating healthy boundaries involves respecting not only the other person but also yourself.

>> **Trust and reliance:** Without trust, there is no security. Trust isn't easy to come by, but it can be fostered within a relationship and within yourself. The more you trust people, the deeper you allow your connections with others to grow; and the more the connections grow, the more trust is fostered.

>> **Open communication:** A sense of security is also cultivated when people communicate with respect and empathy, listening mindfully and being present to another person's wants and needs. The better the communication, the deeper the bonding and the more fluid the communication. In other words, when you feel safe, expressing yourself, your needs, and opinions flow more easily.

>> **Empathy:** Social bonds deepen when you take the time to truly understand another person, to put yourself in their shoes. With empathy, you're driven to care about another person and act on behalf of their welfare, and you're more able to understand the other person's plight, even in the face of conflict.

>> **Reciprocity:** Reciprocal giving of, and to, one another is necessary for the strengthening of social bonds. Whether it's love, time, gifts, or a lending hand, reciprocity is an expression of mutual respect, commitment, and love.

REMEMBER

Trust is formed when individuals know that mutual and consistent reliance exists.

Evaluating Your Relationships

Using these foundational characteristics, you can now evaluate the strength of your relationships. As you observe your relationships over time and collect the data, you come closer to understanding which social connections you want to keep and which areas can use improvement.

Making a list

The first step in the examination process is to take an inventory of your top ten social connections. If you want to add more, you can, if you feel these connections are important to you. You will use this list to help you determine which relationships are most meaningful to you and which bonds you want to build as you go forward.

Write down the name, the category of association (family, work, client, or friend, for example), the basis of your relationship, and the average time you spend with them either in person or talking to them on the phone or via video during a normal week.

This initial evaluation helps you see where and with whom you invest your time when it comes to people you care about. You might realize that you care deeply about someone yet are not investing much time into the relationship. You might also realize that you're spending a lot of time with a colleague because of work demands and spending little time with a friend you care about.

For an example of what your list might look like, here is my client Alice's inventory:

Name	Association	Basis of Relationship	Time Spent
Sarah	Sister	Don't have much in common, but we are blood relatives	A couple of hours a week
Andrea	Friend	Common interests such as shopping, exercising, and dining out	Once a week in person, and talk or text daily
Jill	Colleague	Work interests, especially complaining about our boss	More than five hours a day during the weekday and occasionally in the evenings and on weekends
David	Father	Obligation — an aging father	When I visit once a month

Name	Association	Basis of Relationship	Time Spent
Ruth	Friend	Conversations, with someone you're deeply connected to, that can go on for hours about life and spiritual subjects	Talking on the phone or texting, from once a week to once a month
James	Significant other	Little in common, but a shared love for one another	Most weekends and a couple of nights during the week

Determining your level of commitment

Once you have compiled your list, the next step is to think about each relationship and how committed you are to seeing each one grow and deepen, keeping in mind that strong bonds take work and dedication. Do you want to improve your relationship with your sibling or parent? Does this relationship add value to your life? Is this a temporary social connection, or do you see yourself being connected to this person for the long haul? How dedicated are you? This part of the evaluation propels you to dig deeper into each relationship to help you determine where you might want to put your focus while also showing you what aspects of your relationships can be improved on to strengthen the bonds.

This section looks at three qualities that determine the level of commitment:

» **Mutual rewards** afforded by the relationships, or what each person is gaining from the relationship

» **Mutual investment,** or what each person is putting in or investing

» **Mutual focus,** or whether each person is making this relationship a priority

As you read the following questions, evaluate your own behavior or attitude and then consider the other person's. Take notes in a notebook, and then add columns to your inventory list that look like this:

Name	Association	Basis of relationship	Time spent	Rewards me / you	Investments me / you	Focus me / you	Negatives

Mutual rewards

Rewards come in many forms, big and small. They can be monetary or material, emotional, physical, or professional. In a separate column, list the rewards each person acquires from the relationship, such as in these examples:

>> What rewards do you receive from being in this relationship?

>> What rewards does the other person receive?

>> What is the value of this relationship?

>> How does it support you or them to feel?

>> What does it support you or them to be able to do?

>> Do you feel safe?

>> Do you feel loved and respected?

>> Do they feel the same?

Mutual investment

Mutual investments include the time, finances, love, or interest each person brings to the table. Add another column listing mutual investments.

>> What is your investment?

>> Is the other person investing too? If so, what are they investing?

>> What do you bring to the table?

>> Are you putting in the same amount of effort or time?

>> What sort of emotional contributions do you each put in?

>> Are you doing your part in staying in touch and checking in? Are they?

Mutual focus

Deepening social bonds means being focused on specific relationships and not spreading yourself thin. Evaluate each person, deciding whether your intention is to put more focus on the relationship, and contemplate whether you have been giving this connection enough focus or too much focus. Add another column where you can note whether you want to focus on this relationship. Here are some examples:

>> Is this relationship a priority to you?

>> Do you feel that you're a priority to this person?

>> Is one person focusing on the relationship more than the other?

>> What does making a relationship a priority mean to you?

>> Are you or the other person spreading yourself too thin?

Examining respect and healthy boundaries

Quality relationships have healthy boundaries where all involved parties share *mutual respect*, where you respect yourself and one another enough to create boundaries that support you to navigate the relationship and stay happy and healthy. Further examine your relationships by considering the following questions and continuing to write down relevant notes and comments:

» **Validation:** Do you validate and does the other person validate? List ways you validate one another. Do you honor one another's feelings and needs, whether it's needing more attention or more space or the freedom to be angry? Or do you tend to judge, put down, or belittle?

» **Curiosity:** Are you or the other person curious? List ways you show curiosity. Are you curious about one another? Do you ask questions, wanting to know more about their day, their opinions, or their thoughts, feelings, or beliefs? Or do you tend to focus mostly on yourself and rarely ask questions?

» **Attentive listening:** Do you listen and does the other person listen? Examine how attentive you are when listening to one another. Do you listen without interrupting or tuning out the other?

» **Honesty:** Are you or the other person honest? Do you respect one another enough to be honest, trusting in their ability to handle any kind of news or information? How honest and truthful are you in this relationship?

» **Thoughtfulness:** Are you or the other person thoughtful? Do you make an effort to remember information the other person has told you, what you both might like and don't like? Are you thoughtful when asking one another about an event, remembering what that person cares about or has been working so hard for?

» **Celebration:** Do you or the other person celebrate? Do you celebrate one another's successes, even when you feel down? Are you happy to see one another succeed? How often do you celebrate the other person?

» **Honoring space:** Do you or the other person honor space? Do you respect one another's space and the need to self-reflect and do self-care? Do you respect their space even when you're feeling needy? Do you feel that you're given time and space to reenergize and replenish?

» **Accountability:** Are you accountable and is the other person accountable? Do you take responsibility for the role or mistakes you may have made without casting blame or shame on one another? Are you accountable for your actions?

» **Showing value:** Do you show value and does the other person show value? Do you value one another's opinion, decisions, or actions, even though you might disagree? When do you most value one another? Is it sometimes, never, or always? Is it mutual?

» **Respecting self-care:** Do you or the other person respect the need for self-care? Respect involves taking care of yourself and supporting the other person's efforts to do the same. Do you feel supported to take care of yourself? Does the relationship demand more time than you have? Does the other person respect themselves? Do their actions and attitudes support your self-care or sabotage?

» **Acceptance:** Do you or the other person show acceptance? Do you feel accepted for being who you are? Do you accept the other person for their strengths and weaknesses? What are your expectations of this person? Do you feel you meet their expectations of you?

Assessing trust and reliance

Respect and commitment build trust, and it's this trust that allows you to feel safe, know that you can rely on one another, be vulnerable, and be your authentic self. The following are questions for you to consider, which will guide you to better assess whether your relationship has trust and how well you can rely on one another:

» **Consistency:** Are you or the other person consistent and reliable with your actions and presence? Do you stay true to your word?

» **Showing up:** Are you or the other person showing up? Being consistent involves showing up. Do you show up during the good times and the hard times? When you're together, are you fully present? Are you showing up as yourself or being someone else in order to fit in or to be better liked?

» **Active listening:** Do you or the other person listen? You've already addressed this question, but you can evaluate it with respect to enabling trust. Feeling heard helps you feel safe. Do you listen so that the other person feels heard? Do you feel heard?

» **Vulnerability:** Are you or the other person vulnerable? Can you ask for help? Can you let down your guard? Can you be you without fear of being judged or bashed for making mistakes? Can you admit to making mistakes?

» **Empathic communication:** Do you or the other person communicate empathically? Do you mean what you say, think before you act, and speak from your heart? Do you feel understood? Do you try to understand the other person? Do you give one another space to speak and to be heard? Do they "get you?"

» **Commitment:** Are you or the other person committed? Is this relationship a priority? Do you feel like you're a priority to this other person? Is this person a priority to you?

» **Truthfulness:** Are you or the other person truthful? Can you be trusted? Are you honest and true to your word? Do you keep promises? Do you admit when you're wrong? Are you loyal and/or faithful?

Evaluating communication and empathy

Mutual respect and trust are conveyed when individuals in a relationship listen and communicate with empathy. Good communication is the key to building strong social bonds. The following questions will help you evaluate how effective communication is in your relationship:

» **Presence and listening:** Do you or the other person always listen? In answering this question, think of how often you might daydream, think of an answer as the person is talking, feel annoyed and lose patience, judge, or argue. Are you an arguer? Does the other person tend to shut down, or are they good at listening?

» **Reflecting back:** Do you or the other person ask and reflect back? When you're engaged in a conversation and you're curious about the other person's ideas or thoughts, you ask questions. To show that you're listening and taking in the information, you can reflect back what you have heard. Do you follow this process? Do you confirm what you have heard and avoid misunderstandings? Do you tend to be misunderstood or to misunderstand this person? Do you assume that you know what the other person is thinking, or do you ask? Do you invite feedback?

» **Encouragement:** Do you or the other person encourage conversation? Do you feel encouraged to talk when you're upset? Is this person someone who wants to talk only about the good things? Do you encourage open conversation without judgment with this person?

» **Being silent:** Are you or the other person comfortable saying nothing? How comfortable can you be not saying anything and just allowing the silence, or simply letting the other person speak?

» **Being empathic:** Are you or the other person empathetic? Do you put yourself in the other person's shoes to better understand them? Do you judge or feel judged? Are you able to move through conflict with empathy?

» **Unassuming:** Do you avoid, or does the other person avoid, assumptions? Because you think you understand, do you make assumptions? Do you feel labeled by the other person for having beliefs or thoughts that may or may not be true?

» **Emotional balance:** Do emotions get the best of you or the other person? Do you somehow find yourself arguing with this person often? Do you feel triggered emotionally? Do emotions get the better of either of you when disagreeing?

Taking a good look at reciprocity

You can now evaluate the give-and-take in the relationship, examining whether you're giving or receiving more than the other person or whether it's equal. Giving and receiving refers to everything — time, space, love, financial support, or gentle touch, for example. Asking yourself the following questions will help you assess how balanced reciprocity is in your relationships:

» **Which one are you or the other person?** As you examine the relationship, evaluate whether there's a role that you predominantly play as giver or receiver or both. Who gives more in the relationship? Is it balanced? Are you comfortable receiving? Do you feel safe receiving, or do you feel that taking from this person changes the power dynamic? Do you feel safe enough to both give and receive? Do you see a pattern in this relationship?

» **What do you or the other person get out of it?** What do you get from giving? What do you get from receiving? What is the benefit? Do you expect something back when you give, or expect to give back when you receive? Do you get upset when you give and don't get back? Does the other person do the same? What is the motivation to give or receive?

» **Who has whose back? Do you have their back?** Are you there for one another during hard times equally? During the last hardship, was this person supportive? How did they support you? Did you support them during their last difficult challenge? Do you support one another in the day-to-day struggles or just the big ones or vice versa? Are you reliable? Is the other person reliable? How often do you check in or check up?

» **Is the love flowing truthfully?** Do you give freely of your heart, or do you hold back? How about the other person? Are you helping this person out of obligation or because you want to? Do you often have feelings of guilt or fear when it comes to supporting or not supporting this person? Would they feel this way about you? Do you feel you have to guilt-trip this person into spending time with you?

» **Do you feel lifted up?** How do you feel after spending time with this person? Do you feel energized and lifted up? Or do you feel exhausted and drained? Does it feel like there's an equal energy exchange?

Building Lasting Social Bonds

Relationships can't be perfect because they're made up of humans who aren't perfect. Relationships grow and change just like people do, in other words, so it takes continuous effort and learning to build social bonds that pass the test of time and hardship. Though you can take certain actions on your own, some require all parties to partake in order to strengthen the relationship bonds. Whether you're looking to improve a current relationship that you have evaluated or to create a new one, you can work toward improving the bonds in your relationship by completing practice exercises that I cover in the next few sections.

Communicating with presence and curiosity

Whether it's at business or at home, in my experience, breaks in relationships occur largely because of a break in communication, either talking at, talking down, talking over, or not talking at all. To improve communication, you want to be fully present, speaking and listening mindfully and showing that you care. (See Chapter 9 for more about quieting to listen.) You can do the following 10-minute exercise every day to get you on track to effective communication:

1. Choose a subject.

This exercise begins by choosing a subject that you and your partner want to talk about. Perhaps it's about a situation at work, a conflict you both are having, or a deep desire you each have — or maybe you're simply relaying what happened that day.

2. Set the role.

Decide which of the two of you is the listener and which is the speaker.

3. Set the time.

Set a timer for five minutes or simply be aware of the time.

4. Listen attentively.

If you're the listener, listen attentively without interrupting, thinking of a reply, or offering advice or opinions. Be fully present and allow space for the other person to speak. When the speaker is finished, allow a pause of silence. Then reflect back what you have heard, showing you have listened, and ask questions, showing your interest and desire to know more of their opinion or story.

5. **Ask and thank.**

   When the time is up, the listener thanks the speaker for sharing their story, and then the speaker thanks the listener for listening, unless the listener has more questions, then continue until you have satisfied your curiosity.

6. **Reset and go again.**

   Reset the timer and switch roles so that the listener now can talk about their day, their opinions, their feelings, and so forth while the other person listens with presence and curiosity.

REMEMBER

When you do this practice regularly, communicating with presence and curiosity becomes a habit. The exercise not only helps strengthen your connection with one another but also enhances feelings of respect, empathy, and trust.

Building trust and reliance

You can deepen the bonds in your relationship by enhancing a sense of trust, by trusting more yourself *and* being trustworthy so that invariably both parties believe that the other person is reliable and consistent. Trust, unfortunately, can be easily broken, not necessarily because people lie or are unfaithful, but because they fail to be true to their word, show up late, break their promises, or act self-ishly. By implementing practices that cause both parties to be reliable and consistent, you can build more trust in the relationship. Here are five exercises that can help you build trust in your relationships:

>> **Supply random tasks.** Give one another one or two random small tasks to complete once or twice a week. It may be to pick up your favorite toothpaste, find a good movie, or text a photo of a butterfly. Often, silly random tasks lighten up the mood and take away the feeling that one is being tested. Following through on the task shows that you care and that you're true to your word.

>> **Plan dates and show up.** Plan a date and set the intention that it won't be canceled and that neither person will be late. Make sure that it's a time and an activity you know you can commit to, either once a week or every other week.

>> **Share a fear.** Being able to be vulnerable in a relationship is a sign of trust and trustworthiness. Entrust the other person with something you're scared of doing, being, or feeling. This is a perfect subject for the attentive communication exercise.

>> **Do the surrender embrace.** You may be familiar with the trust fall, which involves standing with your back to one or more people and falling backward, trusting that they will catch you. This exercise is a bit easier to do with one

person, which you can do sitting down or standing up. You sit with your back to the other person and then lean back into them. Completely surrender all your weight so that you're limp, while the other person holds you and rests in this position for five full minutes. It isn't as easy as it sounds!

>> **Listen and be thoughtful.** Each person tells the other person one interesting fact about themselves regarding something they love. You then each have one week to not only remember and recall this fact but also bring something to the other person that is reflective of this love. For instance, you might love pizza and so your partner brings home a pizza magnet or a gift certificate for a pizza restaurant. Being thoughtful shows that you care and that you can be trusted to listen.

Supporting and being supported

Being supportive and supported are of paramount importance when it comes to having strong social bonds. Have you realized that you can be more supportive in your relationships or that you need more support yourself? Sometimes all it takes is being able to communicate your needs. Here are six actions you can employ to build a sense of support in your relationships:

>> **Don't assume.** Don't assume that the other person knows what's in your head and what you need, and don't assume that you know everything, either. Take the time to ask about their needs and what they might want with regard to support from you. Do the same with them.

>> **Get clear on wants.** How is someone else supposed to know how to support you if you don't know what you want or need yourself? The clearer each person is, the better they can support one another. You may want to create a "want list," or a list of ways you want to be supported.

>> **Ask for help.** People can't support you if you don't ask, and if you don't ask, the answer is always no. Take the chance of being vulnerable and ask for support. If the other person supports you, you know that they might be a keeper. Once you have aligned with your wants, ask for help.

>> **Check in regularly.** Life has a habit of making people busy, so they tend to become self-involved and forget to check in on the people they care about. Depending on the relationship, set a time together for checking in, either daily, every other day, or weekly.

>> **Listen and give advice only when asked.** Being able to be present and listen when someone needs to speak is usually what people want most. If they want advice, they will ask. You aren't being supportive if you give advice where it

isn't wanted. Usually, to feel validated, people just want a shoulder to cry on or an ear to listen.

>> **Take care.** Whether it's through acts of kindness or anticipating that care is needed, regularly show that you care. Ask each other questions, pick each other up when someone is down, and bring the person soup when they're sick. Make an agreement and a commitment to one another to be caring and to communicate when you feel that you aren't receiving care so as to be clear about your needs.

Accepting and acknowledging

Everyone has times when they're more judgmental or less accepting of other people or their behaviors, looks, or beliefs, and it's usually when they aren't feeling good about themselves. It's at these times that people also wish their relationship was different, essentially wishing the other person to be something they are not. Such disrespect and devaluing can be the downfall of even a good relationship. The flipside of this behavior is accepting the other person for who they are and sincerely acknowledging their greatness. Here are five ways to practice acceptance and acknowledgement:

>> **Accept imperfection.** Everyone is human and therefore perfectly imperfect. Keep this point in mind before you get upset about the other person not being who you want them to be. There is no perfect person and no perfect relationship. Accept the person for who they are, warts and all.

>> **Let go of expectations.** If you find yourself being judgmental, take time to examine your expectations. Draw on your own inner resources to attract the love and attention you need so that you don't put expectations on other people.

>> **Find the good.** It's easy to find the problems or to point out what might be wrong, and unfortunately, when people become attached to the negative, it's hard to see the light through the thick of the trees in the forest. Find the good and make the effort to remember it. Make a practice together stating three things you're grateful for when it comes to the other person.

>> **Acknowledge regularly.** Boost one another by recognizing positive things about the other person, big or small. Acknowledge their beautiful smile or express your pride in all the hard work they put in to accomplish a task. Recognize small and big efforts, accomplishments, personality traits, and so forth. The key is to be sincere and consistent and to do it because you can and want to, not because you have to.

>> **Be kind and thoughtful.** When you do something kind for another person, you improve the bond not only because that person will like you better, but because you will like yourself better, too. Research shows that when you do something nice for someone, you personally become happier; and other studies show that kindness improves trust and happiness and strengthens relationships.

Settling differences

Being able to navigate disagreements and differences without fighting and acting disrespectfully is another key to building strong social connections. When you have attentive communication skills, trust, respect, support, and acceptance, this ability becomes stronger. In other words, when you're present and mindful, when you respect and accept the other person and their beliefs, and when you trust that you're loved and safe, a disagreement stays just that: a disagreement. Here are eight steps you can take to help you settle differences in a peaceful way:

1. **Pause it.**

Before you both lose your cool, agree to take a pause. Use this time to breathe deeply, calm your emotions, and take care of yourself. It may take moments, hours, or a day. The more you practice emotional regulation on your own, though, the quicker you find your calm. When you're quieter, you're better able to be present, open, empathic, and respectful.

2. **Lose the ego.**

As you get ready to enter into a conversation, set the intention to lose your ego and be humble and willing to be wrong — or, if nothing else, to relinquish your need to be right or to win. Decide that winning comes only by deepening your connection and understanding.

3. **Communicate attentively.**

Use the attentive communication exercise to ensure that you stay mindful and attentive, allowing each person to speak their truth.

4. **See value.**

Give value to your feelings and opinions as well as the other person's. Everyone has the right to feel the way they do and to hold their respective opinions. It's people's differences that bring them together and enable them to learn from one another.

5. Step back.

Try to see the bigger picture. This situation is one scene in the bigger movie. What is the underlying theme? What is the greater issue or desire? Stepping back helps you put the situation into better perspective.

6. Let go.

You usually hold on to an opinion or belief because doing so helps you feel more validated, and you feel less so when others disagree with you, especially if you value their opinion. By honoring your own and the other person's feelings and beliefs, you let go of the need to be validated by another person or to be right. You're both valued, regardless.

7. Agree to disagree.

When you take care of your emotions and see value in everything, you're less attached to the outcome. You can agree to disagree.

8. Forgive.

Practice extending compassion and forgiveness to one another. Everyone hurts, and everyone is human. People make mistakes and act without thought sometimes. Trust that there is no intention to harm and then let go of the issue. Holding on to resentments and allowing past mistakes to dictate your feelings can ruin the relationship. Love, let go, forgive, and see the situation as an opportunity for growth and getting closer as you learn more about one another.

Investing time in and time out

Strong relationships require an investment of your time and care. They also require that you take time out for yourself, to ensure that you aren't getting lost in the relationship and giving up the time you need to rest and reflect. In a partnership, this often means setting healthy boundaries that help determine the time you put in and the time you step out to take care of yourself. It also means assessing the quality and quantity of your time together and apart. Here are ten ways to manage and invest your time in and out of relationships:

>> **Add meaning.** Add meaning to the relationship by having meaningful conversations, sharing dreams and goals, or making special excursions that bring you greater understanding or growth.

>> **Lighten up.** Keep joy and play high on your list. Remember to laugh, including at yourself. Let down your guard and do silly and ridiculous things. People who have fun together are better able to stick together.

>> **Be excited about the good.** Practice being present with one another and appreciating every moment together, as though you're seeing a long-lost friend.

>> **Support through the hard.** Invest in the relationship with care and support, through the good times and hard.

>> **Enjoy the quiet.** Enjoy silence together. Treasure the quiet and be present with one another without the need for words or other distractions.

>> **Savor the ordinary.** Create routines that you do together, and enjoy the process, especially when it's something ordinary, like cleaning the house or making dinner. Cherish the time together, no matter the activity.

>> **Be comfortable being uncomfortable.** Spend time doing things the other person likes even when you don't. It shows that you care and are interested in their interests.

>> **Be thoughtful.** Perform random gestures of kindness and do thoughtful things for one another. Life can get crazy and people tend to take other people for granted. Be mindful and do one thing a day that is thoughtful and kind for one another.

>> **Be comfortable being alone.** You don't have to be together all the time to know that you're cared for. Enjoy your alone-time and see it as an opportunity to have space to reflect, regroup, practice self-care, and assert your own wholeness. The small stuff adds up.

>> **Encourage personal self-care.** You may enjoy doing self-care practices together — like exercise, healthy nutrition, restful sleep, meditation, and being out in nature — but ensure that you take Me Time to take care of yourself. You're not responsible for the other person's self-care habits — only your own.

Strengthening Bonds by Sharing

Research shows that sharing activities with people improves social bonding. I personally find that pleasure is often tripled when I am sharing something enjoyable with someone I care about. I feel good not only because I've helped bring joy to another person but also because I am being cared for — because the other person is witnessing and participating in this event with me. Whether you engage in physical fitness activities together, share a meal, or simply share interest in a conversation, when you share, it's an expression of caring and it brings you closer.

Sharing news and gratitude

Sharing your days with one another can help strengthen your relationship bond, especially when you're both attentive and curious. Many people, especially as they endure stressful experiences, however, spend much of their time together complaining or talking about their problems. Though being able to share your misery and being heard by another person is important, you want to balance it out with sharing positives that lift you up.

TIP

One exercise that I find my clients enjoy is the practice of sharing news and gratitude, where you take a few minutes each, attentively communicating and sharing what happened in your day, starting with the highs that you're grateful for and followed by the lows, if there are any. This exercise also teaches you to look for silver linings and stay positive, even during hardship.

Sharing goals and dreams

How do you feel when someone asks you and is truly interested in knowing your goals and your dreams? It's a good feeling that attracts you to this person, because you feel that they care about you. Sharing your goals and dreams with one another helps you engage in meaningful conversations as you understand what is important to each of you and how you're inspired, and it also engages the other person to support and be involved in making your dreams come to life.

TIP

The relationship can further strengthen when you share a dream or vision together. Create a vision board together that outlines a dream, a project, or some plans you want to make together. Map out activities and action steps you can do together that can bring you closer to your goals.

Sharing worries and fears

Life isn't all roses and sunshine, and getting to know someone means learning about their hopes and dreams as well as their worries and fears. Being able to be vulnerable with one another improves trust and strengthens social bonds.

TIP

Engage in meaningful conversations where you share your past and what you have experienced and learned, in addition to your hurts and disappointments and where or when you might need support.

Sharing adventures

Doing activities together that are memorable and exciting will surely seal your social bond. Whether you take a trip, try out a new dive for dinner and drinks, or try a new sport, sharing unique experiences together will help you create special memories together that bring positive associations and your relationship closer.

TIP

Choose an activity that is out of both your comfort zones so that you can share the thrill of the challenge with one another as well as the risk. Plan it out or be spontaneous and go for it!

Sharing the mundane

Talk about the weather, the show you watched on TV, what you ate for dinner, or the state of traffic on your way home. Go grocery shopping together, share a meal, or clean the house. The key is to not take the mundane activities for granted. You get to be together, so whatever the activity, it's something that can bring you closer.

TIP

Set an intention to take a moment every day to be grateful for what you get to do together. Remember that you're getting to do this very basic activity with *this* person.

Sharing physical contact

Each relationship is different, of course, but whether it's a friend or a lover, some form of physical contact is sure to bring you closer. Physical connection is a human need and can raise levels of the feel-good love hormone oxytocin as well as other happy chemicals, like serotonin and dopamine. The more pleasure you experience, the more likely you go back for more, enhancing the social bond.

TIP

Check with one another to find out what the preferences are when it comes to physical contact. Check your own comfort level and needs, and express these to the other person. This includes a gentle touch when you're checking in to see whether the other person is okay, a hug when you greet one another, or being sexually intimate.

Sharing hearts

Deepening the bonds of your relationships means opening your hearts to one another, to share yourself and your hopes, dreams, worries, doubts, interests, history, and adventures — and the mundane. When you feel safe and you trust, you can better surrender your heart to another person, bringing more richness to the relationship.

TIP

I have found the following heart sharing exercise to be a profoundly effective way to practice surrendering your hearts with one another:

1. Sit face-to-face.

2. Look into each other's eyes.

3. Smile.

4. Breathe in as deeply as you can.

5. Exhale as completely as you can.

6. Bring your breath to your heart center, and breathe in and out through your heart center.

7. Breathe infinite love into your heart center until your heart is so full that it opens like a flower and the love begins to overflow as you exhale, without effort.

8. As the love overflows, imagine that it's flowing out of your heart to your partner's heart. As that person is doing the same, a circle of love flows between both of your hearts.

9. Place your right hand on your own heart and your left on your partner's heart, showing that you're both receiving love and giving love.

10. You may want to each say to one another, "I feel you. I see you. I hear you. I am with you. I cherish you."

This is a wonderful exercise to do regularly because it sets the stage for love and trust to be solidified in the relationship.

Chapter **14**

Building a Resilient Community

ndividual resilience is influenced by the circles of support that you're connected to. These networks of support — which can consist of your family, neighbors, friends, colleagues, or spiritual community — are instrumental in providing you with emotional, practical, and material support, especially when you're faced with challenges. The more resilient the community that supports you, the more you benefit. The resilience of this community is dependent on the strength and cohesiveness of the social bonds between members and on the levels of cooperation, collaboration, mutual respect, trust, and effective communication. (For more details on what makes a resilient community, see Chapter 8.)

This chapter focuses on helping you examine your social support networks and guides you to evaluate and build a community that is also resilient.

Determining Who Your People Are

A *community* consists of a group of people who share values, goals, obligations, duties, responsibilities, and interests, and who essentially feel that they belong together. The community can be a family unit, a neighborhood, a sports team, a group of friends, or a network of colleagues. The resilient community is the group of people you want to belong to that also has your back in times of need.

Until my early 40s, I had a hard time sticking to an exercise regimen and a healthy diet. In and out of physical therapy for back problems, I easily lost motivation to keep exercising, and my weight yo-yoed for over 25 years. Finally, in my mid-40s, I joined CrossFit, a fitness community made up of like-willed people who want to become more fit and be supported by their peers in getting there. Together, the community celebrates accomplishments and supports individuals to meet their goals. Whether sweating and suffering together, following the same nutrition guidelines to improve well-being and performance, or supporting one another in times of personal hardships, the community provided me with social support that helped me stick with my training, follow a healthy diet, maintain positive emotions and outlook, and develop a more resilient attitude. They also provided me with emotional support and care when my mother suddenly took ill and was hospitalized for over a month. I learned that I could not only become physically fit and mentally tough but also be vulnerable and lean on people for emotional support — actions I had always avoided.

REFLECTION

Do you know who your people are? Does a specific group come to mind? Whom do you turn to in times of need? Do you feel part of a community?

If you read this entire chapter, you'll have the opportunity to assess your social support networks, communities, or teams and to evaluate whether you feel you can count on people, whether you share the same values, whether you share a sense of trust and respect, and how well you collaborate. You will also find strategies to help build stronger and more resilient communities. As with your close relationships, building a strong community takes time and effort because social bonds need to be nurtured and trust built.

Evaluating Your Communities

This section guides you to thoroughly evaluate your communities, particularly focusing on the traits that make a community resilient, which includes shared values, goals, and resources; the effectiveness of collaboration; defined roles and communication; and the existence of empathy, encouragement, fairness, and trusted leadership.

Making a list

Make a list of the groups you belong to. You can include your family, spiritual group, sports team, business network, and others.

Once you have made a list, the next step is to make an assessment. Your goal is to evaluate each of the above mentioned (shared values, effective collaboration, leadership, and so on) qualities by answering questions and doing a variety of exercises. I recommend you keep a separate working notebook for each group, so that you can add ideas and observations on a regular basis.

Sharing values

Most communities form because the members of the group share the same values. Certain values — such as respect, commitment, compassion, cooperation, and reliance — reflect a community that will likely be more resilient in tough times. What are the shared core values that enable the group to bond? Do the group's values match your own values?

The following exercise guides you to assess your own core values as well as the group's:

1. **From the following list of words, choose as many relevant ones that describe the group's core values.**

2. **Choose as many relevant words as describe your core values.**

3. **Choose three or four words from each list that get to the heart of the group's and your values.**

4. **See how they match up.**

5. **Write a few sentences describing the shared values of your community.**

Appreciation	Advocacy	Accountability	Boldness	Be the best	Caring
Challenge	Charity	Commitment	Compassion	Cooperation	Collaboration
Contribution	Credibility	Consistency	Creativity	Curiosity	Decisiveness
Dedication	Dependability	Diversity	Empathy	Enthusiasm	Ethics
Excellence	Fairness	Family	Friendship	Freedom	Fun
Generosity	Growth	Happiness	Health	Honesty	Humility
Humor	Inclusiveness	Individuality	Innovation	Inspiration	Joy

Kindness	Knowledge	Leadership	Learning	Love	Loyalty
Mindfulness	Motivation	Optimism	Originality	Passion	Performance
Professionalism	Recognition	Relationships	Reliability	Resilience	Responsibility
Security	Service	Spirituality	Stability	Success	Teamwork
Thoughtfulness	Tradition	Trust	Uniqueness	Versatility	Vision

Committing to shared goals

You've come together for a reason. Are you clear on what is bringing you together? Try to see whether you can delineate the purpose or the commitment your community might have. Perhaps you're committed to improve your skills in a particular sport or hobby, a political platform, or a neighborhood safety group. You might also want to use this opportunity to inquire whether there's a purpose that you want the community to build or strengthen or move toward.

The following questions guide you to evaluate your own goals as well as the goals of the group:

Examine your own goals first:

>> Why did I join this group?

>> What purpose does it serve for me?

>> What am I getting out of it?

>> What do I want to achieve?

>> Do the goals align with my core values?

Then examine the goals of the group:

>> What are the goals of the group?

>> Is the group successful in achieving these goals?

>> Is the group taking action as a group to achieve those goals?

>> Do the group's goals align with its shared values?

REFLECTION

Most people know what they don't want but not what they want. Do you know what you want? Do you have a set list of goals? Or do you tend to focus on what you don't want?

Combining resources

After you commit to shared goals, the next step is to evaluate what kind of resources the community offers its members and whether the group shares resources among one another. Resources are material needs or equipment, social support, advocacy, and emotional support, for example.

The following questions can serve as a guide to evaluating resources. Don't feel that you need to be limited by these questions. Write down whatever comes to mind:

>> What are the material resources?

>> What are the emotional resources?

>> What other types of resources are available?

>> Does the community offer everyone equal resources?

>> Are resources equally available?

>> Who provides the resources?

>> What role do I share when it comes to resources?

Contributing and cooperating equally

You can now look more closely at the roles people have in your community. You can assess the roles and contributions of the members, whether the contributions are equal, whether people cooperate well, and whether they value one another's roles. Here are some questions to evaluate contribution and cooperation:

>> Do I have a clearly defined role?

>> What are the roles within the team or community?

>> Is everyone given equal value?

>> What are my responsibilities?

>> Do people follow through in their given responsibilities?

>> Is there clarity or confusion when determining who-can-do-what?

>> Can we rely on one another to fulfill our roles or duties?

>> Do we cooperate well?

>> Are all contributions valued equally?

Communicating effectively

Effective communication is essential for a group to work together toward a common goal and be successful. Evaluate ways that your group communicates — by email, phone, or newsletter or in person, for example. Evaluate whether people listen to one another respectfully and how they speak to one another. Use these questions to evaluate effective communication:

>> Are people clear when they speak?

>> Do people interrupt one another, or are respect and attentive listening obvious?

>> Do I feel heard when I speak?

>> Do I feel safe to speak my mind or ask for what I want?

>> Is our way of communicating effective?

>> Do lines of communication get crossed often?

>> Has communication been an obstacle, or has it been helpful in enabling success?

Displaying sensitivity and empathy

Sensitivity and empathy are qualities that strengthen social bonds and help people feel safe to express their needs and concerns. Evaluate whether members of your community care about one another and display mutual empathy, warmth, and sensitivity to the needs and well-being of every member. Examine how people treat one another and think about how you feel when relating to other members. You can ask these questions to examine sensitivity and empathy:

>> Is a sense of unity and trust evident as a result of the caring and empathy the people display?

>> Are empathy and sensitivity lacking?

>> Are some members empathic and others aren't?

>> How does negativity affect the balance of the group?

>> Am I empathic?

REMEMBER

Empathy and the ability to understand someone else can involve imagining that you are in their shoes and seeing their point of you.

Encouraging and celebrating

Members who care and believe in one another encourage one another, whether it's to keep moving during hard times or to simply continue being who they are as unique individuals with value. Evaluate the level and frequency of encouragement and people-celebration in your community. Look for ways that members show they care, believe in one another to succeed, or support one another during challenging times or times of failure. Use these questions to examine encouragement and celebration:

» Are wins or gains recognized?

» Are birthdays celebrated?

» Do I feel encouraged by my community to keep pushing when I'm tired?

» Do I feel celebrated by my community?

» Do I make the effort to encourage and celebrate others?

Exemplifying fairness and inclusivity

Resilient groups celebrate differences, knowing that it's these differences that make them stronger, and guidelines are followed to ensure that people feel secure, supported, and valued. They work toward making sure everyone is treated equally, and they are always looking toward ways to improve on being more just and fair. Using the following questions, evaluate your community for inclusivity and fairness and for established guidelines that ensure people feel safe, know their roles, and feel supported and valued.

» Do we follow guidelines that establish fairness and inclusivity?

» Are differences celebrated?

» Are people judged if they don't meet a given criteria, or is everyone accepted?

» Do people feel safe to give feedback and voice their opinions?

» Do I feel that I have to conform to fit in?

Having trusted leaders

Strong leadership helps build trust, respect, and cohesiveness within a community. If there are leaders in your community, evaluate their effectiveness and their roles and whether they are strong and resilient leaders. (For more on leadership, see Chapters 8 and 15.) You can ask these questions to evaluate leadership:

>> How many leaders are there?

>> What are their roles?

>> Are they effective?

>> Are they trustworthy?

>> Are they role models for resilience?

>> Do they listen well, engage, promote respect, and help the group achieve their goals?

>> Am I a leader?

>> If I'm a leader, can I be trusted and relied on to lead?

Creating the Foundation for Your Community

Having done your evaluation, you will have a better idea of your community's strengths and weaknesses. The stronger your community, the better they can provide social support, resources, knowledge, quality relationships, joy, value, and meaning to your personal and professional lives. Whether you want to build a community from scratch or improve one of the existing ones that you have evaluated, the key is to ensure that these five foundational objectives are strengthened:

>> Buying in of shared goals

>> Agreeing on shared values

>> Making sure the right people are on the team

>> Upholding effective communication

>> Creating guidelines that ensure safety, fairness, and inclusivity

As you read on in this section, I give you some exercises you can do as a group to build on these foundational objectives.

Getting everyone to buy in on the goals

As a group, you want to come together to establish the purpose of the community and the shared goals, both short-term and long-term. These goals inform future actions, strategies, roles, ideas, and the expected behaviors of the group. You also want to take time for each individual to establish their personal goals and share them with the group. This gives people a better idea of how to support one another.

You can use the same or similar questions as posed to you in the earlier section "Committing to shared goals," and incorporate them into the following exercise, which is extremely powerful in bringing people together. It involves the sharing of personal stories and desires, collaboration, and the finding of similarities that help people interrelate.

Setting community goals and purpose

If the group is larger than six to seven people, split into smaller groups (try to keep the size of each group no bigger than six or seven people) and follow these steps:

1. **Brainstorm on goal-setting.** The brainstorming session is for everyone to throw out ideas and general thoughts. Everything counts. A designated person keeps notes or writes potential goals on a whiteboard. Each person in the group offers ideas and beliefs regarding the objective of the group. Contemplate these questions:

    - Why are we here as a group?

    - What is our purpose?

    - What do we want to achieve?

    - Where do we want to be in one year or in three or five years?

2. **Summarize the common themes.** Once ideas have been gathered, discuss common themes and summarize them in a way that concisely establishes the group's purpose and goals. For instance, perhaps you have come together with other business owners to form a networking group. A couple of ideas for goals that have been thrown out to the group include "Growing our businesses," "Success and more money," and "Making connections." The summary is then, "Our goal is to strengthen connections among business owners to help individual businesses grow and succeed." Start general and then get specific.

3. **Determine the smaller goals.** Once the larger goals are established, discuss the how-to aspect of getting there and agreeing on the smaller goals that need to be achieved to reach the larger goal. Brainstorm first, and then work together to come up with the smaller goals that will form the basis of future action plans.

REMEMBER

Focus on what you want to achieve rather than what you want to avoid. It's okay to think big!

Setting individual goals

People join a community because they have personal desires or goals and believe that the group or community can help them achieve them. Once the team or community goals are established, engage every person in establishing and sharing their personal goals. Follow these steps:

1. **Write a story.** Begin by having each member write out a story of why they are present, what has brought them to this community, and what they are hoping for. You might have them contemplate such questions as these:

   - What keeps you up at night?

   - What do you need help with?

   - What do you think a group of people might help you accomplish?

   - What are your passions?

   - What do you have to offer that you want to share with others?

   - What do you want most?

2. **Share the story and summarize.** Each person takes a turn telling their story while the rest of the group listens attentively. The group can then help the individual solidify their goals into a concise summary.

3. **Support for success.** Once individual goals are established, the group then offers specific ways that each person can achieve their goals and ways the group can be supportive.

Aligning core values

After you set individual goals, the next step is to confirm the group's core values and ensure that these values are aligned with personal core values. You can use the same list of values and questions posed to you in the earlier section "Sharing values" when working through the following process that sets the stage for creating a resilient group culture.

Personal reflection

Each person is given time to reflect and list their core values followed by what they believe the core values of the group are — or want them to be. Here are some questions they may ask:

>> What do I value?

>> What is meaningful to me?

>> What values do I believe I have that help me succeed?

>> What values influence my behavior?

>> What values influence my relationships and how I interact with the world?

>> What values would help the group succeed?

>> What values would influence the group's behavior, actions, and plans?

>> What values would influence the relationships within the group and how the group interacts with the world?

Once answers have been compiled, create a list of all the values. You can use examples from this list or add whatever comes to mind.

Appreciation	Advocacy	Accountability	Boldness	Be the best	Caring
Challenge	Charity	Commitment	Compassion	Cooperation	Collaboration
Contribution	Credibility	Consistency	Creativity	Curiosity	Decisiveness
Dedication	Dependability	Diversity	Empathy	Enthusiasm	ethics
Excellence	Fairness	Family	Friendship	Freedom	fun
Generosity	Growth	Happiness	Health	Honesty	humility
Humor	Inclusiveness	Individuality	Innovation	Inspiration	Joy
Kindness	Knowledge	Leadership	Learning	Love	loyalty
Mindfulness	Motivation	Optimism	Originality	Passion	Performance
Professionalism	Recognition	Relationships	Reliability	Resilience	Responsibility
Security	Service	Spirituality	Stability	Success	Teamwork
Thoughtfulness	Tradition	Trust	Uniqueness	Versatility	Vision

Brainstorming as a group

Come together as a group and share your thoughts. Every person shares their list of values while a designated person keeps notes or writes potential values on a whiteboard.

Summarizing and prioritizing

Choose the top ten values that represent you as a group, and discuss why these values are most important so that you can eventually list the values in priority from most important to least. Keep in mind that this is a collaborative effort where all opinions are welcome. Be open to disagreements and to learning from one another.

Matching values with goals

Match your values with the established goals. Set the intention to ensure that your values are taken into consideration anytime you devise strategies and action plans toward achieving goals. Discuss examples of which action plans to achieve your goals would be coherent with your values and which ones may not.

Putting the right people in the right roles

I often think about the magic that happens when watching athletes on a successful sports team work together. Each one is different, with a different skill set and role, yet they communicate as if they can read each other's minds. If one person falters, another person has their back. Each person is in the perfect role, coming together, in perfect harmony.

Whether you're creating a team of your own or looking to strengthen the ones you're on, you can work toward putting the right people in the right roles and ensuring that everyone feels valued. When the right people are in the right roles, you will find that your community is that much more harmonious and resilient.

I was asked to help a company because its team members were having trouble getting along, communicating effectively, and, ultimately, managing customers well. After an evaluation, I discovered that each person individually was quite caring and motivated. The problem was that the company grew fast over a short period and many people were unclear on who was responsible for what task. A plan was then instituted to clarify roles and responsibilities that best fit each person's competencies and desires, and accountability charts were created — as were opportunities for professional development and growth — so that employees were set up to succeed. Within six months of implementation, morale improved, as had communication, flow of work, and customer satisfaction.

The same guidelines apply for families, sports teams, or community groups. When your people are clear about roles, expectations, and responsibilities and they share values together, they are more likely to cooperate and to be better motivated to work together toward the shared goal.

When you think about any group you might belong to, including the company you might work for, are the roles defined? Do you know who you can turn to for specific issues? Is there any confusion in your own role? Would you prefer to have a different role?

There are many routes that communities, companies, or teams can use to evaluate the roles and responsibilities. I find the process in the following section to be effective.

Performing a needs assessment

After you create a vision for your community by establishing goals and values, you can then figure out what skill sets you need in order to accomplish these goals, the roles and responsibilities, and the kind of people that would fit in with your community's culture. Evaluate these aspects:

>> **Skill sets and structure:** What skill sets do you need in order to accomplish your goals and to ensure that processes are smooth? What type of work structure is needed?

>> **Roles:** What positions need to be filled? What are the roles? What are the responsibilities of each role? Expectations? What is the role of the leader?

>> **Personalities:** What type of personality type fits best for which role? What are the values the members need to have? What type of personalities blend well together in a way that will best achieve your goals? What is the personality of the leader? What is the personality deal-breaker that would ruin team cohesion? Is the person dependable, reliable, empathic, and enthusiastic?

>> **Communication skills:** What communication skills are necessary? When it comes to communication, what is the expectation for each role? What is the policy on handling conflict? Are emotional intelligence and empathy required? What sort of interpersonal skills should they have?

Appraising the people

When you appraise the members of your team, approach every person with the assumption that they have value. Rather than look to have a particular person fit a specific role, examine what qualities that person may have that are a fit for the community. The key is to

>> **Match values and goals.** Assess whether each person shares the community's core values. If you see a lack of alignment, you know from the start that

this relationship is unlikely to work, whether the person has the skills or not. It won't be a good fit.

» **Review competencies.** One person may be competent at many tasks, and it's always good to have people of diverse skills on the team. Allow members to list their talents, say what they believe they excel in doing, and talk about their success stories.

» **Assess motivations.** It's not enough for someone to be competent at doing something — they have to want to do it, and you want them to be internally driven to achieve both their own individual goals and the goals of the community. You therefore want to figure out what each person actually wants to do, is inspired to do, and is motivated to do. Have members specify their heart's desire, say what they love to do, discuss a skill they want to improve, or indicate that they want to be recognized for something.

» **Ensure that you have team players.** You may meet someone who is a rock star — an expert in their own right who has the exact right skill set that your community needs. The problem is that this person is pompous and judgmental and shows a lack of trust and respect for other people and their abilities. Look for people who are dependable and show that they care about others, and see whether they consider themselves lone wolves or prefer to team up with others.

» **Appraise for positive attributes.** Positive attributes include dependability, collaboration, respect, good communication, leadership, motivation, adaptability, flexibility, maturity, accountability, empathy, creativity, and hardworking. Some attributes are apparent when you first meet someone, and others show up over time. You want your members to be on the same page, share values as well as the ability to care about one another, and be accountable and empathic.

Ensuring that roles, responsibilities, and milestones are clear

It's always better when people are clear about their roles and responsibilities and are given defined objectives and goals that they can shoot for. Within your community, you can assess whether members are clear about their roles. Here are some suggestions:

» **Write it out.** Each person can write out their role description and responsibilities. This reflects their perception of what they believe they are doing, can do, and are answerable for.

>> **Make a comparison.** Review the individual's description and compare it to the defined roles you established in the needs assessment. Look for similarities and discrepancies and then determine where clarification is needed, or even a change to the role description.

>> **Give support.** Ask and advise on ways the person may need help in meeting the responsibilities and the role.

>> **Chart progress.** Create milestones and goals so that progress can be evaluated.

>> **Stay open.** Keep an open dialogue for continued reevaluation of the role and any concerns or questions that might arise, or changes that need to be made.

Improving communication

Have you ever played the game broken telephone? In it, one person whispers a secret to another person who then goes on to whisper the secret to another person who then does the same to another person, and so on. When the secret reaches the last person, that last person says the statement out loud and it's compared to the original statement. Invariably, it's never the same.

Communication between two people is tricky, let alone with a large group. No two people hear that exact same thing in the exact same way. Everyone comes to the table with different perspectives and ways of interpreting and remembering what they hear.

Many companies have communication issues, for instance, mostly because a set system hasn't been put in place, from my observation. Verbal agreements don't get documented to ensure that everyone is on the same page, email communications aren't clear, agendas aren't be created before meetings take place, or formats have not been established that give team members an opportunity to be heard.

REMEMBER

Effective communication is paramount for the success of a team and the resilience of a community. It supports the strengthening of social bonds, facilitates better cooperation and efficiency, avoids errors and misunderstandings, and supports the community's ability to work together to adapt and manage adversity. When effective communication is established, cooperation and efficiency are improved, as are engagement, motivation, and bonding of community members.

Ensuring that communication is effective and sound is a multilayered process. It begins with solidifying values, goals, roles, responsibilities, expectations, and milestones. Once established, guidelines can be created that provide all individuals with a clear understanding of effective communication practices.

Making sure voices are heard

Every person's voice must be heard and respected. Whether they have feedback to give, complaints, or questions, each person needs to feel safe that their opinion is valued. When communicating, asking questions such as these may be helpful:

>> Would you like to share your thoughts?

>> Do you have any feedback?

>> Is there something you think I missed?

>> What is your opinion?

>> Do you have anything to add?

Encouraging feedback

Allow an open-door policy for all members to provide feedback on anything from ongoing goals and processes to how leadership may be performing.

Regularly send out emails or notices to remind members of the open-door policy to offer feedback.

>> Ask your team members how they think you're doing.

>> Set up regular quarterly meetings for members to provide feedback in a group setting, where issues can be discussed and positives can be celebrated.

>> Regularly review milestones with members and provide feedback.

Giving meetings purpose and direction

Create an infrastructure so that meetings take place on a set schedule. Some meetings may occur annually, quarterly, monthly, weekly, or as daily check-ins, and each one has a given purpose. Goals are reviewed and decisions are made with clear instructions for the next action steps and goals. They key is to

>> **Generate a rhythm for meetings.** Setting up regularly scheduled meetings ensures that members are regularly checking in with one another, assessing needs, reviewing processes, and understanding what they're accountable for and when. Having a rhythm to meetings can improve efficacy, efficiency, and collaboration of the group. Individual members may set up daily check-ins with specific teammates, weekly reviews, monthly assessments, and quarterly or annual strategic planning.

>> **Create agenda templates.** Agenda templates can be followed for each given meeting to ensure consistency and efficiency and to allow people to be prepared.

>> **Encourage participation.** Engage members in providing ideas, opinions, feedback, or updates.

>> **Set a time limit.** People lose interest when meetings continue for hours on end, when one person talks incessantly, and when no clear takeaways have been established. Time limits need to be set for the meeting, the amount of time spent on each item on the agenda, and how long each person has the floor.

>> **Make takeaways.** Before the close of the meeting, summarize the takeaways of the meeting, which include recommendations, milestones, goals, or action steps.

>> **Agree.** Ensure that all people present agree on the takeaways.

>> **Share the minutes.** Upon conclusion of the meeting, minutes of the meeting are shared with the participants, including members who were unable to attend.

Documenting and confirming

Just like the game broken telephone, rarely does everyone in the meeting hear the exact same things. To reduce the risk of confusion and miscommunication:

>> Document conversations and especially decisions.

>> Send follow up emails to confirm decisions and action plans.

>> Have all parties involved confirm or validate documentation.

Being mindful

No matter the format of communication — whether it's email, text, group, or one-on-one — one person's tone can affect the outcome of a conversation. A person who speaks negatively, rudely, and with arrogance, for example, will have quite a different discussion than a person who speaks with respect, interest, and courtesy.

Steps you can take to communicate mindfully include:

>> First and foremost, always be mindful that you're speaking or communicating to someone of value.

>> Ask questions and for clarification, without assuming the negative to gain clarity.

>> Show gratitude or thanks.

>> Reflect back what you have heard and understand and avoid blaming or shaming.

>> Check your attitude before responding.

>> Regulate your emotions before responding if you find yourself upset.

Understanding communication styles

People have different ways of communicating, depending on their comfort levels and their personalities. Whether you choose to use a personality test like the Myers-Briggs Type Indicator (MBTI) or the DiSC Assessment, a tool that measures people's behavior differences, it's important to honor and understand the way different individuals communicate. According to the DiSC Assessment, people have four primary communication styles:

>> **Dominant:** This type tends to see the big picture, gets straight to the point, focuses on the bottom line, is results oriented, and speaks with confidence.

>> **Influencer:** This type, which enjoys collaborating, tends to be optimistic, open, enthusiastic about hearing other people's views, focused on influencing or persuading others, and eager to be heard.

>> **Conscientious:** This type tends to want expertise, quality, and competency; is independently minded and prefers objective reasoning; and focuses on details to ensure accuracy to prevent getting something wrong.

>> **Steady:** This type tends to be dependable, sincere, methodical, calm, and steady, and focused on cooperation and supporting others.

TIP

Your community may find it helpful to do such an assessment because it enables members to better understand communication styles. By accepting that Joe tells it like he sees it, for example, people may take less offense when he speaks in a blunt manner.

Establishing guidelines for fairness and inclusivity

A group works best together when each individual feels respected and valued, and where trust has been built and fairness exemplified. People who feel that they aren't being treated fairly or justly will lose trust and become less motivated, productive, and helpful. In building a resilient community, therefore, you must establish guidelines that support and ensure that members are treated fairly; people act with respect, care, and honesty; and the group itself is intolerant to intolerance. It takes three foundational steps to create a fair and just culture.

Treating everyone equally

Here are ways to ensure that people are being treated equally:

» Collaborate with all the members to establish rules of fairness that apply to everyone with the expectation that everyone will be held accountable.

» Meet regularly to review the rules and ensure accountability.

» Equally distribute rewards to individuals who have worked hard and especially met their milestones.

» Hold everyone equally accountable.

» Give everyone equal voice to be heard and voice opinions.

» Offer everyone training to be able to excel and succeed.

Ensuring inclusivity

Ways to improve inclusivity include the following:

» Encourage diversity and welcome all people who share your core values and goals, no matter the gender, race, or creed, for example.

» Ensure that all voices are heard and all opinions matter.

» Recognize bias among members and instill de-bias trainings for all the members, after which everyone is held accountable.

» Provide support and sponsorship for those individuals who may be less fortunate and have fewer resources.

Practicing open communication and transparency

You can make certain that channels of communication stay open by doing the following:

>> Be clear in any communication regarding expectations, responsibilities, and guidelines, especially regarding fairness and justice practices.

>> Be accountable for errors or mistakes.

>> Create a format for members to feel safe to work through conflicts, with a facilitator who doesn't choose sides but rather helps the individuals come to a resolution.

>> Encourage regular constructive feedback.

Chapter **15**

Becoming a Resilient Leader

eaders are responsible for crafting change and growth for their communities, making responsible decisions, and guiding people through uncertainty. At some point, leaders have to face challenges and setbacks, and the resilient ones not only successfully adapt and bounce back stronger but also help their teams do the same. Capable, confident, optimistic, and open, resilient leaders embrace change and navigate their communities through the complexities of life's twists and turns.

This chapter focuses on the makings of a resilient leader so that you can be inspired to evaluate and build your own resilient leadership skills.

The Making of a Resilient Leader

Resilience is a quality that today's leaders can't afford not to have, as pandemics rage throughout the world, the stability of the economy wanes, and high stress is the rule rather than the exception. Leaders need to know how to remain strong, adapt, and bounce back despite adversity, and influence others to do the same. They need to stay positive and optimistic, despite struggles, hold on to a larger vision and perspective to find pathways for success, and have a positive belief that a way exists, even if it isn't clear, to forge ahead.

Resilient leaders have five qualities that set them apart from other leaders:

>> **They embrace change and seek out opportunities.** Resilient leaders are eager to learn and grow. In addition to not fearing failure, they are curious to learn, willing to take risks, eager to create and invent, and always in search of new strategies and ideas — therefore, they encourage the team to be innovative, creative, and open. They learn to ask questions, embrace uncertainty, and accept not knowing everything they need to know.

>> **They communicate effectively and openly.** Resilient leaders are commanding when they speak yet also clear, empathic, and transparent. They are distinct about what they want and therefore clear when relaying expectations, goals, and objectives. Their empathic, approachable, and authentic nature builds trust and opens pathways for discussion and feedback.

>> **They build healthy networks of support and trust.** Resilient leaders aim to cultivate strong social bonds within the community and to build trust, share goals and core values, and connect through shared purpose. They recognize strengths and weaknesses, ensure fairness and justice within the group, help individuals develop and grow, and facilitate the group to work together and collaborate so that, collectively, they can be stronger.

>> **They willingly learn from others.** Resilient leaders are confident yet also humble, knowing that they have much to learn. They stay open to feedback from the community and are coachable because they reach out for advice from trusted sources, counsel, classes, and other networks of support.

>> **They are self-aware and take care.** Resilient leaders are calm and emphasize their own work-life balance, taking care of their mind, body, and spirit. They take care of their physical health and work toward better self-awareness, emotional regulation, and stress management.

REFLECTION

Effective leaders regularly take time for self-reflection to review themselves and their actions. This self-reflection allows them to adjust their leadership style when needed and take note of ways their performance may need improvement. Do you regularly carve out time to self-reflect?

What Is Your Style of Leadership?

You may or may not consider yourself a leader, but I am telling you that you are. You influence the people around you, whether you appreciate that fact or not. Your sphere of influence goes either wide or narrow, but it still goes. You may not be the CEO of your company, nor a manager or captain, but you may be a parent or a part of a community, team, or group made up of like-minded individuals. As I mention elsewhere, a boulder and a pebble both cause ripples in the water — one larger and one smaller. The key is that they both cause ripples. There may be other people in your life who look up to you, and others who rely on you to help make decisions. You may be a boulder or a pebble, and, either way, you have influence on other people.

Questions regarding leadership to ask yourself

Take a moment to reflect and answer the following list of questions. It's a wonderful way to self-examine your own beliefs regarding leadership:

>> Do I consider myself a leader or a follower?

>> How do I define each of these roles?

>> Whom do I consider a great leader?

>> What do I consider to be the key characteristics of a leader? (List as many as you can think of.)

>> How many of these characteristics do I possess?

>> What qualities do I think I lack?

>> What actions have I taken recently that reflect me as a leader?

>> Do I have a vision for my future? For the future of a group I belong to?

Appraising your sphere of influence

You can assess your sphere of influence by examining where in your life, personally and professionally, your opinion and actions hold weight. The sphere includes family, friends, peers, and colleagues.

1. Make a list of the different people you regularly interact with, and group them into the specific network that they may be a part of (feel free to add another category):

   - Family = **F**
   - Close friends = **CF**
   - Colleagues = **C**
   - Peers in a group = **P**
   - Teammates = **T**
   - Neighborhood community = **N**
   - Social media = **SM**

2. Read the following statements and rate them using the following scale and list the groups that apply:

   - I strongly agree: 5
   - I somewhat agree: 4
   - I am neutral / not sure: 3
   - I somewhat disagree: 2
   - I strongly agree: 1

3. Add up your score and notice for which group (if not all) the numbers are higher. The higher the score, the greater your influence.

Statements	Rate	Groups
I often try to influence change at home, like getting my children, parents, or siblings to eat healthier.		
I often try to influence change at work, like getting my colleagues or staff to implement new ideas or strategies.		
I often work on persuading my coworkers, colleagues, or teammates when I am hoping to get them on board to make a change or listen to a new idea or disagree with how something is being done.		
I enjoy encouraging other people to stay focused, motivated or keep doing a great job.		
I am eager to share my knowledge with other people.		
I often help other people get organized or to figure out their plans or goals.		
I enjoy telling stories to groups of people and seeing them learn and be entertained.		

Statements	Rate	Groups
I often find myself giving advice.		
I often find myself coaching and helping other people learn and develop skills.		
I often enjoy creating a strategy that will support my team, family or colleagues.		
I believe I create an environment where people feel safe, relaxed, and creative.		
I often delegate tasks to other people.		
My actions influence at least one to two people in my personal life.		
My actions influence at least one to two people in my professional life.		
I believe people listen to me and do as I recommend.		
I believe people look to me to be a role model.		
I need to practice what I preach because I set an example for others.		
The decisions I make impact a lot of people.		
A lot of people follow me on social media.		
I often inspire people on social media with my posts.		

You have more influence than you might realize. No one lives or exists in isolation. How you behave, act, and even feel can influence many people around you.

Evaluating your resilience as a leader

You may have come to realize that your sphere of influence is larger than you first thought, and perhaps you're more of a boulder than a pebble. The more resilient you can be, therefore, the bigger and greater your positive impact on the people around you.

You can evaluate how resilient you are as a leader by using the following Resilient Leader Checklist to see how you match up when it comes to embracing change, effectively communicating, building trusting networks and relationships, being willing to learn, and taking care to be self-aware.

Take the time to reflect and answer the following questions as authentically and truthfully as you can. Once you have answered yes or no, extrapolate why or how this answer is true for you, keeping your spheres of influence in mind.

The Resilient Leader Checklist

Leadership Category	Yes/No
Embracing change	
Do you push yourself beyond your comfort zone?	
When faced with adversity and needing to adapt and create change, can you stay calm and manage your stress?	
Do you have the ability to create a vision that can encourage others to embrace change?	
Do you have the strength and the ability to stay calm, which is necessary to lead others to change?	
Do you consider yourself a bold risk taker?	
Are you open to new ideas that might lead to drastic changes?	
Do you feel excited and optimistic at the prospect of making a change, even when difficult?	
Do you trust in your own competency to be able to make adaptive changes in difficult situations?	
Can you make decisions that involve heading in a new direction under pressure?	
Do you sign up to do the things other people are afraid of?	
Communicating effectively	
Do you have strong communication skills, and are you able to relay your thoughts, expectations, and decisions in a clear fashion?	
Do you make sure people understand your direction, expectations, and ideas?	
Do you listen attentively, allowing people to feel heard and not interrupting, cutting them off, or disregarding their opinions?	
Are you able to take control and command others to follow direction in challenging times?	
Do you show empathy when listening to others when they communicate their thoughts, complaints, or needs?	
If miscommunication happens, do you try to fix the issue and find out why the miscommunication happened?	
Do you work toward creating alignment in communication when using multiple modalities such as email, text, or verbal conversations?	
Building networks of trust	
Is it important to you to nurture your relationships?	
Do you inspire others to reach higher limits and work hard?	

Leadership Category	Yes/No
Do you encourage people to share their opinions, including when they're different or conflicting?	
Do you encourage people to collaborate?	
Are you adept at recognizing people's strengths and weaknesses?	
Are you adept at knowing how to get the right people and resources together?	
Are you able to be fair and just when it comes to mediating between people?	
Do you feel you're trustworthy?	
Do you create a safe place for people to open up and give honest feedback?	
Do you encourage activities to enhance the connectedness between people?	
Willing to learn	
Do you enjoy learning new skills and gaining new knowledge?	
Are you comfortable knowing that you don't know everything you need to know?	
Are you open to hearing other people's ideas and thoughts?	
Are you coachable?	
Do you tend to take credit for successes because they're a result of your efforts or because of the efforts of several people working together?	
Are you open to receiving feedback?	
Do you see challenges as opportunities to learn and grow?	
Do you engage in classes or ways to improve and learn?	
Are you always on the lookout for strategies and tools that can make you and others more effective?	
Taking care and being self-aware	
Are you aware of the influence your attitude, words, and actions have on others?	
Are you aware of the influence your emotions have on your behavior and decision-making?	
Are your actions aligned with your core values?	
Are you aware of your own limiting beliefs?	
Are you able to regulate your emotions during difficult times and stay calm?	
Do you take care of yourself with regular exercises, healthy nutrition, and restful sleep?	
Do you have a meditation practice?	
Do you feel you're connected to something greater or larger, including a higher purpose?	
Do you try to set an example for others?	

Having answered these questions, you will have a better idea of your own leadership presence and perhaps of the qualities or traits you want to further develop or build. As you read on, this chapter offers you tools that will help you become a more resilient leader.

REMEMBER

Leaders are great partially because they are constantly evolving. This questionnaire helps you learn more about yourself so that you can continue to evolve as your life changes.

Embracing Challenges and Change

Change happens daily whether you like it or not, and even though you might think you're in control, for the most part life happens with or without your being in control. You might believe that you detest change and not being in control, but feeling this way simply leads to being miserable. Because change is going to happen anyway, you may as well choose to at least tolerate it and, if you want to be a resilient leader, embrace it.

Embracing change means that you look forward to it. You look forward to being challenged and actually seek out challenges. Rather than run away from discomfort, you head right in. You have a sense of control of your own destiny, a belief in your own competence to handle adversity, and an eagerness to learn and grow, even if doing so is difficult. You believe that life happens to you and for you, so rather than ask "Why me?" you prefer to ask, "Given what is, what can I learn and what can I do?"

Becoming more adept at embracing change involves following this list of suggestions:

>> Get comfortable being uncomfortable.

>> Face the fear of doing something a little risky.

>> Get lost.

>> Start with a clean slate.

>> Go the other way.

>> Go with the flow.

Becoming comfortable being uncomfortable

Your body is wired to seek comfort and to avoid pain or discomfort. It's automatic. You shift positions when you're uncomfortable, and you avoid placing your hand on a hot stove. You also may shift away and avoid difficult situations, conflict or uncertainty. Now, I'm not suggesting that you put your hand on a hot stove or walk on hot coals or fire, which many people have done. However, you must learn how to be present while you embrace and move through discomfort – rather than run away from it or avoid it altogether.

>> **Exercises you can do alone:** You may choose to sit with anger or negative feelings and simply be present with them. Observe them as they come and go. You can choose to do a somewhat physically strenuous exercise and be present with the physical discomfort. Breathe through it and pay attention to the spot where the discomfort is coming from, and then use the information to shift positions slightly, without stopping what you're doing. (Do not push yourself to the brink of pain and injury. This is a gentle exercise of being aware of discomfort, accepting its presence, and breathing through it).

>> **Activities you can do as a group:** As a group, you can lead participants into having a difficult discussion that will likely instigate conflicting ideas, elicit intense emotions, and guide people to be present and mindful with their feelings and experience. This type of exercise helps people bond and develop empathy and support for one another while learning to accept different opinions and find constructive ways to work through the differences.

Facing the fear of doing something risky

Becoming more resilient involves getting comfortable making decisions under conditions of uncertainty and risk. Try doing something new that slightly scares you and requires you to make a decision involving some kind of risk.

>> **Exercises you can do alone:** Try out a new sport, take a dance class, attend open mic night, learn a new language and try to speak in it, or sing karaoke for the first time. Try a new activity and, without judging yourself, let yourself be uncomfortable and scared and then, of course, push through the fear.

>> **Activities you can do as a group:** As a group, decide to try out a new activity, whether it's ziplining or another outdoor adventure or visiting an escape room where you're part of a group that needs to figure out how to work together to escape from a room. This type of activity enables people to support one another to overcome fears and meet challenges together.

Find your way home after getting lost

A great challenge to test yourself is to see how well you can figure out how to get home or to a place you have never visited. This activity challenges you to think out of the box and to be creative and resourceful.

>> **Exercises you can do alone:** Turn off your GPS and let yourself get lost. Your goal is to use only a compass or maybe one of those old paper maps that requires you to read city and town names, names of roads or routes, and figure a way home.

>> **Activities you can do as a group:** Have someone drop off the group somewhere blindfolded and work together to find your way back. This is a great exercise to do with other people because it emphasizes teamwork, communication, resourcefulness, and leadership.

REFLECTION

When is the last time you felt lost? Can you remember a time you couldn't find your way home or to a particular destination? What emotions do you experience when you feel lost about a certain situation in life? How do you manage the emotion?

Starting with a clean slate

Being resilient means being comfortable with uncertainty and ambiguity and being open to learning. Most people worry about not having the right answers or not knowing everything they need to know — rather than enjoy the process of not knowing and learning. Get curious, throw out everything you think you know, and learn something new.

>> **Exercises you can do alone:** Take on a new project, like building a piece of furniture from scratch, learning a new language, or understanding a new concept. Imagine that you're a child and your mind is a blank slate. Be curious and ask a lot of questions, especially of other people so that you can also gain new perspectives.

>> **Activities you can do as a group:** Embark on a group project or challenge that involves learning a new skill or concept. Read a book together on a new concept or in a new language, or work on a project together, making sure that the jobs people have are new to them and not part of their wheelhouse or standard skill set. Ask one another questions and learn about the other's perspectives, especially if one person has the skill set you need to learn.

Heading the other way

People often get used to a routine: taking the same route to work, watching the news at the same time every day, or being steadfast about their opinions or beliefs. Getting comfortable with change means learning how to gain a new perspective and being flexible. Follow these steps to change up your life a little, and do things in the opposite fashion from your norm.

>> **Exercises you can do alone:** Take a different route to work, eat dinner at breakfast, walk backward, write with your nondominant hand.

>> **Activities you can do as a group:** If you're at work, sit at different desks. Can you manage without having everything you need? Meet as a group and do role plays, also known as reversing roles, an exercise that allows you to put yourself in another person's shoes. Meet as a group and sit in a circle. In the center, place an object that each person separately draws and describes. Change positions so that each person is sitting on the opposite side, and then draw and describe what you see. The group then compares perspectives.

Going with the flow

Your ability to embrace challenges and change is dependent on your being open and receptive, flexible, and adaptable. This is hard to do when your mind is busy being negative, your body is tense, or your emotions are so charged that you can't think clearly. The key is to quiet your mind and calm your emotions so that you can go with the flow, like a river that gently maneuvers around a boulder as it keeps moving.

>> **Exercises you can do alone:** Develop a meditation or mindfulness practice where you regularly clear the mind and relax the body and then engage in some kind of passive movement, like floating on the water and letting your body drift, walking mindfully as you engage your senses in the experience and walk without a goal or definitive destination, or perhaps dance without thinking, letting your body move to the rhythm of the music. Have you ever danced with abandon, feeling like you're completely at one with the music, only to start thinking about what you're doing and then screw up? Don't think. Just go with the flow.

>> **Activities you can do as a group:** These are wonderful exercises to do as a group, because they help build trust and are also a lot of fun. You can dance with abandon as a group, go on a mindful walk, or empty your mind and close your eyes and allow another group member to move your body, either stretching or walking.

Creating Your Vision

Great leaders use their vision to give people direction and encourage them to keep pushing forward together. Their vision provides community members with a sense of shared purpose and common goals and enhances trust and social bonds. Because it's broad, the vision takes in the full scope of a given situation, which ingredients are needed to achieve said goals, the wisdom to know when to act and what to ask and whom to bring in, and the ability to clearly communicate this vision to others.

Creating a broad vision necessitates clearing out fears and limiting beliefs so that you are able to see the big picture, better delineate goals, draw out a strategic plan, and clearly communicate the vision to your team or community in a way that gets them engaged and enthusiastic. The process I spell out in the following sections will help you create a broad and clear vision for your community. You can do this on your own and then engage others or do it together with the whole group or with key leaders. When you do come together as a group, I recommend that you break up into smaller groups of five or six and sit at a circular table, if your group is large, and then choose one person as the representative and facilitator.

Clearing and opening the mind

Because the aim is to remove preconceived notions and be open to new ideas, you want to start off by clearing and quieting the mind. You might choose to sit in silence for a moment or two, state an intention or a prayer, or even literally shake your entire body for a minute or two.

REFLECTION

You may want to try the shaking routine out for yourself. What happens when you stand up and shake your entire body? Wiggle your torso, kick out your legs, and bob your head in different directions for 30 to 60 seconds. Then stop and be still. How do you feel?

You can also try this exercise. Give the group five minutes to do the following steps, using a chime or soft bell to signal that time is up.

1. **Sit quietly and close your eyes.**

2. **Take a deep breath in, breathing in through your nose, and then exhale completely, breathing out through your mouth.**

3. **Bring your focus to the breath, observing the sensations you experience as you breathe in and out.**

   Notice what you feel and sense with each breath.

4. **If thoughts arise in your mind, allow the thoughts to be absorbed with your breath and watch them come and go with your breath.**

5. **Begin to count 1-2-3 as you breathe in and 1-2-3-4-5-6 as you breathe out.**

6. **Count to 3 on the inbreath and 6 on the outbreath for the next ten cycles of breath, allowing all tension in the body and thoughts in the mind to be cleared with the breath, released out into the wind or air.**

7. **Observe your body, noticing any sensations you might be experiencing.**

8. **Appreciate the silence.**

   Appreciate your breath. Appreciate the opportunity you have right now to be silent.

9. **Breathe in appreciation and then exhale, letting go of everything else for another ten cycles of breath.**

10. **Sound the bell or chimes to gently bring everyone back into the present moment, and instruct them to keep their eyes closed.**

Visualizing the future

The next step is to engage the imagination and your sense of curiosity and creativity by visualizing what you want the future to look like. Doing so helps you connect with desired objectives and goals while also enhancing a sense of confidence and the belief that success is possible. The following exercise will guide you to envision the future of the team or community in ten years:

Setting the timer for another ten minutes, instruct the participants to follow these steps:

1. **Begin by closing your eyes or keep them closed.**

2. **Imagine that you can see ten years into the future and you're watching TV:**

   A news flash soon comes on and the headline announces a cover story about your community or team.

   A reporter then comes on the screen, reporting on the story of the amazing group of determined people who beat the odds and are now the top in their league and receiving an award for their accomplishments.

   The reporter then goes on to file an in-depth report, interviewing members, asking about the strategy, and showing the trials and tribulations that were overcome, where they came from, and where they are now.

3. **Allow yourself to see the vision clearly.**

What is the reporter saying? What do you see and notice? What action steps were taken?

4. **When the bells chime, come back to the present moment and open your eyes.**

Writing out the story of success

The next step is to write down the story of how you envision success happening. If you completed the exercise in the earlier section "Visualizing the future," write the story down. Try to record as many details as possible. As a group, ask each person to write down their vision in a story format following these guidelines: Focus on writing a full story from beginning to end, as if you're writing a newspaper article, starting with a headline. Here are three good questions to work with to guide you:

>> Where did we come from?

>> Where did we go?

>> Where did we end up?

Set a 10-minute time limit. If you're with the group, give each individual in the group a turn to share their story, as a facilitator writes down key headlines, actions, or points on a whiteboard. As each person relays their vision, details are added to the story of success, revealing the variety of headlines and ways that success was achieved.

REFLECTION

How does it feel when you visualize the story of success? If you think about it, many people spend their time worrying about the future rather than conceiving ways to feel good about it.

Defining goals and objectives

A big part of your vision involves defining clear goals and objectives. You can brainstorm together to strategize on formulating goals that also align with your core values. (See Chapter 14 for info about setting goals to build a resilient community.) You can also use the information you gathered from writing down the story and completing the following exercise:

Examine the story of success and tease out realistic goals and objectives from which to base future action plans. Stay in the small groups first to determine goals and objectives, and then convene with the larger group to share and decide which ones are most relevant and apt:

1. Using the details from the story, tease out the broad and long-term goals and put them into categories. You might ask questions such as these:

   - What do you want to accomplish?

   - What is the destination? Where are you going? What does it look like?

   - What is the long-term outcome that you envision?

   - Where do you want to be?

   - What do you want to feel?

2. Examine the story for the ways in which success was achieved to formulate some key objectives that will lead to the larger goal, and ask questions like these:

   - What did you need to do to get there?

   - Where did you need to be?

   - How did you need to behave?

   - Who did you need to have on your team?

   - How did you measure success?

   - What are the targets?

Creating the strategic plan

Once you have set goals and objectives, you can brainstorm on possible strategies and action plans. You know your destination, and now you want to figure out how you're going to get there. What does your story of success tell you? How did you get there?

1. **Define the specific categories for the plan, which will clarify priorities.** Examples are information technology, supplies and resources, business development, training and development, and maintenance.

2. **Split into smaller groups of three to work together on one (or more) categories.**

3. **With each category, map the situation, asking**

   - Where are we now?

   - Where did we start?

- Where do we want to go?

- How do we get there?

4. **Reconvene as a larger group and have a spokesperson from each group present their discussion summary and recommendations.**

5. **Have the group discuss each topic until everyone buys in on specific strategies for each goal.**

Communicating the vision

If a vision is created by the leaders or leader, it eventually needs to be communicated to the rest of the community members. The vision needs to be exciting and compelling enough to get everyone to buy in, and it has to be communicated well. Think about a time you had an idea and wanted to persuade your family or peers to get on board. What convinced them to buy in?

You want your vision to inspire people and to have them believe in it, to motivate them to want to push forward in the face of the challenge together. You can take your story of success, defined goals, and objectives and strategy-play, or write out a vision that is clear, of high impact. The five key ingredients for successfully communicating your vision and getting buy-in from others are described in this list:

>> **Keep it simple.** People have short attention spans, for the most part. Start with a headline and follow through with a concise and short story, telling the Why. Remember that less is more. Keep the story to a few minutes long. Figuring out a way to use fewer words to describe your vision, like an elevator speech, also forces you to get clear — so it's a win-win.

>> **Stay consistent.** No matter in which channel the vision is communicated — conversations, newsletters, emails, or message boards — keep the language and story consistent.

>> **Press Repeat.** Words and headlines are easily forgotten. Find ways to remind everyone of the vision by way of videos, vision boards, slogans, and meetings.

>> **Stay open to feedback.** You're more likely to get people on board if you give them an opportunity to have an opinion and offer feedback. Nothing is set in stone, and all opinions need to be welcomed, regarding not only the vision but also how well people think the group is doing in abiding by the vision.

>> **Stay true.** More people will buy in when you stay true to the vision yourself. If you don't believe in it, after all, why should anyone else? It's like telling your family that the vision is for everyone to be healthy and fit by the end of the year and then eat ice cream for dinner every night. Being consistent and authentic with your beliefs and actions motivates others to align with you and do the same.

REMEMBER When you can translate your vision into a powerful reality, people will follow.

Being a Trusted Leader

Communities are made up of people, and a resilient community is composed of people who have strong social bonds, trust, and shared goals and purpose. I've seen countless groups and companies dissolve because of a lack of trust within the group, and much of this was a result of poor leadership, reflected in lack of authenticity and transparency, lack of respect for other's opinions, and lack of fairness. Great leaders drive the strengthening of these relationships because they instill trust, interdependence, fairness, and justice.

As a leader, it's your role to build and ensure this trust, and therefore be a trusted leader. To become a trusted leader involves knowing yourself, being self-aware, being able to regulate your emotions, remaining authentic, and becoming the best expression of yourself — caring and still commanding. Following the trusted-leader "B" list will help you get there:

>> **Be supportive.** Support people to know that they're heard, reward them when they contribute and succeed, and offer training and guidance when they make mistakes.

How can I support you to succeed?

>> **Be consistent.** Actions speak louder than words. Always align your behavior with your words and be a role model for others to follow. Do as you say you will do consistently and keep to your commitments.

Am I practicing what I preach?

>> **Be honest and transparent.** Even when you fear that people may lose confidence in you, if the news you have to report is bad or unpleasant or if you don't know all the answers, be truthful. Being transparent and honest shows your respect for other's strengths and their need to know, and also shows your humanness and vulnerability, which builds trust.

Am I telling the whole story?

>> **Be an attentive listener and be empathic.** Be present and listen attentively by reflecting back what you have heard, avoiding interrupting, asking questions, and being concerned. Show that you care and that you understand, even if you disagree or have an opposing view.

Do I understand how and why they are feeling this way?

» **Be dependable and accountable.** Do as you say you will do, and work hard and earn respect. Be accountable for your mistakes and your promises and follow through.

Have I done what I said I would do?

» **Be approachable.** You aren't better than anyone else. You just happen to have leadership qualities that can facilitate the group to achieve a shared goal. Keep an open-door policy, and allow open discussions where people can express their opinions to you and feel safe.

Am I standing on a pedestal or my high horse?

» **Be open to feedback.** In this same light as being approachable, encourage open dialogue and feedback from others. Be open to criticism and to learning from others' opinions and feelings.

How can I learn more from others?

» **Be connected.** Set time aside to relate and connect to people socially, both within your group and outside. The more widespread your networks of support, the more as a leader you can support others, and strengthening social connections comes with being social.

Have I spent time socially with friends or colleagues this week?

» **Be human.** You will make mistakes, and you can use those times as opportunities to forgive your humanness and find ways to share and learn from the mistakes with others. Being okay with being wrong also makes you more approachable.

Am I comfortable being wrong?

» **Be calm.** Staying level-headed and calm, especially during a time of crisis or stress, is essential for a leader because people look to you for direction and decision-making. Work to quiet your emotions and clear your mind of negativity so that you can be trusted to make decisions in uncertain times.

Am I in control of my emotions?

» **Be focused.** When you're calm, you can focus and act decisively. People depend on you for that when you're the leader. Focus on clear objectives and goals that are in your control to actualize.

Am I focusing on what I can control rather than on what I can't?

» **Be optimistic.** A resilient leader has an optimistic attitude toward the future and is able to rally others to feel the same. You want to have a positive belief in your own abilities and the capabilities of the group to handle uncertainty and be able to push through, despite obstacles.

Am I having doubts?

>> **Be fair.** Be an advocate for others, and be fair and just. Listen openly to all ideas, respect all cultures, and reward people equally.

Have I been open-minded and fair?

>> **Be grateful.** Show gratitude to people for their contributions, presence, or hard work. Give credit where credit is due. Encourage people to get into the practice of starting meetings or conversations with each person reflecting on something they're grateful for.

What can I do to share gratitude?

If you think about your job, home, or another group you belong to, would you say that people are treated fairly? Are people held accountable for their actions? Are they rewarded for their contributions and successes? Are the leaders dependable and accountable themselves? Is there trust?

Taking Care and Being Self-Aware

You're of no use to anyone if you're dead or sick. How can you effectively show up and support your team if you aren't taking care of yourself?

Leaders tend to carry the weight of many on their shoulders, which prompts them to work harder and care even more. If work-life balance isn't intact, the result can be burnout and fatigue, and sometimes worse. In addition, leaders who don't take care of themselves set an example for others to do the same, leaving everyone feeling burnt-out and undervalued, which only grows worse during stressful times. On the flip side, when leaders are more self-aware and they fuel themselves with restful sleep, exercise, good nutrition, time in nature, or quality relationships, they build their resilience and act as role models for others to do the same.

If you want to be a great leader, you want to be a role model for resilience by creating an optimal work-life balance and adopting self-care and coping practices that will especially fuel you during times of stress. When you're self-aware and you value self-care, you encourage others to value their own self-care as well. One resilient person can thus encourage the entire community to be resilient.

I noticed this happening in my own life. When I became more serious about my fitness, I found my body changing. My body got muscular, and I became more vibrant and energetic. People around me wanted to have what I was having (to borrow loosely from the movie *When Harry Met Sally*). They wanted to know my secret, and before I knew it, people who normally didn't exercise were exercising and taking their health more seriously.

Because you likely have a busy and stress-filled life, you'll want to incorporate self-care practices into your life that you will actually do. Don't, for instance, make yourself meditate for 30 minutes if you feel you don't have a lot of time in the day. Start slowly and build your way up to doing more of the things you enjoy. If you don't enjoy it, you won't do it. This is why self-awareness is necessary.

Examples of key practices for self-care are restful sleep, exercise, healthy eating, meditation, spending time outdoors, spending time with loved ones, and having fun.

TIP

I encourage you to keep a journal so that you can jot down observations about how you feel, questions you might have, or ideas that arise. For full details on improving vitality and self-care, see Chapter 16.

The 5-minute morning meditation

Rather than jump straight out of bed and before you look at your smartphone, lie in bed for five or so minutes. Start your day waking up mindfully.

>> **Appreciate the feel of the blanket, sheet, or comforter and the feel of the pillow beneath your head.** If light is coming through the window, notice the sunlight as it shines. Can you feel the warmth on your skin? What sounds do you notice? Are the birds singing?

>> **Appreciate your breath as you breathe in deeply and exhale completely.** Think about something you feel grateful for.

>> **Slowly pull off the covers.** Notice the difference in the temperature of the air and how you feel.

>> **Place your feet on the ground.** Then you can better appreciate your connection to and support by the earth.

>> **Slowly stand up.** Become fully aware of the weight of your body and any other sensations you feel.

>> **Stretch your arms as far as you can, reaching for the sky.** Breathe in as deeply as you can, and when you exhale, allow your body to loosely fall forward, bending at the hips as your arms dangle to the floor. Breathe in deeply and exhale a few times completely as you release any sleepiness into the earth.

>> **Take a deep cleansing breath.** Slowly rise up, take the breath, and start your day.

Practicing gratitude

Stress can build up and negatively affect your state of mind and mood. Taking the time to remember why you're lucky and what you're grateful for can help keep your mood and mindset more positive while also lowering your stress level.

>> Keep a gratitude journal and, before going to sleep, write down three things you're grateful for that happened during the day.

>> Be thankful every time you eat, grateful for the food and for the farmers or people in the market.

>> Talk to your plants and thank them for being beautiful and gracing your home or garden.

>> Thank yourself every morning for waking up.

>> Take a mindful walk and thank the earth for the divine beauty around you.

>> Show gratitude to the people you work with, live with, and interact with.

4
Putting Resilience into Action

Harness your body's innate ability to heal and thrive by providing it with the best possible fuel.

Improve resilience by organizing and harmonizing your mind and physical space.

Maximize your ability to succeed in the workplace and establish work-life balance.

Share the resilience and enhance happiness, optimism, communication, and connectedness in your family.

Chapter **16**

Fueling the Mind and Body

L ife's hardships are difficult enough as they are, let alone having to manage them when you're sick. Being resilient means being able to bounce back from hardship and setbacks, often stronger and better, not just mentally but also physically. This means being hardy enough to recover quickly from any kind of stress, including injury, surgery, or viral illness, fueling your mind and body so that you can fully enjoy life and thrive.

This chapter guides you to evaluate your physical vitality and gives you the tools you need to help you thrive. (For more details on physical vitality, see Chapter 3.)

Making Fitness a Priority

If you were to be given the choice between being sick, feeling okay, and being fit and having an abundance of energy to conquer hardship and still maintain your vitality, which would you opt for? I would imagine it's the last one. The problem is that being fit takes work and mindfulness, which many people don't make time for, so they settle for the second option, feeling okay.

Unfortunately, settling for feeling okay may not support you to be resilient when push comes to shove. If you don't exercise, eat nutrient rich foods more often than not, get restful sleep, find time to shut off to relax and play, or partake in other healthy behaviors, your body may not be ready to withstand as much stress as you might need it to during challenging times. You can be on the verge of feeling sick and not know it until you actually get knocked down and can't bounce back readily.

To truly be resilient, you need to fuel your mind and body so that you can be vibrant and strong every day of your life. It means making fitness a priority, learning how to listen to your body, and being self-aware so that you can take care.

Taking care of your body's whispers before it screams

The presence of aches and pains — whether annoying or debilitating, acute or chronic — indicate that something's out of balance. What they don't mean is that you should drink more caffeine, eat more fried food, stay up all night, or pop a bunch of pills so that you can keep going. You have feelings for a reason, and those feelings, which include your emotions and any other bodily sensations, are meant to signal you to pay attention and take care. If your body tells you it's tired, for example, it may be asking you to take care and sleep. If it tells you your left hip is aching, it may be asking you to take care and stretch, move around, and avoid being sedentary. If it tells you that you're sad, it may be asking you to take care and let out your grief and nurture yourself. If you don't listen and you don't take care, these whispers can eventually become screams that lead to more problems.

Ellen came to me complaining of constant lower back pain. It had been going on for months, and the pain was starting to radiate down her left leg. She said it started out as a little tweak in her lower back after a long day of meetings and carpooling. She had taken some ibuprofen at the time for about a week, which helped, but the next morning she could barely get out of bed. She had meant to go get it checked out, but she didn't have time. She complained that her days involved one meeting after another, carpooling, getting the kids ready for their activities, and generally being the wife, husband, mom, and everybody's go-to person at the office.

I said, "Wait a minute. I thought you had a husband and that you were an accountant. Why aren't you getting any help?" That's when the tears started flowing. It turned out her husband had been laid off over six months previously, so she had increased her hours at work to full time. At first, he was busy looking for work and the more he got rejected, the more depressed he became. She thought with his being home he would take on more responsibility, but instead he was withdrawing, and she was left to do most of the work at home. She was exhausted all the time, buying takeout meals and avoiding cooking healthy meals, and she was frustrated. She felt badly for her husband, but at the same time she was angry and worried. When I asked her if she had asked family or friends for help, she said she was too embarrassed. I said, "I am so sorry you have had to go through so much distress. I am guessing your back knew you had to get some help before your brain did. I am not saying that there isn't something structurally misaligned in your lower spine, but generally, the body can handle some misalignment, but not when it is bearing so much stress and weight. Often, back pain is telling us we need to be supported and to slow down and nurture."

I showed Ellen a relaxation technique using her breath that would help her relax the tension in her body and once she felt more calm, we discussed and agreed on some better coping strategies: She was going to ask her mother to help with the home; have a long, empathic talk with her husband and let him know how she was feeling and then urge him to seek counseling; assign him specific tasks he could accomplish; and create a routine for herself within the time that she had to stretch, walk, relax a bit, eat healthier, and get more sleep. Two weeks later, Ellen reported that her mother agreed to help three days a week, and her girlfriend was taking over the carpooling two days a week. Her husband agreed to get help and apologized for not being more helpful, and she had gone for a walk twice, meditated daily, stretched before going to bed, and started cooking meals again and was therefore being more mindful about eating healthy food. And, Ellen reported that she had no more back pain.

Ellen's story is just one example of the thousands of clients I have worked with who have had similar experiences. Your body is wise and will let you know when you're out of balance and in need to take more care. Do you take care?

REFLECTION Do you listen to your body? Are you too busy to improve your self-care habits, like exercising or cooking a healthy meal? Do you take medicine so that you can continue living your usual lifestyle? Do you ignore pain? Do you ignore symptoms, hoping they will go away? Is your excuse that you dislike going to the doctor? When you're anxious or stressed, do you face the issue head-on, or do you drink, eat, take pills, or work harder in an attempt to numb yourself?

When you take care of your body's whispers, you can not only prevent subsequent problems but also be proactive in helping your body become stronger and fitter. Taking care of your body's whispers means that you have to make a concerted effort to listen and be attentive to any sensations or feelings you experience throughout a given day. It's akin to staying alerted to a baby's needs. Listening and taking care involves these actions:

>> **Be mindful.** Without judging anything as good or bad, regularly scan your body from head to toe, appreciating any sensation you might be experiencing and labeling that feeling. You might notice, for instance, "Lower back tight" or

"Stomach gurgling" or "Right buttock relaxed, left buttock numb." Also scan your emotional state. Your labels may be "Feeling sad" or "Feeling excited" or "Feeling anxious."

>> **Check for patterns.** If you notice an area of tension or discomfort in your body, assess that area for an emotional component. If you notice that you're feeling an emotion, check to see where the corresponding tension or discomfort shows up in your body.

>> **Have a conversation.** Talk to your body. Ask areas of tension or discomfort (in a curious frame of mind rather than a judgmental one) why they are there. Listen to what it has to say. It can be quite eye-opening!

>> **Fuel and nurture.** Decide to fuel and nurture your body in the ways it's asking you to. If you're tired, sleep. If you're hungry, eat food that will fuel you. If you need support, call a friend or counselor. If you need to grieve, let yourself grieve. If it hurts a lot, stop.

>> **Not being scared, take care.** When in doubt, get professional help. Healthcare professionals are much better able to help you when you can be clearer about what is bothering you. When you take care of your body early on, it's that much easier to get the right care that you need.

>> **Err on the side of choosing love.** Be empathic toward yourself. Do not judge. You aren't bad for being in pain, having to slow down, or feeling angry. You're human, and your body is brilliantly communicating to you that you're in need of love. So choose to love yourself and your body.

Evaluating your vitality

Part of the process of listening to and taking care of your body is to regularly assess your state of vitality, which includes both how you feel and what lifestyle habits you're engaging in. You want to look for ways that you're fueling your health to thrive or ways you're creating leaks in your fuel tank that might be causing your health to dive. Doing such an evaluation can give you a better idea of what you might need to improve on to feel more energized and physically resilient.

The first step is to look at your daily routine. What happens during the average course of your day?

The time pie exercise

Draw a circle on a page. Imagining that the whole circle represents a 24-hour day, divide the circle into sections relegated to your activities, giving a time frame to each one. Activities should include sleep, exercise, relaxation, work, hobbies, eating healthy, eating junk, spending time with friends, volunteering, worrying, feeling stressed, procrastinating, playing video games, and reading.

This exercise is meant for you to become more self-aware of how you might spend the average day. There is no judging, right or wrong, so be as truthful and authentic as possible. You may want to make separate time pies for an average weekday and one for the weekend.

Once you have completed the time pie, evaluate what activities or habits fuel you and which ones may drain you. Could you replace actions or activities with more fun and vitalizing ones? The next assessment exercise will help you evaluate your self-care habits and your level of vitality.

The vitality self-assessment

Try to rate the statements as honestly and authentically as you can. The assessment may seem long, but trust me, it's worth getting to know yourself better. The more you know and understand now, the more useful the ensuing tips will be for you as you forge ahead on the path to improving your vitality.

Use the following scale to rate the following questions or statements. Never true: 1. Rarely true: 2. Sometimes true: 3. Often true: 4. Frequently or often true: 5.

Statement	Rating
I describe myself as feeling vibrant and full of energy.	
My energy stays high throughout the day.	
I have the energy to run around with little kids.	
I rarely get colds during the course of the year.	
I consider myself fit and healthy.	
I rarely need to visit a healthcare professional.	
I rarely cancel my appointment when I have an issue that requires a healthcare professional.	
I do not take any medications.	
The last time someone checked, my metabolic profile (cholesterol, blood pressure, heart rate, and weight) was perfect for my age group.	
I rarely complain of aches and pains (including muscles, bones, and headaches).	
I rarely complain of feeling tired.	

Statement	Rating
I rarely feel irritable or moody.	
I feel my body is quite flexible.	
I rarely feel stressed.	
My weight is stable.	
I rarely eat processed foods or foods that are high in sugar and fat.	
I eat at least five to six servings of fruit and vegetables a day.	
I rarely drink sweet soda, fruit drinks, energy sport drinks, or beverages with artificial sweeteners in a given day.	
I rarely snack on processed (hydrogenated fat) chips or crackers or refined sugary foods like candy, desserts, chocolate, ice cream, or cookies during the day or evening.	
I regularly walk places rather than drive.	
I regularly take the stairs rather than take the elevator or escalator.	
I take regular breaks to stand, stretch, or move my body to avoid sitting for long periods.	
I do vigorous exercise (aerobics, high interval training, running) two or three days a week.	
I do resistance or weight training exercise two or more days a week.	
I do moderate sport activity (biking, swimming, tennis, or long walk) five or more days a week.	
I regularly engage in stretching exercises or exercises that help me be more flexible, like yoga or Pilates.	
I get very good-quality sleep.	
I feel rested when I awaken in the morning.	
I rarely drink caffeine to have energy in the morning — I don't need it.	
I rarely wake up during the night.	
I fall asleep easily.	
I keep my bedroom quiet and peaceful.	
I relax at least an hour or two before I go to sleep.	
I regularly enjoy relaxing and having fun throughout my week.	
I have many hobbies that help me relax that I use during the day or week.	

Statement	Rating
I take time to meditate and quiet my mind by doing mindfulness or another type of meditation, yoga, or tai chi.	
I often allow my mind and body to just be quiet or silent.	
I regularly go on retreats or take vacations.	
I get out into nature every day in one way or another.	
I regularly take time to visit a beach, park, or forest or to hike or picnic or engage in another activity out in nature.	

Add up your score. If you scored low, I encourage you to focus on being more pro-active in making the changes that will support your body to thrive. If your score is high, I congratulate you for taking care of yourself. Keep it up, but read on — you might learn something new! You may also score high in one area and low in the next. Take note so that you can know where to focus your efforts.

Improving Your Metabolism

Do you ever wonder why you feel tired even though you've slept or why the "tire" is growing in your midsection even though you've been exercising? The likelihood is that you aren't fueling your body with the right nutrition, and your body is stressed and inflamed, which is shutting down your metabolism.

In today's modern world, fast food, foods high in sugar and trans fats, processed food loaded with chemicals, overeating, and a lack of physical activity have led to an increase in obesity, diabetes and other diseases, inflammation, and poor metabolism. When metabolism is slow or not working efficiently, it means that the body, especially the mitochondria that produce energy, are having a hard time making energy out of the food you consume.

Understanding metabolic flexibility

Normally, your body has the ability to make energy out of the carbohydrates, proteins, and fats you consume. Because your human ancestors would go for long periods without food, the body was designed to metabolize carbohydrates when the food was plentiful and to metabolize fats when food wasn't available, or when they were forced to fast. The ability of the body to go back-and-forth between metabolizing carbs and fats is called *metabolic flexibility*.

WHAT ARE YOUR EATING HABITS?

REFLECTION

Think about your eating habits and answer these questions:

How many meals do you eat in a day?

At which times do you usually eat?

How often do you snack?

What is your usual choice of snack?

Do you get up at night to eat?

How much coffee or tea do you drink in a day?

How many alcoholic drinks do you have in a day?

Do you eat when you're stressed?

Do you eat until you're full?

Do you ever fast?

What is the longest period that you go without eating?

How many hours per day do you fast between your last evening and first morning meals?

When you listen to your body and fuel it appropriately with balanced amounts of carbohydrates, proteins, and fats, while also giving it periods of rest from eating, you will find that you have more energy and your body's metabolism improves. If you have a preexisting medical condition like diabetes or problems regulating blood sugar, I recommend being monitored by your healthcare provider when making dietary changes.

The body prefers sugar over fat because it's easier to metabolize, so if sugar or carbohydrates are present, your body will use this fuel source first and store the fat away in your fat cells for future use. During periods of fasting or starvation, the body calls on this stored energy, first using the stores of carbohydrates (glycogen stores) and then the fat stores. The longer the fasting period, the more the body will eventually revert to lipolysis, or the breakdown of fat to fatty acids to use for fuel. As such, when you go through periods of eating as well as fasting, the body is able to maintain metabolic flexibility, or the ability to shift back-and-forth from using glucose (from carbohydrates) or fatty acids (from fat) for fuel or energy.

In today's modern world, people eat all the time, and often the food is laden with additives like refined sugar, partially hydrogenated fats, and artificial sweeteners. The result is that fats end up being stored in your fat cells (especially in your midline), and the carbs you're consuming stimulate insulin levels to rise. Eventually, the mitochondria that are producing fuel can become less efficient in their ability to switch back-and-forth between carbohydrate and fat metabolism so that you lose your metabolic flexibility. The mitochondria also end up getting tired, which translates to your metabolism being tired. The result can be weight gain and the slowing down of your metabolism and a propensity to develop other problems, like diabetes, metabolic syndrome, high cholesterol, or heart disease.

Taking charge of your metabolism

If you have trouble going long periods without eating, feel like you need to take a big snooze after a meal, feel lethargic more often than not, or have a hard time losing weight despite dieting — you may be experiencing metabolic inflexibility or at least the need for a metabolic boost. Here are five ways you can take charge of your metabolism (for more details on improving your nutrition, see Chapter 3):

Cutting down on sugar

The fewer carbohydrates you ingest, the more often your body will have to rely more on fat for its fuel source. You want to cut out refined grains or sugar (even juice), processed foods, and dairy and eat one to two pieces of fruit a day to start. (You can increase this number after a month or so.) You may also want to try following a paleo diet for three to four weeks and see how you feel, which essentially involves eating only vegetables and proteins, nuts and seeds, and some fruit. After a few weeks to a month, introduce carbohydrates slowly, starting with whole grains. If you're prone to inflammation or have an inflammatory disease or history of cancer, you may also benefit from trying a ketogenic diet, which is also low in carbohydrates. Unless you have a medical condition that requires you to stay on a particular diet, I recommend eventually shifting to a balanced diet composed of whole grains, lean proteins, plenty of vegetables, certain fruits, and nuts and seeds — and void of processed foods and refined sugars.

Boosting your metabolism with antioxidants

Poor metabolism has been closely linked to oxidative stress and inflammation, and the use of antioxidants in nutritional plans has been shown to have a positive influence on this. Oxidative stress has been linked to a myriad of health problems including cancer, heart disease, dementia, and autoimmune disorders. Antioxidants are naturally occurring immune cells that neutralize free radicals (oxygen molecules missing an electron) that are responsible for oxidative stress.

You can increase your intake of antioxidants by eating dark leafy greens, berries, and other fruits and vegetables that come in a variety of colors. You can also add in spices or supplements containing curcumin and green tea extract, two of the many different antioxidants that are powerful in aiding metabolism. Examples include Brussels sprouts, broccoli, tomatoes, carrots, spinach, grapefruit, cauliflower, cabbage, dark leafy greens, lemon, lime, blueberries, red grapes, green tea, dark chocolate, coffee, cinnamon, cloves, black pepper, turmeric, and oregano.

Trying intermittent fasting

You may want to check how long you can go without eating by fasting for short periods. Try starting with 12 hours, eventually extending it to 16. For instance, if your evening meal is completed at 8 P.M., you have your next meal at 8 A.M. Over the course of the next week, extend that window to 16 hours so that your last meal is at 5 or 6 P.M., for instance, and your next meal is at 9 or 10 A.M. the following day.

By consuming all your calories in the morning window when your metabolism is supposed to be most active and then fasting from early afternoon on, you can improve your metabolic flexibility. Some people choose to fast for 24 hours or more, which you may want to try — make sure that you check with a healthcare professional if you have underlying health problems. It isn't right for everyone.

Keeping the microbiome happy

The bacteria living in your gut support your metabolism by helping your body break down, absorb, and digest food and nutrients. They prevent inflammation and support your body's antioxidants to do their job well. Introducing foods into your meals that are high in these bacteria can boost the flora or natural bacteria in the gastrointestinal tract and reduce inflammation. Such foods can include kefir, miso, kimchi, olives, pickles, sauerkraut, or yogurt that is very low in sugar. Prebiotic foods also support and feed the bacteria. Examples include garlic, dandelion greens, chicory root, onions, Jerusalem artichoke, leeks, asparagus, bananas, barley, oats, apples, flaxseed, and seaweed.

Challenging your body with a variety of physical exercises

The more active you are, the more energy you need, which pushes your body to break down fuel sources. After the body depletes the glycogen stores, it begins to catabolize (break down) the fat stores. When you push a little harder, move faster, or do something new and different, your body also has to reset itself. For this reason, you want to create variability in your workouts and every now and then throw in an activity your body isn't used to doing, such as hiking, swimming, or dancing.

Getting Functional with Your Movement

As the old saying goes, "If you don't move it, you lose it" — literally. If you don't move your body, you can lose muscle mass as well as brain cells. If you want to stay resilient, age well, and keep your wits about you, it behooves you to get your body moving and get your fitness on.

Your human ancestors exercised daily because they had to move from one place to another, pick up stuff, put stuff down, climb or run to obtain food, run fast so as not to become food for another animal, or jump high to reach fruit hanging from a tree branch. In the modern world, you don't have to move to survive. No predator is chasing you, and you can visit a drive-through, order in, or dine at a restaurant. If you want to exercise, you go to a gym or hire a trainer, and if you're motivated, you move outdoors for a jog or a bike ride. For many people, it's hard to motivate and exercise, especially when other things in life take precedence.

Whether you enjoy exercising in a gym or outdoors, with weights or without, or if you simply don't like it at all, you can get your fitness on by incorporating movements into your daily life that improve your functioning abilities, employing similar functional movements that your ancestors used to survive. These movements involve squatting, lifting, pulling, pushing, or twisting. By incorporating these movements into your life, you can build muscle mass and improve your metabolism as well as your coordination and flexibility. In fact, you might find that doing these functional movements regularly can be as good as or better than weight training in helping you become stronger and leaner.

Integrating five key functional movements

In addition to walking, you can incorporate at least five basic functional movements into your daily routine throughout the day — or do them all together for 15 to 20 minutes.

Step 1: The squat

You squat throughout the day as it is, whether you realize it or not, like when you go to sit down on a chair or a commode and then get back up.

The movement: Start by bending forward at your hips, sticking your buttocks back and then down, and letting your knees follow until you're in a squat position. Avoid starting the bend from your knees. Your knees will follow as you bend from your hips. When you're ready to stand up, press your heels into the floor and squeeze your buttocks as you rise.

TIP

Suggestions: Do 10 squats every day and work your way up to 50 every day, adding 1 to 5 squats to the rep scheme per week. You can also practice your squats by doing the get-up-and-go, which means you slowly sit down so that your buttocks tap the edge of a chair and then get-up-and-go ten times.

Benefits: This movement helps your hips, quadriceps (in your thighs), glutes (in your buttocks), back, and abdominal muscles.

Step 2: The lunge

You may not think you lunge much during the day, but you do — every time you walk up the stairs and sometimes when you go to pick up an item from the floor. It involves transferring your weight from one leg or another as you're moving forward or backward.

The movement: Step forward with one leg about two-and-a-half feet ahead, and then bend both knees, until that knee of the back leg touches the ground. Make sure that when you bend the knee of the front leg, it doesn't extend past the toes of your foot.

TIP

Suggestions: Do five to ten lunges anytime you move from one room in your house to the next, or do 10 to 20 lunges (5 to 10 on each leg) every minute on the minute for five to ten minutes.

Benefits: This movement strengthens your glutes, quadriceps, abdominals, and back.

Step 3: The push

If you can do a push-up, you're already on your way to adding this valuable move-ment into your life. If you can't, not to worry: You're pushing every day when pushing the grocery cart, pushing the door open, lifting something over your head, or putting something up high on a shelf. It takes coordination, stability, and some upper body strength. To push intentionally, you can get yourself a household object, like a broom or book.

The movement: Keep your feet shoulder's width apart. Hold the object with both hands in front of your chin. Tighten your buttocks and imagine that someone is about to punch you in the gut (it makes you tighten your belly), and then press the object upward, using your shoulders and moving your head back slightly, toward the sky until your elbows lock and the object is above your head. Slowly bend your elbows and bring the object back to a resting position.

Suggestions: Do the push movement with an object ten times a day and, work your way up to three sets of ten, taking 1-minute breaks between sets.

Benefits: This movement benefits your shoulders, triceps, and back.

Step 4: The pull

You pull regularly, too. You pull on your pants, pull on ropes or blinds, pull out your laundry, and so on. The pulling motion can be done with your arms overhead or with your arms closer to your body.

The movements: Get a bag and put grocery items in like a bag of rice or four or five oranges to create a light weight. Hold the bag with your arm extended at your side. Keep the abdominals tight and your shoulder stable, and then bend your arm and pull your elbow upward, as if you're rowing, and then slowly straighten the arm, letting the bag return to starting position.

Suggestions: Do this movement five times with each arm, for three sets, taking 1-minute rests between sets.

Benefits: This movement benefits your biceps, shoulders, and back.

Step 5: The hinge

The hinge is probably the most common of the movements when it comes to your daily activities, because you bend at the hips to pick things up, empty the dishwasher, and even sit. Learning how to do this movement correctly can have many benefits, including strengthening your back and improving your balance.

The movements: With an object on the floor, bend at the hips, and with a flat back and tight abdominal muscles, bend forward, allowing your knees to bend as you reach for the object on the floor. Pick up the object and then press your weight into your heels, squeeze your buttocks as you straighten your knees, and raise your back to the upright position.

TIP

Suggestions: Do this movement five times for three sets, resting one minute between each set. Work your way up to five times for five sets.

Benefits: This movement benefits your glutes, lower and upper back, shoulders, quadriceps, and hamstrings.

REMEMBER

The more you engage your body in doing functional movements, the stronger you can become and the more energy you might find you have to have some fun in your life.

Playing isn't just for kids

Are you having enough fun in your life? Playing isn't just for kids, after all, and it's just as important for your health and well-being as exercise, healthy nutrition, and restful sleep. Playing can be anything from playing a sport, an instrument, or a game like Monopoly. It involves taking a time-out from your serious and focused life to enjoy yourself, laugh, be amused, and become engaged in something that is enjoyable to you. Adding play to your life can enhance your outlook and improve your flexibility, creativity, productivity, and sociability, and more importantly, help you manage stress.

Many of my clients often find it challenging to sit still and meditate in order to relax. They do find, however, that they have an easier time complying with instructions to add more play into their lives, and they do find that it helps dampen the impact of stress on their lives. The reason is it supports them to maintain a more positive outlook and use the coping techniques they're learning.

Did you know that play deprivation can be a real issue? I'm sure you have personally met people who are so serious that it seems they have forgotten how to laugh, play, or be happy. Dr. Stuart Brown discussed the concept of play in his TED Talk and said, "The opposite of play is not work; it's depression." Imagine if we could get the curmudgeons of the world to just play a little. What a happier, more resilient world it would be!

You can choose from a myriad of ways to play, and of course the ones that give you joy are the ones you want to partake in. In general, though, here are seven ways you can add play into your life:

>> **Find activities you love.** If you don't love it, it won't be fun. Set time every week to engage in an activity that you enjoy — whether it's alone or with other people. Do you enjoy painting, dancing, playing cards, or singing karaoke? Schedule at least one hour a week to engage in this fun activity.

>> **Go back to being a kid.** What did you love to do when you were a kid that you stopped doing as an adult? Did you play an instrument? Play catch or Frisbee? Did you collect baseball cards or play dress-up? Travel down memory lane and engage in a fun pastime activity.

>> **Embark on an adventure.** When you were a child, everything was new and somewhat of an adventure. Either go with your friends or family on a real adventure, like skydiving or ziplining or another adventurous outing, or create your own adventure, like putting together a treasure hunt or pretending that going to the grocery store is a treasure hunt.

>> **Have a laugh.** Make an effort not to take yourself so seriously. Imagine that you're an alien who has landed on Earth and your time here isn't just an adventure but is also quite comical. Your body, your life, and everything around you is a bit upside-down and silly. Go to comedy shows or watch funny movies. Stimulate your funny bone regularly.

>> **Schedule game night.** What is better than having fun with friends on game night? Schedule a game night once a week or every other week with the same group of people. You can play charades, trivia, or spin-the-bottle. Take your pick!

>> **Pick up a new hobby.** You can always challenge yourself by picking up a new hobby or an activity you've always wanted to try. There's no time like the present!

>> **Have play dates.** Play dates aren't just for kids. People's lives can become so busy that by the end of the week they aren't sure how time flew by so quickly. Schedule play dates with people you enjoy being around at least once a week.

Taking Time Out for Recovery

Most people are used to going 100 miles per hour every day, all day. There's always something to do and so much to get done. Can you sit still? Most of my clients claim they can't. They say they grow restless, uneasy, or anxious. They feel guilty and think they *should* be doing something. This belief also keeps them from getting all the sleep they need. Then they wonder why they feel burnt out, tired, or depleted.

Your brain and body need a time-out for rest and for quiet, to refuel and to regenerate. Even your car needs to have pit stops to refuel, get the tires changed, and give the engine a chance to cool off. When you embrace the opportunities to take a time-out — to rest, sleep, meditate, let yourself off the hook, or simply be — you build an even stronger foundation within yourself that supports your resilience.

Losing guilt and embracing love

For some reason, people have convinced themselves that it's dishonorable to rest and do nothing. They feel guilty and push themselves often to the brink of exhaustion. If you want to be resilient, you have to give your brain and body time to recover and give your cells time to replenish themselves. Lose the guilt and follow these guidelines:

>> Be gentle with yourself. Don't "should on" yourself or shame or blame yourself.

>> Ask yourself, "If I loved myself, what would I do?" Then do it.

>> Let yourself be pampered. Take a relaxing bath, get a massage, or luxuriate in your bed. You deserve it.

>> Think of helping others with a full tank. You're of no use to anyone if you're sick, so if your tendency is to think self-care is selfish, think of the resting period as a time to fill up so that you can help others.

>> Practice self-compassion.

All the wealth and success in the world mean nothing if you're dead.

Quieting the mind

One of the best ways to quiet your mind is through meditation. Over the past several decades, there has been great interest in studying the benefits of meditation, especially its effects on the mind, emotions, and physical well-being. One key benefit of meditation is that it calms the mind and relaxes the body, allowing you to stay in the present moment and away from worries of a future that has yet to happen or from rumination of the past that is already gone. (For more details on quieting the mind, see Chapters 9 and 10).

Getting restful, quality sleep

Resilience won't happen unless you sleep, because it's during sleep that your brain cells regenerate, memory is consolidated, hormones are released into your body that keep you healthy and strong, and your immune system cleans out the waste, especially in your brain. (For more details on sleep and sleep hygiene, see Chapter 3.)

Chapter **17**

Organizing Your Environment

The environments you create reflect and affect your physical, mental, and emotional health — and therefore your resilience. If your external world is messy and disorderly, it can have a negative impact on your mental and emotional health, on your coping behaviors, and on your time efficiency. Likewise, if your mental world is cluttered, it negatively affects your coping abilities, emotional health, and likely also your personal space. Decluttering and creating more organization in your environment and your mind can, in turn, help keep your mind clear, reduce your stress levels, create a feeling of more spaciousness, and, ultimately, enable you to feel more energized, capable, and resilient.

This chapter focuses on describing ways that you can better organize your thoughts as well as the physical space where you spend most of your time, and in a way that supports you to develop better habits and feel more in control and empowered.

Benefitting from Being More Organized

The lack of organization can trump your ability to be efficient and productive. It can cause you to waste good energy, experience more stress, have less clarity of mind, and put a damper on your resilience. In contrast, organizing your environment as well as your thoughts can help you be more efficient with your time and energy, feel productive and in control of your life, support your mental clarity, and give you more time to have a happier and richer life. You can

>> **Become more productive.** The more organized you are, the more efficient you can be, as well as productive, because you aren't wasting time looking for things, and you have more time to focus and get tasks done. Being organized enables clearer thinking, less distraction, and better communication. The positive results are the proof in the pudding.

>> **Feel less stressed.** Whether it's being unable to find an item of clothing or feelings of overwhelm and confusion when your thoughts are muddled, becoming more organized will help you feel more in control and better able to manage any stress. You're more likely to feel calm and grounded and in control or on top of things.

>> **Make better decisions.** Good organization can lead to better decision-making when you feel less stressed and less distracted, as your thoughts and priorities are clearer, not to mention that you have ready access to the right tools and information. Your concentration will improve, as will your ability to absorb new information.

>> **Feel better about yourself.** When you're late, forgetful, overwhelmed, or incapable of completing a task from a lack of organization — or if you can't get something done because of one small task you forgot or an item you misplaced — you can end up feeling badly about yourself and frustrated, which can lead to losing self-confidence and self-respect. By becoming more organized, you might find that you're more punctual; better able to complete projects in a timely manner; clearer and therefore making better decisions; and feeling good about your accomplishments; all of which result in more self-confidence and self-respect.

>> **Enjoy a happier life and better relationships.** When tasks no longer feel like they're piling up, you will notice that you have much more free time. You'll also enjoy boosts of confidence because you're able to complete tasks more efficiently and communicate more clearly. You will find that you get to enjoy more freedom, do things you love and enjoy, and have more time to grow your social connections. Your relationships will thank you.

» **Experience better health.** The less worry or feelings of overwhelm you have, the better you will sleep, the lower your stress response, and the more time you have for self-care behaviors and Me Time. Your environment will also be cleaner, meaning that you have less exposure to toxins like mold or other allergens.

Taking Stock of the Obstacles to Organization

Did you know that women who describe their home as messy have higher stress hormones than women who describe their home as relaxing or having a beautiful outdoor space? It makes sense if you think about it and about all the time you have wasted in your life looking for something you misplaced. Or how about the anxious feeling you might have experienced when coming home to a messy house or being late to a meeting or an appointment because you actually forgot about it?

If you're like many of my clients, either your home is disorganized, your desk is full of clutter, or your brain is full of to-do items, which causes you to feel overwhelmed, unable to focus, or feel out of control. If you relate to my clients, then the idea of getting organized and cleaning up is daunting, which means that you procrastinate and put it off. The more you put off organizing, the more clutter you accumulate, and as the clutter increases, you feel more overwhelmed. In addition, your ability to think clearly, process information, or make decisions can be negatively affected.

My client Suzanne described herself as a capable and strong person who "got stuff done" and that's why people — her family and co-workers — depended on her. The problem, she complained, was that her mother had recently fallen sick and, between her caretaking and work responsibilities, she was feeling increasingly overwhelmed. She had no time for herself, so to soothe her nerves, she was overeating and shopping online. As a result, she reported, she had gained close to 50 pounds in less than a year, and the way her house looked made it clear that she was becoming a hoarder. In addition to helping Suzanne overcome limiting beliefs (see Chapter 11) to strengthen her self-value and develop self-care behaviors that would better soothe her nerves and cope with stress, I worked on helping her become more organized. We created a daily schedule for her to relieve stress by throwing things out, which turned out to be quite cathartic. We organized her calendar, prioritizing the action items of most importance and delegating responsibilities to people in her life who were actually waiting for her to ask. We also created a system that helped organize her thoughts, which involved writing things down and mind mapping so that she could create a 360-degree view of any given situation. Within weeks, Suzanne reported feeling lighter and freer, in mind, body, spirit, and closet space.

When you take stock of your tendencies and the obstacles that may be keeping you from being organized, you can take the appropriate measures to fix the problems. Common obstacles to being clutter-free include these:

>> **You don't know what being clutter free feels like.** You're used to the clutter, and you don't know what it might feel like to be organized.

>> **You're feeling overwhelmed.** You're overwhelmed because you have so much stuff.

>> **You have no free time.** You don't have the time.

>> **You have too much going on in the head.** You can't get organized in your head in order to organize your environment.

>> **You're addicted to accumulating possessions.** You have an addiction to accumulating things, called *hoarding,* which is a reflection of a deeper mental health issue.

>> **You're unable to delegate.** You can't say no, you take on too much, and you're unable to delegate.

Freeing Up

It's possible to take control of your clutter and reap the rewards of a more organized life, both professionally and personally. The more ordered and calm your life is, the better able you are to think clearly, act decisively, take better care of yourself, be more efficient and productive, de-stress, and enjoy your life.

Decluttering involves not just organizing your external environment but also discovering ways to organize your thoughts and ideas. One act supports the other, and you might find that creating ways to organize your mind helps you then tackle your external space. You might also discover the reverse to be true: When the physical spaces where you spend most of your time are clutter-free and harmonious, you can think more clearly. Being more organized, in short, sets your mind fee and your time free.

Freeing up your mind

When your mind is overloaded, it can be overwhelming, which adds to stress and inhibits good decision-making and being present, focused, and happy. A variety of tools are available to you that can help you free up the clutter in your mind and organize your thoughts so that not only are you less stressed, but you're also more creative, present, curious, insightful, and innovative. You can start by following my suggestions in the following sections.

Keeping a notebook

Keep a notebook and journal your thoughts, observations, and questions as you go through the day. If something pops into your mind, write it down. Use colorful pens or markers, doodle, or draw. If it's in your mind, it may be taking up space, so get it out on paper. Keeping a notebook helps clear your mind while also engaging your sense of curiosity and creativity as you let ideas and observations flow out. Mark the time and date you're making your notes or observations so that you can go back and read them when you need to. Use your notebook to write down key points from conversations or meetings or ideas that pop up while you're doing something else.

Creating a list

Using the notes from your notebook, other observations, and the obligations you know you have in your life, create a to-do list, categorizing action items (household, work, children, and self-care, for example). Then itemize your list according to level of priority. You might have different lists — one for the day and one for the month.

Mind mapping

Though the list is helpful, it's still a linear view of your life and your obligations. When you have a 360-degree view of any given action item, you're better able to see what needs doing, what items you need to be responsible for, and what you can delegate to someone else — essentially, to be more creative and better at solving problems. Mind mapping is a wonderful technique, developed by Tony Kuzan, that helps you do just that — it helps you organize your ideas, plans, goals, or thoughts by stimulating both your left brain and right brain. It involves placing your ideas on paper, using color and free association.

These are the rules for mind mapping:

>> **Start with a symbol or picture that represents your topic in the center of the page.** This allows your mind to open to a full 360 degrees of association. Symbols and pictures are also more stimulating and easier to remember than just words alone.

>> **Write down key words.** They act as your "information-rich nuggets" to enable you to recall and do creative association.

>> **Connect the central image with the key words.** Connect the words with lines that radiate from your central image so that you can see the image and words relate to one another.

>> **Print your key words.** That makes them easier to read and remember.

>> **Print only one key word per line.** This strategy forces you to find the most appropriate word that will cover all associations or as many as you might need.

>> **Print the key words on the radiating lines so that the length of the word is the same length as the line.** This enables maximum clarity and encourages you to use the space economically.

>> **Use colors, pictures, dimensions, and codes, which allow for greater association and emphasis.** Highlighting and using color helps your memory, stimulates ideas and associations, and helps you prioritize what is most important and what is secondary.

You can pretty much use mind mapping for everything — from summarizing a chapter, thinking about retirement, problem solving an issue at the office, or planning a vacation or dinner for friends. This technique lets you see the big picture and understand which ingredients need to go into a recipe so that you can better accomplish your goals.

Breaking the big into little

Mind mapping helps you see what steps need to be taken to accomplish goals so that you can break the bigger goals into smaller action items. Focusing on meeting smaller goals can reduce your feelings of overwhelm and increase your self-confidence and self-value because you're better able to meet your goals.

Celebrating your wins

As you allow your ideas to flow and form a clear picture of your priorities, celebrate yourself when you scratch something off your list. In fact, schedule celebration time in every day to congratulate yourself for one or two accomplishments. When you reward yourself in these ways, the positive feelings encourage you to partake in the same actions again.

Managing your time

The need to "manage time" is a funny concept if you think about it. People are so busy "doing" that they have no time to "be," so they need to manage it. It may be a strange concept, but, unfortunately, the struggle is real. There just doesn't seem to be enough time in the day to get all the tasks done, let alone get organized, or mind map. The deal is that when you take a little bit of time to organize, you find that your life actually frees up to "be."

Managing your time more effectively is crucial to feeling more in control of your life and more effective in it. You want to create a system that enables you to feel confident about what you can do and when, and one that helps you stay calm as you flow through your busy day. It may take a little time to create the system initially, but once it's done, you will only need to review and update as you go forward. The following seven sections can help you manage your time more effectively.

Creating a template

Start by creating a template of typical to-do categories from your to-do list. For instance, categories might include work projects, communications (people you need to follow up with or correspond with), finances, home repairs, child care, self-care, housekeeping, or cooking and eating. The categories stay the same, for the most part, from day to day and week to week. The itemized lists beneath the categories will change, however.

Prioritizing your list

Separate the action items according to their level of priority and when they need to be completed. When does this task have to get done? Is it a short-term or long-term goal? Can you take your time and do a little every day, or does it all have to be done today? Write down a date for when you think this action item needs to be completed.

Delegating responsibilities

Review your list and think about what aspects of the action items you need to do and what you can delegate to someone else. (Mind mapping at this point is helpful.) Many of my clients find that they're doing more than they need to, and plenty of people, especially colleagues and friends, are willing and wanting to be involved or to be asked to help.

Transferring to your calendar

Once you have created a list with priorities, put the details in a calendar so that you can view a week or a month at a time, noting the items that need to be done daily, starring tasks that are a priority, and estimating how long action steps might take. Follow these general rules for keeping your calendar organized:

>> **Sync your calendars:** Keep a desk calendar that allows you to view your entire week or month as well as a digital calendar to send you alerts and reminders. Make sure the two are synced.

>> **Everything goes into the calendar.** Whether it's scheduling a dental appointment, needing to call a contractor, having a deadline at work, or planning to call a friend, put it on the calendar.

>> **Complete high-priority tasks in the morning.** That's likely when you're at your best.

>> **Do lower priority tasks that you have time to complete in the afternoon.** Make sure you set aside at least 30 to 60 minutes for this task so that you will find that when the time comes for this task to be completed, you're pretty much done. Slow and steady wins the race!

>> **Include daily tasks in your calendar.** You have to put everything in there, not just the new stuff.

>> **Keep open time slots in your calendar.** Then you can accommodate the "anything goes" tasks or events in the middle or end of your day.

>> **Don't forget to schedule Me Time.**

Having fun with sticky notes and color

Create a color scheme for your input that reminds you of which actions or tasks are of higher or lower priority. Use sticky notes if you need reminders, though you should be sure to place them in designated areas so that your wall space or desk space isn't cluttered with them. You may want to consider having a bulletin board on a wall in your home and office where you can keep a calendar and sticky notes.

Staying flexible

The best-laid plans can get thrown out the window when the unexpected shows up at your door. Don't get too upset if your plans get screwed up. Make sure you give yourself wiggle room every day to be able to handle emergencies or unexpected delays. This way, if nothing happens, you have more free time for yourself.

Creating timed distractions

Don't feel badly if you can't focus — it happens to the best of us. When you have a lot going on in your life, staying focused can be even more challenging. I find scheduling timed distractions into your day always helps. Most people try to force themselves to focus and end up procrastinating or being useless because they can't focus. You're better off scheduling breaks every 20 to 30 minutes to get up and stretch, take ten cleansing breaths, go for a walk, get something to drink, cruise the Internet, or play a video game. Give yourself anywhere from 1 to 15 minutes to be distracted with something else and get it out of your system. When the time is up, you will find that you can better focus on the task at hand.

Decluttering Your Physical Space

A chaotic home and office can ruin your productivity and your mood. It can zap your motivation and add to your stress. You know that you need to declutter, but where do you begin? It can be overwhelming! Remember to always start small, doing a little at a time, and follow these ten decluttering steps:

1. **Gather containers to put stuff in.** Get yourself plenty of trash boxes, inexpensive containers, or bins in which to store things.

2. **Set aside time.** You might set aside 15 minutes a day to start and maybe more time on the weekends. You probably want to start with small blocks of time so that you don't feel overwhelmed. You're better off being consistent with your efforts over time than trying to do it all at once.

3. **Start small.** Start small and focus on one space at a time in a specific room. You might start with the drawer of a desk and then slowly move on to clear the entire desk, followed by the area surrounding the desk, the closets, and other cabinets, for example.

4. **Completely pull everything out.** Whether it's a drawer, a closet, or the trunk of your car, pull everything out all at once. Clean the area thoroughly, and then begin sorting through the stuff.

5. **Separate everything into piles.** As you clear items, put them into one of five piles, labeled accordingly:

   - *Trash:* It has to go — it's not worth anything.

   - *Donate:* Give it to charity or give it to a friend: It has to go, and it's worth something, so it should go to someone who can use it.

   - *Sell:* It has to go, but it's worth a lot. I recommend this category only if you're adept at selling things, and you have the time to do it. Don't even attempt to put things in this category if selling used items isn't in your wheelhouse.

   - *Keep:* I need it or I love it.

   - *Not sure:* I can't decide what to do with this item. I'll set it aside for later.

6. **Put your Keep items back.** The Keep pile can be split further into two piles — one for storage and one to use regularly. If it's meant for storage, like your tax files, put it in labeled storage bins to be set aside in your designated storage area. Keep only the items that you know you need to store, like your taxes for the past seven years. If the paper is ten years old, chuck it. If it's something you use regularly, place it back in the drawer, and so on.

7. **If you don't use it, let it go.** If you love it but never use it, bless it and think about the person who will be grateful to have it and use it. Give it away. You can take a picture of it if you need, but if you really can't let go, put it in a storage bin and label it.

8. **Ask for help.** You may be uncertain whether to keep or let go of specific items. When in doubt, get a second opinion by asking a friend or family member. You can always hire an organizing professional if you're overwhelmed and confused. If you feel that you can't let go of anything and suspect that you're hoarding, seek help from a mental health professional.

9. **Maintain upkeep.** As you declutter and become more organized, make a concerted effort every day to keep it up; here are my suggestions:

   - Set aside five to ten minutes a day to put away all stray items.

   - Make a habit of cleaning dirty dishes.

   - Clear your desk or even your computer desktop when you're done using it.

   - Keep a balanced karma in your closet. Basically, if you're going to get something new, you give away something you have or get rid of it.

   - Regularly shred papers you don't need.

   - Regularly file papers according to a labeling system that makes sense to you. Do the same with files on your computer.

   - On your desk or where you do most of your work, designate an area where you keep the things you need for the current project you're working on. Everything else should be stored away in your filing system.

   - Regularly review your emails, delete old or unimportant ones, and create files for the ones you need for the future. Label them in levels of priority.

10. **Celebrate.** Reward yourself when you have completed a big task, like fully organizing your desk, a closet, or an entire room. Treat yourself to a relaxing bath, massage, nurturing dinner, or fun event with friends. Organizing needs to be a balanced process, where you dig in and then take time to relax. Over time, this rhythm of organizing and then enjoying free time should become the habitual flow in your life.

As you improve at eliminating clutter and becoming more organized, you'll find yourself feeling more relaxed and positive, and you'll eventually have more time for yourself and the people you care about.

TIP

You can also focus on beautifying and creating an environment around you that supports you to be healthy and thrive.

Harmonizing Your Environment

A harmonious and relaxing environment supports your body and mind to also relax and be harmonious. Have you noticed how differently you feel in different spaces or rooms? Science does show that bringing nature into the home, in the form of plants or scenes of nature, can improve health and well-being.

Feng shui is the ancient Chinese practice of harmonizing your environment with nature. Practiced for over 6,000 years and originating from Daoist beliefs, feng shui involves strategically designing your surroundings and placing objects in specific locations in such a way that it creates a feeling of harmony and flow. The belief is that if your home has an imbalance, it will show up in your life — and if you create balance in your home, it will balance your life. Feng shui has been touted to improve well-being, relationships, energy flow, and success, and to clear negative energy. As it becomes quite popular in today's modern world, proponents of this practice claim that it helps people feel stronger and healthier.

Though I am not an expert on feng shui, I can offer you general takeaways that can help you create an environment that's not only more organized but also more healing and harmonious. (And, of course, you could always hire a specialist to help you, or you can, for more information, refer to *Feng Shui For Dummies,* written by David Daniel Kennedy and published by Wiley.)

REMEMBER

You don't live in isolation from your environment, which means that whatever is happening around you — including personal environments like your workplace, home, and car — can influence your mood, behaviors, health, and ability to manage stress.

Clearing and creating an open space

You may have already read about decluttering your environment, and with feng shui, it's especially important to clear plenty of open space as well as remove clutter from hallways and entrances. Removing clutter allows energy to flow in and out. You especially want the entryway of your home to be welcoming and open — to you, guests, and new opportunities. Keep the area clean, add a mirror on the wall or a beautiful light fixture, or add a plant or flowers that add a feeling of openness and welcome. The key is to remember that the space welcomes opportunity!

Placing furniture or key items facing the door

Ultimately, you want your bed, table, or desk to face the door, though not be directly in line with it. Known as the *commanding position*, placing your key furniture facing the door allows you to be able to see who or what is coming your way without being in the line of danger or blocking the energy flow. According to feng shui principles, this improves your sense of control and the flow of energy in your space.

Letting the light in

Light brings with it new possibilities. Allow natural light in through windows, and make sure you keep the windows clean so that you can stay open to seeing new possibilities and opportunities. Feng shui also recommends adding lighting to staircases or touches of art to balance out the energy and, literally, lighting the way.

Shutting the lid where water drains

In feng shui, it is believed that water represents abundance and wealth and that keeping the doors closed if it's a room where water drains, like bathrooms, prevents your wealth from running down the toilet or down the drain. Make sure that the toilet seat is down (ladies, you can tell the gents that this will improve their finances), and put plants near the kitchen sink or in the bathroom because it's believed that plants soak up water.

Bringing in green

Plants are always welcome when it comes to feng shui, because they represent a positive life force and energy and bring nature into your home. Science also confirms the health benefits of bringing plants into homes, workplaces, and even hospitals.

Balancing with nature's elements

The Daoist premise is that everything in nature (including plants, rivers, mountains, animals, galaxies, and us humans) is made up of five elements — wood, fire, earth, metal, and water — that interact with one another to sustain life. Each element has a role in the cycle of life and has its own characteristic, relating to the seasons, colors, movements, shapes, and other aspects of life.

The following sections present some examples of colors and shapes you can bring into your home or office to support the energy you desire. The key is always balance, never overdoing it on any particular color or element. The following few sections provide guidelines and examples of ways you can improve the balance in your home or workplace using nature's elements.

Wood: Creating a feeling of new beginnings

The wood element is associated with growth, optimism, and renewal and the season of spring. It represents opportunity, enthusiasm, new beginnings, and positive energy and is especially helpful when you want to turn over a new leaf, get out of a rut, or move something in your life forward, like your career or relationship.

>> **Bringing wood into your space:** Bring in furniture made of wood, use wood flooring or wood cabinets, or accessorize with items that are green as well as ones that are shaped in the form of a square or triangle. Examples include green plants, throw pillows with green accents, and wooden furnishings.

>> **Best rooms:** Hallways and entryways.

>> **Best combination:** Combine this element with the fire element to enliven the energy and create positivity and flow. Throw in a beautiful lamp with a wood base in the hallway.

Fire: Bringing in passion and productivity

The fire element represents productivity, passion, romance, joy, success; the energy of the life-giving sun; and the season of summer. The energy is bright, bold, and happy, and it can bring warmth, joy, and sensuality, like an open and loving heart. It brings in creativity, empowers relationships, and enhances the feeling of connection.

>> **Bringing fire into your space:** Bring in reds and oranges, candles or fireplaces, and items that are shaped in the form of triangles or pyramids. Examples of the fire element are fireplaces, candles, pillows with red accents, crystals in the shape of pyramids, the addition of lighting to dark rooms, and the opening of window shades to let in light.

>> **Best rooms:** Bedrooms, family rooms, office spaces, and workshops.

>> **Best combination:** Combine this element with earth to add stability, like adding exposed bricks to your fireplace, or accent the family room with earthenware or weaved baskets.

Earth: Establishing warmth and stability

The earth element is associated with the warmth and stability and the season of late summer. This element supports your connection with yourself and your strengths and aligns you with being able to appreciate all that you have and are.

>> **Bringing earth into your space:** When you bring in earth colors like browns, yellow, and reddish orange as well as square shapes, you enhance the feel of stability, security, and nurturance. You can paint walls, bring in items that share the earth colors, use stucco or paint walls beige, use ceramic tiles, or accent with earthenware or weaved baskets.

>> **Best rooms:** Living rooms and dens.

>> **Best combination:** Combine this element with metal to produce a grounded and productive energy, like having a living room table that has a stylish metal base or adding modern art to the walls.

Metal: Creating space for creativity and thoughtfulness

The metal element aligns industriousness with creativity and is considered to be a conductor for the soul because it's associated with the season of fall. It supports organization, attention to detail, and thoughtfulness.

>> **Bringing metal into your space:** You can bring in anything metallic or round, or anything that has colors like gray, gold, silver, or white. You can add stylish tables and chairs that have a metal basis, modern art, or appliances or have items like countertops with marble or copper finishes.

>> **Best rooms:** Kitchens, bathrooms, and workshops.

>> **Best combination:** Combine this element with water to enhance productivity, like adding blue accents to the backsplash in the kitchen.

Water: Allowing in peace and flow

The water element is associated with creativity, inner peace, reflection, and flow — like moving water — and is associated with the season of winter. It supports you to feel peace, to be more in the flow of your life, and to be reflective.

>> **Bringing water into your space:** You can bring in colors like blue and black, items made of glass, items that contain water, and shapes that have no real form but create the feeling of expansion and flow. Bring in fish tanks, indoor fountains, or glass vases or tabletops or mirrors, and bring in items that have a variety of blue accents.

>> **Best rooms:** The study or the meditation room.

>> **Best combination:** Combine this element with wood to enhance the feeling of growth, flow, and reflection, like putting a plant in the study.

REMEMBER

Working toward being better organized, both in your mind and where you spend most of your time, invariably supports you to be more resilient.

Chapter **18**

Resilience in Action at Work

When it comes to work, resilient people are better able to handle the demands that are placed on them, prioritize their workload, and also find time for personal care and renewal. This is no easy task in today's modern world, especially when people are constantly connected by email or text, the workload never seems to diminish, and job security is often in question.

The World Health Organization describes stress as *the* global health epidemic of the 21st century, and the Center for Disease Control and Prevention states that one-quarter of all employees feel their job is the number one stressor in their lives. Burnout from work stress isn't uncommon, and because it doesn't look like anyone's work stress will ease up anytime soon, it behooves you to build resilience in order to manage it and still thrive.

Being resilient at work involves persevering despite setbacks, believing in your capacity to handle challenges as they arise, knowing how to prioritize, getting support when you need it, and delegating responsibilities when you can. It also entails being organized and being able to continue taking care of yourself so that you have the energy and fortitude to maintain your health, emotional balance, and mental clarity — no matter the stress.

My client Marie thought she would never be free of the anxiety she felt daily at work. She worked for a large company and felt it was hard to "turn off" the workday, because she was hyperconnected and had to be responsive to work anytime and anywhere. She felt tired all the time, had trouble sleeping, and complained that she had little time for herself or for self-care. On closer evaluation, I discovered that Marie had a deep fear of failure. She feared that if she didn't respond to emails right away, she would appear incompetent and that she believed her identity and sense of value resulted from putting her heart and soul into work.

I asked her then, "Is it true that the job or what you do defines who you are? Are you only your work? Are you only you when you're working hard at work?" She reflected for a moment and then answered, "When you put it that way, no, it doesn't define me, and it's not who I am."

Upon further discussion, Marie realized that she was basing her sense of value on her work successes and on working hard in general. If she wasn't working hard, she understood, she doubted her worth. If she succeeded, she felt valued and worthy, and if she failed, she felt the opposite about herself. We therefore focused on helping her strengthen her self-value (covered in Chapter 12) and developing a more optimistic attitude, especially toward failure. Rather than view failure as a negative event, she was to practice seeing it as an opportunity to learn, and grow stronger. As Marie's belief in herself and her capabilities grew, she was better able to establish balance between her work life and personal life. She began delegating responsibility to other people and leaning on her networks of support for help, recognizing that she didn't need to work so hard, or all alone, to know her value.

Like Marie, you too can enhance your work resilience. It takes fostering a sense of self-value along with optimism, creating balance within yourself and your life, and strengthening your networks of support. This chapter focuses on how you can better cope with the pressure and adversity that come with workplace stress and guides you to develop strategies and habits that can help you improve your resilience at work.

Fostering Optimism

When I worked my job in primary care medicine from 8 A.M. to 6 P.M., going back to work every Monday felt like a huge challenge. I *dreaded* Mondays. Come to think of it, I dreaded Tuesdays, Wednesdays, and Thursdays, too. Fridays I enjoyed because I knew I would get to take a break on the weekends, if I weren't on call at my job — and those weekends caused even more distress. Finding myself on the verge of having an anxiety attack one day, I decided I needed to do something — I had to check in on my attitude.

When I checked in, I realized that my negativity was causing me to despise my job, minimize my compassion for patients, lose sleep, and become lazy about taking care of myself. My job was filled with plenty of stress on its own, and I was adding to it with my attitude so that work was becoming practically unbearable. I understood then that I had to make a choice:

Change my attitude and stay at this job or change my attitude and leave this job.

Either way, I had to change my attitude to one that was more positive or at least less stress provoking. I had to remember that the job was providing me with an opportunity to learn and grow and that I chose to be in medicine for a reason. I decided to focus on why I got into medicine, what I loved about it, and what I loved about my patients. I reestablished my sense of purpose and value and chose to change my attitude to be more positive and open. This attitudinal change enabled me to discover new strengths and make loving connections with my patients. And, after a few years, it led me to discover the next path I was to embark on, because I was open to it. The whole experience taught me to see challenges as opportunities.

REFLECTION

Can you think of ways your attitude positively or negatively affects different situations in your life? Do you look at life differently when you are in a good mood versus negative?

Seeing challenges as opportunities

It may sometimes feel like you're trapped in your job. You're unhappy, you feel stressed, and you worry that you will never be able to leave, because you need the money. Your negative thinking leads you to feel increasingly helpless and hopeless. Your job may suck, but your attitude and negative thinking are making the situation worse. What you may not realize is that your job isn't an endpoint — rather, it's a bus stop on the journey of your life. You may not like it, but you do have the option of viewing it differently, as one of many bus stops along the way that provides you with the opportunity to explore new grounds and uncover new discoveries about life and about yourself.

Cultivating optimism and a positive attitude involve seeing value everywhere and opportunity for growth in every situation. Rather than resist change, you look forward to it. Rather than fear failure, you accept it as part of your process for getting better and growing stronger. Rather than ruminate about having problems, you decide that the problems are opportunities for you to master skills, learn about yourself, and build new achievements.

Developing the habit of using challenges as opportunities involves doing the following:

» **Choosing your attitude.** Check your attitude at the start of each day and throughout the day. Are you dreading work? Are you pessimistic, judgmental, or negative? Don't judge yourself; rather, acknowledge your mental state. Have compassion for yourself and the way you feel. Tell yourself, "Given what is, what can I do? I can choose to stay miserable and negative-sounding, or I can choose to shift my attitude."

Then make a choice if you want to make the shift. You can choose to stay in a negative state of mind, or you can choose to shift into a more open and positive mental state. First make the choice.

» **Looking for opportunity.** Decide to focus on at least one reason that work is presenting you with an opportunity. Will you have the chance to learn something new? Can you test out a new theory? Is there a challenge you can think of that will teach you how to become stronger or better at something? Can you put yourself in your colleague's shoes and learn more about how that person might feel?

Take your time to come up with the opportunity that will motivate you most. You might discover several different options, so make a list, setting the intention to go through your day seeking ways to learn and grow.

» **Staying curious.** Ask questions and be curious about everything, like a child who is learning about something new and interesting, especially looking for ways to delve deeper into making the most of the opportunities you have written on your list.

Choose to be in a state of wonder when something goes awry or when you find yourself frustrated. Being curious helps you let go of any fear around making mistakes while also diminishing feelings of overwhelm. Remember that you're looking forward to the opportunity to learn.

» **Keeping a notebook.** You might find more than one opportunity, and as you go through your day, observations and ideas will invariably come up. Write it all down. Keep a notebook on hand and jot down whatever comes to mind.

This process can also ignite your curiosity and creativity. You might find that you're better able to solve problems and find creative solutions to complex situations.

» **Being proactive.** Welcome assignments that are out of your comfort zone as you continue to seek opportunity for growth and learning. Believe in yourself, and believe that you're up to the challenge of doing something different and new. Be proactive; talk and seek support from people who can help you along the way.

Seeing value everywhere and in everyone

When you feel overwhelmed, negative, or victimized by your circumstances, you're more likely to be judgmental of others and yourself. You can flip the switch on your negativity by choosing instead to see value in others and in yourself. Like Marie, when you recognize your value, you don't view your accomplishments or failures as representing who you are. You can have compassion for yourself and be able to accept your weaknesses. You also may have more compassion for others and be able to see value in everyone and everywhere. The reverse is also true: When you choose to see value everywhere in everyone, you own sense of worth increases.

You can improve your sight so that you can see value everywhere by

REMEMBER

>> **Nurturing a positive self-view:** Believe in yourself, your value, your contributions, and your ability to find solutions to complex problems. At the end of your day, write down three or four characteristics or behaviors you feel proud of, positive traits you learned about yourself, or positive actions you took toward nurturing yourself that day.

>> **Avoiding self-flagellation:** Beating yourself up serves little purpose, other than to make you feel worse and to sabotage your resiliency.

You're human, and you will make mistakes. Forgive yourself, and accept yourself as you are. If you find that you're getting upset with yourself, take a break and choose instead to nurture yourself.

>> **Celebrating your wins:** When you take time at the end of your day to journal, make sure you include what went well that day and congratulate yourself so that you can train yourself to focus on valuing rather than devaluing yourself.

>> **Cultivating compassion and empathy:** Being more compassionate toward yourself and others enhances positive emotions, improves your sense of well-being, and helps lower stress levels. The key is to remember that everyone is human and that everyone is suffering and trying to learn in some way. You can practice compassion meditations (see Chapter 9), work toward self-acceptance (see Chapter 12), or develop the habit of putting yourself in other people's shoes to help you gain empathy (see Chapter 13).

>> **Relishing gratitude:** Enhancing your sense of gratitude will certainly improve your mood and your attitude. When you're compiling your list at the end of the day, also write about what you feel grateful for or the reasons you feel lucky.

Embracing failure and setbacks

A setback doesn't confer being a failure, nor does it determine your worth. As frustrating or upsetting as it may be to experience one, neither does a setback have to ruin your day. It can instead be the reason you decide to do something a little differently, learn something new, or finally take a break. Having this kind of attitude helps you stay positive and view every situation as fodder for growth and learning.

When you hit a roadblock or a setback, it's okay to take a few minutes for a pity party. Once you've gotten it out of your system though, flip your attitude, and start realizing that the situation is giving you a chance to take a break, breathe, make some space, and reexamine and reset your priorities, paths, or ideas. You can decide to embrace the setback by

» **Seeking meaning:** Opportunities are everywhere, especially in setbacks. Look for meaning. What is there to learn? What can you do differently? Is this the right path? Seeking meaning doesn't mean you decide that everything happens for a reason — rather, it means that you look for reason with regard to why things happen. Milk the situation for what it's worth, and discover more about yourself, why people behave in certain ways, or why life happens as it does. Read up on different literature, ask for advice, or use your favorite search engine to find more meaning in your situation.

» **Using rejection to reflect:** There are many reasons that your proposal was rejected or a plan didn't work out. It isn't personal. Use the rejection as a chance to reflect, learn, and start again in a different way. If rejection occurs again, reflect again. You may find that you're going down the wrong path and instead discover a path of lesser resistance and better success.

» **Embracing change:** Remember that change is part of life and some of these changes may screw up your carefully laid out plans. If this happens, take a pause and figure out a way to adapt. Remember that this change is presenting you with an opportunity to grow, ask questions, hear advice, and be okay with receiving the support you need in order to take a different path or do things differently.

» **Redirecting your focus to something positive:** When you find that you're upset or frustrated and hyperfocusing on what's wrong, decide to redirect your focus to something else temporarily. You can focus on a work-related issue or not, but make sure it's something positive that celebrates a victory, something you feel grateful or lucky for. As you connect with positive emotions and thoughts, you improve your sense of wellbeing and self-value, allowing you to lower your stress levels and be better able to view the situation more objectively.

>> **Keeping it in perspective:** Take note of your emotions and your thoughts. Notice when your thinking is irrational or limited, when you focus on why everything is wrong or nothing is going your way, or when your tunnel vision disables your ability to see the big picture. Take a pause and remind yourself that you're not a victim of life and that you have resources within you and around you to handle the situation. Clear your negative emotions and balance yourself, and you will find that your perspective will shift. You may even gain new insight. (See Chapter 10 for details on how to gain deeper insight.)

>> **Getting back at it:** Your bigger perspective will help you gain better insight and ideas about potential solutions, goals, strategies, and even new pitfalls. Devise a plan and ways to forge ahead with a new direction. Meet with your colleagues, boss, or customers, and present your ideas, keeping in mind that if your ideas are rejected, you're again being given an opportunity to learn.

Choosing Balance

With technology at your fingertips, it's extremely challenging not to be constantly connected, and it might often seem that you need to work around the clock as a result. Throw in a pandemic that keeps you working from home and literally scared for your life, and the boundaries between personal life and work life become that much hazier. As life stress and the workload increase, self-care behaviors, positive emotions, and life-balance can be lost. To build and hold on to your resilience, though, you will want to make the choice to find and create more balance.

REFLECTION

How much time do you set aside to take care of you? Do you feel selfish when you do take the time?

Creating and finding balance within yourself and your life translates to having more physical and emotional space to take care of yourself and your relationships. It involves regulating your emotions, letting go of limiting beliefs that are driving maladaptive behaviors, and asserting boundaries and structure in both your personal life and work life. When you choose to take care of yourself, you fuel yourself so that you can have the capacity to handle the stress that is present in your life. Choosing and creating balance involve these actions:

>> **Acknowledging that an imbalance exists:** Recognize that your work-life balance ratio is out of whack. Do not wrong, blame, or shame yourself or anyone else. Simply acknowledge the existence of an imbalance.

>> **Taking a pause:** Decide to get off the hamster wheel for a moment, and take a pause so that you can examine yourself and your life more closely. Take five

minutes or five days to reflect, breathe, and clear your mind of your list of tasks and your worries.

» **Regulating your emotions:** Examine your emotions and the fear that is driving your behavior. Choose any technique that helps you calm your emotions and quiet your mind. (See Chapter 9 for exercises on quieting.)

» **Shifting your mindset:** As you feel quieter and calmer, choose to shift your mindset. (See Chapter 11 for more on shifting the mindset.) Think about ways to fuel yourself that will support you to have more energy and enhance your ability to perform and strive for excellence. Ask yourself, "What can I do to support myself to thrive and perform at my best?" This means evaluating your self-care habits, organization, support, boundaries, values, time for rest and relaxation, and so forth.

» **Taking action to take care:** Choose to start taking action to take care. Knowing that the more energy you have, the bigger your bandwidth, start making sure that you're getting restful sleep and putting nutrient rich fuel in your body. Give yourself breaks to exercise, meditate, walk, or be with friends. Look at how better to organize your time and your space, and make yourself a priority.

Bringing meditation into your work life

You can better manage your time, your emotions, and your thoughts by bringing meditation into your life. Having a meditation practice helps reduce stress levels, regulate emotions, improve communication skills (see Chapter 9), focus and have great insight (see Chapter 10), and enhance performance. I know this sounds like another task to put on your to-do list, and you might think you don't have enough time, which is why I am also suggesting that if you can't take time to meditate, you can bring meditation into your work life. This means you don't necessarily take a chunk of time to sit quietly in the lotus position and meditate, and instead, take pauses throughout your day to breathe, lower your stress response reactivity, and be mindful. You can bring meditation into your life by following these four action steps:

» **Breaking to breathe.** Take a 5-minute break in the middle of your day to meditate. You can choose any type of meditation that works for you. You may want to listen to a guided meditation on an app, do some yoga, pray, or sit silently as you gaze out the window at nature. You may also choose to go for a mindful walk. Start with five minutes, and build your way up to 20 minutes, if you can.

» **Setting reminders.** Set your watch or calendar to alert you every hour to remind you to breathe. For at least ten cycles of breath, count 1-2-3 as you breathe in and 1-2-3-4-5-6 as you breathe out. The more breath cycles you do, the better.

>> **Making your mornings mindful.** Start your day being mindful so that it carries over into your time at work. Eat your breakfast mindfully or take a shower mindfully. Be present, in the moment, in appreciation, without judgment. You can appreciate the aromas of your breakfast meal, the colors on the plate, the textures of the different foods, and appreciate how it's fueling and nurturing you to achieve excellence today.

>> **Practicing workplace mindfulness.** Set the intention to be mindful throughout the workday. When you take the breath breaks, use that time as an opportunity to reset and be more present, aware, curious, appreciative, and nonjudgmental throughout your day.

Getting unplugged

Being more mindful helps you take note of your energy and identify when it's time to unplug and take a break, knowing that when your energy runs low, your ability to be productive and efficient diminishes greatly.

REMEMBER

Typically, your ability to concentrate and perform at a high level lasts anywhere from 90 to 120 minutes. For some, focusing for longer than 20 minutes is challenging.

By giving yourself short breaks to detach and reset, you can refuel yourself enough to improve your mental clarity, focus, emotional balance, and resilience. When you take breaks, you benefit most if you totally unplug from everything and everyone. This means being off the clock and turning off notifications, emails, or any technology that will grab hold of your attention and draw you back into work or into the big wide web that can be so addicting and brain-zapping.

Here are some tips to help you unplug:

>> **Time your breaks.** While at work, remind yourself to take at least a 5-minute break every 90 minutes with phone reminders, calendar alerts, or emails. Go for a walk, stretch, meditate, grab a bite to eat, or chat with a friend or colleague.

>> **Take timed distractions.** If you find that you can't focus more than 15 or 20 minutes, add in short timed distractions to your day. Every 20 minutes, give yourself a 5-minute break (set a timer) to distract yourself. You might choose to do your meditative breaths, stretch, call a friend, or close your eyes.

>> **Stick to an unplugging schedule.** Decide on a set time to unplug emotionally at the end of your day and stick to it. When you unplug, set the intention to focus on yourself and on your relationships, hobbies, and whatever you enjoy.

>> **Go on holiday.** Taking extended time off for rest and recovery, even if it's just a day, provides you with fuel that helps you go that extra mile. Go away for a day, a weekend, or a week. Attend a retreat, go fishing, or take a staycation.

Establishing an organized approach to managing tasks

Creating more balance in your life involves getting organized in how you approach your work life as well as your home life. You can remove activities from your life that are wasting your energy, for instance, split projects into smaller goals that you can manage, engage in activities that you love and really want to do, and delegate tasks to other people who might be better equipped. When you restructure how you go about doing things and get better organized, you will find that you have more time for you and for engaging in pleasurable activities. (For detailed organization tips, see Chapter 17.)

Setting smaller, more attainable goals

When you set manageable goals, you're more likely to feel less pressed for time and better able to set boundaries between your work life and personal life. Setting smaller and more achievable goals also supports your sense of achievement and ability to celebrate yourself and your successes, which enhances your self-value and your sense of well-being. Take any project and establish a set of small goals that will take you toward accomplishing your task. Estimate how much time each small goal will likely take and add a few hours or a day to give yourself some wiggle room. Prioritize which goals need to be done first and mark your calendar for when you plan to attack each goal.

Wasting no energy

Pay attention to activities that may be wasting your time and energy and are taking away your ability to focus, to enjoy what matters to you, or to be productive. Note that if you're engaging in something that feels like it's wasting time yet it's serving as a distraction that enables you to focus better later, you can simply create boundaries around how much time you spend doing this activity (like surfing the Internet, playing video games, or texting). Nothing is wrong with engaging in activities that seem to have no productive value — unless they're preventing you from being more efficient and focused or they're draining your energy. If you enjoy these activities, do them during your timed distractions so that you stay within a time limit. Pay attention to your energy level after engaging in these activities. If you feel energized, great. If not, and they have no productive value, stop engaging in the activities.

Setting boundaries and priorities

Learn to say no, focus on what matters to you and what plays to your strengths, and prioritize people, projects, activities, and your self-care. Before you throw yourself into a new project, ask yourself whether the subject really matters and how important it might be. Figure out whether the project is one you have time for, given your current schedule and commitments. Evaluate whether the project or activity will fuel you or drain you. If you think it will drain you, either don't do it or set limits on when you will. Make sure to set limits for work hours and create a clear separation between your work life and home life as well as Me Time.

Delegating responsibilities

Let go of projects and activities that are not your priority or that don't play to your strengths, and delegate them to people who can manage the tasks instead. Though delegating can lighten your workload, it can also increase it if you don't assign tasks to the right people or if you don't communicate your needs clearly. You want to think of delegation not as a way to pass the buck, if you will, but rather as a way to build trust and show respect to someone else, in that you believe in their ability to help and contribute. I realize that sometimes it feels like tasks will take longer to complete if you don't do them yourself, but this attitude doesn't decrease your workload, nor does it enable others to learn, grow, and improve in their skills and confidence.

Getting a life

You can't have work-life balance if you have no life. I remember having this thought the day I finished my first *grueling* year of residency. I had just worked for 30 hours without sleep and, having just ended my shift, I decided to walk around town and enjoy a nearby summer fair. I remember walking around like a zombie, observing people laugh and talk to one another without a care in the world and thinking, "I just lost a year of my life. I did nothing but work. I am going to make sure that when my residency ends, this type of lifestyle is an exception, not the rule. What good am I to anyone if I am a zombie?"

REMEMBER

Your life is meant for you to enjoy, and that work is just part of your life's journey. It might pay the bills and it might fulfill your passions, but nevertheless, it does not determine your value. It still involves doing rather than being.

Your value grows when you choose to value yourself and your life and you engage in activities that also fuel your life and support you to thrive. This means you take the time to unplug and focus on you and your health, passions, joys, interests, and relationships. Make yourself a priority and take the necessary measures to fuel yourself so that you can perform at your best while also having a great life. Now, 25 years later, I no longer walk around like a zombie. Instead, I try to live by these four general rules:

>> **Take care of you.** Take care of your health. If your goal is to be productive, happy, and vibrant, it behooves you to fuel your body. Be physically active, and make sure you're getting restful sleep and nutrient rich foods. You should partake in other self-care habits to improve and enrich your physical and mental health, as I explain in Chapter 16.

>> **Find a hobby that brings you joy.** Whether it's a sport or a creative endeavor or project, being active in your community, or volunteering, engage in an activity that takes your mind off work and brings happiness and fulfillment into your life.

>> **Nurture and be present in your relationships.** Nurture your relationships and spend time with people outside of work and, if you enjoy them, with your colleagues. Enjoy a dinner out, a movie, a hike out in nature, or an entirely new and different endeavor. Make it a rule not to talk about work. Cherish those you love, and be fully present when you're with them. Turn off notifications on your phone and consider putting it away altogether when you're with people you care about.

>> **Be.** I dare you not to *do* and try just to *be*. Be completely unplugged. Give yourself the luxury of doing nothing in particular. Roam around in nature, immersing your senses in the present moment, in full appreciation of the beauty around you. Luxuriate in a relaxing bath. Stare into space. Take a nap. Give yourself the space to simply be and not do, even if only for five minutes a day. I recommend getting into the habit of *being* at least 20 to 30 minutes a day, if you can.

Strengthening Networks of Support

The stronger your support networks in both your personal life and work life, the more resilient you can be. You can lean on your family and friends, cry on their shoulder, or celebrate interests together. At work, your colleagues can offer advice, assist you in projects, serve as sources of emotional support, and be mentors in helping you manage uncertainty or difficult situations. To strengthen your networks of support, I recommend these actions:

>> **Make a list.** What sort of support do you need, and what kind of support can you give other people? Is there something you want to learn? What goals do you have? Being clearer about your goals, both personal and professional, will guide you to figure out whom to turn to or what groups you might want to join, work related or not. Make a list of your goals and then make a list of resources of people or groups who can support you to achieve these goals.

>> **Nurture your existing personal relationships.** The people you're close to are the people who will support you during the hard times. Nurture your friendships and make them a priority. Set aside time daily or weekly to see the people you care most about. Reach out regularly, not just in times of need, and invest in your existing relationships so that you can make them stronger.

>> **Build relationships with your co-workers.** You can only talk so much about work with your friends and family. It's important to be able to feel understood and heard, and also be able to turn to peers for advice or mentorship. Building your relationships with your coworkers helps you enjoy your job and keeps you engaged. Take time to chat with them during breaks, and make time to meet up outside of work.

>> **Expand your professional connections.** You benefit from building your professional connections by also looking outside of your workplace. Join professional networking groups or meetups and schedule time to meet individuals for coffee or lunch regularly. Doing so provides you with more diversity, knowledge, sources of support, and even possible work opportunities.

Chapter **19**

Resilience in the Family

R esilient families flourish and thrive despite adversity. They grow together as a result of confronting difficulty rather than fall apart. Relationships are nurtured, and the adults of the household act as role models for their children, staying level-headed, compassionate, calm, and resilient in the face of hardship.

It's one thing to be resilient as an individual — it's another thing for an entire family to be resilient, because often families are made up of individuals who are vastly different. Is it possible to cultivate resilience when each individual is so unique, circumstances change, and resources and family dynamics vary?

This chapter focuses on how to cultivate a resilient family, how to set an example for your children and create structure for them, and how to work together as a family to solve problems and develop positive coping skills.

Developing the Core Framework

Whether you're part of a biological family or a group of individuals who have come together, it's possible to cultivate resilience as a family unit. According to Dr. Froma Walsh, a leading researcher in family resilience, families — whether formal or informal kin networks — can shape their ability to respond to adversity by applying a structured framework for resilience. This framework, according to Walsh, involves nine processes that fall into one of three categories: sharing beliefs, being organized, and employing effective and compassionate communication practices. These nine processes are covered in the following sections.

Sharing beliefs

These three processes make up the framework that enables families to share beliefs:

>> **Maintaining a positive outlook:** Resilient families work together to maintain a positive and optimistic outlook. They encourage one another to be optimistic, to look for silver linings, and to accept that there are some things in life they can't control.

>> **Making meaning:** Resilient families find meaning in difficult challenges. Members evolve together as they work through hardships to turn them into transformative opportunities for growth and learning.

>> **Connecting to spirituality:** As a unit, resilient families connect to faith, hope, and a sense of purpose to something bigger than just themselves and their immediate issues. They may follow certain religious or cultural traditions or find ways to nourish their spirituality through other endeavors, such as connecting to nature or music, or reading spiritual literature together.

Being organized

The framework for helping the family be organized consists of these three processes:

>> **Being connected:** Members of a resilient family can rely on one another and have a strong sense of connection, respect, admiration, and healthy boundaries. They appreciate their togetherness while also respecting the need to be unique individuals.

>> **Staying flexible:** Resilient families stay open to change while also being stable and secure. They collaborate and work with one another to reorganize the

family structure in the face of challenges while still maintaining structure and consistency.

>> **Building networks of support:** The resilient family knows that they aren't an island onto themselves, and they build networks of support including extended family, neighbors, friends, and organizations that can provide emotional, educational, financial, or other practical support.

Effectively communicating

These three processes make up the framework that encourages the family to communicate effectively:

>> **Being clear and consistent:** Resilient families are able to communicate clearly and effectively. Messages are consistent, and members feel safe to express their views and be honest.

>> **Expressing and talking about emotions:** With mutual trust and empathy, members of a resilient family express their emotions and are able to talk about their feelings. They're able to comfort one another, laugh or cry together, and take time to enjoy activities together to recover and revitalize.

>> **Solving problems together:** The resilient family works as a team when it comes to addressing problems and finding solutions. They brainstorm together, set goals, and work on learning skills that can help them achieve their goals and be prepared for the future.

Though all families are different, it's possible to enhance resilience at home when you cultivate these nine processes. Throughout this chapter, I go into more detail on each of these processes, but before I do, remember, that if you want your family to be resilient, it starts with you setting an example.

Setting an Example

Being a role model for your family is the first step in cultivating resilience at home. If you practice what you preach, it's that much easier to foster positive shared beliefs with the rest of the family members and encourage very different individuals to support one another, cooperate, and communicate effectively.

Much of human learning, especially for children, occurs by way of observation of others. People learn by example. If you want your family to be more resilient then, you want to set an example for them.

I'm not saying that everyone has to be perfect, mind you — you will make mistakes and so will they, which is exactly how you want it to be. Making mistakes and being okay with making them is a key factor in building resilience. Your role is to strive to be a consistent role model of resilience so that you can lay down a foundation for everyone else to follow suit.

My client Martha complained that she was unhappy in her marriage but couldn't leave because she was worried about her daughter. She told me that her husband had had multiple affairs and had a sex addiction. They had been to countless therapists and marriage counselors, to no avail. She worried that her daughter would be unable to cope with a divorce and also feared being on her own.

I asked Martha if she could think of a female role model whom she looked up to and why. She answered that Oprah was her role model, having beaten the odds and become a successful leader in her own right. "When you think about Oprah," I asked, does she inspire you to forge ahead and try to beat the odds yourself? How do you want to be viewed by others?"

I went on to ask Martha to think about what sort of role model she wanted her daughter to have and what she wanted for her. I pointed out that children learn by example and that when people love and respect themselves, their children can learn to do the same. The same goes for when people *don't* respect or value themselves.

Martha understood that she needed to work on her own sense of self-value and respect before she could make any decisions about her marriage. Over the next six months, she became increasingly more confident and decided that she was ready to become more financially independent, and so she went from working part-time to full-time. She joined a support group and got her daughter working with a therapist. Eventually, Martha did decide to leave her marriage and, with the help from a family counselor, both mother and daughter were able to thrive and are much closer as a result.

REMEMBER

Relationships aren't easy, and even without marital trouble or addictions in the mix, people navigate a lot of challenges when it comes to family.

As with any relationship, improving the bonds and making it resilient starts with you taking care of you. You have to learn to do the following:

>> **Have love and respect yourself.** Show your family that you respect and love yourself by engaging in self-care practices like eating nutrient rich foods, exercising, meditating, and getting restful sleep. Make sure you take care of your needs so that you can be fully present for everyone else. Teach your family that you're fueling yourself so that you can give more (versus being selfish) and that self-discipline is a form of self-love. Be forgiving toward yourself, avoid admonishing yourself for making mistakes, and minimize self-criticizing. Work toward being comfortable in your own skin.

>> **See value in everyone.** People learn that they're loved and respected by the way they're treated by others, especially as children. Be kind and respectful to every family member, including your partner or your children's father from whom you're divorced. Teach your family that everyone has value, even when their actions aren't favorable or their beliefs differ. Be fully present when speaking with them: Put away your phone and your work, and let them know you care and respect what they have to say.

>> **Give back.** Show your family how to do good for others who are less fortunate, and show them that resilience comes with supporting others and being supported. You can volunteer at a shelter, your child's school, a religious institution, or a farm. Engaging the family to join you is also a meaningful way to spend time together.

>> **Express and regulate your emotions.** Articulate how you feel, and encourage discussions on why you might be feeling the way you do. Show them that it's possible to feel and express emotions while also staying calm so that an emotional charge doesn't lead to hurtful actions or words. Because you won't be perfect at this endeavor, you want to be able to discuss openly why you reacted in a given way, showing them how to reflect and learn from your emotions.

>> **Persevere despite failure, conflict, or criticism.** When faced with failure, conflict, or criticism, show your family how to use the situation as a transformative opportunity to learn and grow. Do not avoid or run away from conflict — show them instead how to embrace criticism and conflict as lessons for improvement. It's okay for your family to see you struggle. It's important for them to see you fall or falter and then get back up and persevere.

>> **Stay open and positive.** Because you don't see your setbacks as failures but rather as transformative opportunities, you stay open and positive when faced with challenges. You regularly search for silver linings and actively exemplify a positive attitude when times are tough. This doesn't mean that they never see you upset or unhappy, but rather that they see that you don't stay in a negative state for long.

>> **Seek support.** It's important for the family to see that no one has to be strong all the time and that strength also comes from the support everyone gets from others. Seek support from friends, family, neighbors, or organizations. Show them how to be resourceful by building and accessing networks of support.

>> **Be consistent.** Say what you mean and mean what you say. Match your words to your actions. Be consistent in the way you treat people, in how you take care of yourself, and in the structure you provide for the family. Show up when you say you'll show up, and always be present when they're speaking to you. Consistency breeds structure and trust, and also helps imprint resilient coping habits.

Adopting Shared Beliefs

It can be challenging to influence people to change their beliefs and attitudes if they aren't open to making changes. As hard as I may have tried, I have not always been successful in convincing my own family members to let go of negative beliefs or adopt healthier behaviors. I have found, however, that when I accept and love them for being exactly who they are, they're more open to listening to suggestions, to being influenced by my personal choices and behaviors, and to developing a more optimistic outlook. Of course, I'm referring to my parents and siblings and not to my children, and it's often more difficult to influence adults than children. Having said that, though, it's still possible. You can still work toward enhancing family optimism, making meaning together and making spirituality a family affair.

Enhancing optimism

According to research, encouraging optimism in children is associated with improved physical and mental well-being, life satisfaction, ability to cope with stress, and a greater sense of purpose.

REMEMBER

Instilling an optimistic attitude in your home doesn't mean sugarcoating hardship, being a Pollyanna, or being blindly optimistic. Rather, it involves encouraging everyone to maintain a realistic view of situations while also upholding a conviction that no matter what, things will work out.

You can enhance optimism at home by

» **Nurturing a positive self-view:** Being optimistic is easier when you have a positive self-view, or when you believe in yourself and your abilities to succeed despite hardships. As such, you want to do what you can to encourage members of your family to feel good about themselves, trust in their strengths, and help them see weaknesses as human. Instill in them the belief that asking for help and working on weaknesses is a positive character trait.

» **Loving family members unconditionally:** No matter how old people are, they want to feel loved and valued, and to know that their behaviors don't determine their value. Separate behavior from love, take care not to withhold love because you're upset with someone's behavior, and openly express love and affection. If you find this difficult to do, take a timeout and balance your emotions so that you can remain objective and clear.

» **Letting family members succeed on their own:** It's often tempting to "fix" things to protect the people you love. Fixing things, though, doesn't help people, especially children, learn to handle challenges or develop self-confidence in their skills. Encourage family members to work toward achieving success on their own so that they can experience pride in their abilities. Support them when needed and avoid expressing fear and worry, because this tends to send the message that you believe they're too weak to handle difficulty.

» **Celebrating one another:** Celebrate successes, big and small moments, birthdays, good ideas, or the willingness to try something new. Reward family members for their unique contributions and creative form of self-expression. Such celebrations foster more self-confidence.

» **Spending quality time together:** A sure way for your family to feel valued is to spend quality time with them. Set time every day for the family unit to be together without distractions. Ask questions and get to know one another as if for the first time. Find out what ignites passions, causes fear, or makes them laugh. Do fun activities together and enjoy one another's company.

» **Empathizing and emphasizing:** It's natural for people to be disappointed with themselves if or when they fail, but it isn't helpful if disappointment persists into negative self-talk and self-limiting beliefs. Empathize and talk about feelings. Emphasize that mistakes and failures don't determine value. Encourage replacing negative self-talk with positive statements and affirmations.

» **Encouraging gratitude:** Make expressing gratitude a daily habit in your home. Everyone can share one thing they're grateful for at the dinner table or write in gratitude journals at night, before going to sleep. Express gratitude to your family members when they have been helpful and when going through difficult challenges, and work together to list reasons you can be grateful as a result of the situation.

Finding meaning together

I worked with two different sets of parents who each had a child who was being bullied at school. Both cases involved verbal and physical assaults, a poor response by the school administration, and the need for police authorities to be drawn in. Rightfully so, both sets of parents were extremely upset, initially overwhelmed, and horrified by the school's inadequate response. Both families had the financial means to seek legal help if necessary, but only one family chose to go down that path. For the purpose of this explanation, I'll designate one set of parents as the Smiths and the other as the Johnsons.

I counseled both sets of parents — at separate times, of course. We worked on regulating emotions, finding ways to use the situation to help their sons grow and become stronger, and coming up with ways to help the school system improve its bullying policies to prevent future episodes. I encouraged them to speak with the other families and to reach out to the community to work together to help the children and parents alike become more aware of the problems and for parents to communicate with one another and their children about it. The Smiths were eager to build their connections with the community and did just that. They found that the situation brought them closer to not only their son but also one another, the school administration, and the community.

The Johnsons felt too distraught to see any silver linings, felt angry and betrayed by members of the school administration, whom they believed weren't responding appropriately, and chose to pursue legal action. Subsequently, disagreements and arguments occurred (us-versus-them) between parents of the schoolchildren as well as between school administrators. Even though their son seemed to be okay and was getting along with other students, they remained angry, worried, and vigilant. While Mr. Johnson complained of worsening migraines, Mrs. Johnson complained of insomnia, anxiety, and palpitations. I continued to support them by teaching them tools that could ease their anxiety and improve self-care so that they could endure the hardship.

Please know that I don't believe there is a right or wrong way to handle bullying or any other difficult situation, especially one that involves the safety of your child. It may well be that the schools and communities were markedly different, and that one community was less cohesive and resilient than the other. It may also be that for the Johnsons, pursuing legal action was the course of action that would lead to lasting policy changes in the community.

REMEMBER

In the end, you want to choose the path that keeps your family safe and makes a difference in the world while ensuring that your family is being supported and is able together to continue to make meaning out of the situation.

Though there is no single right way to get there, ways to nurture meaning in the family include the following:

>> **Being empathic:** Show compassion for yourself and for your child or family member who is hurting. Avoid making statements like "Toughen up" or "Don't cry." Emotions and feelings need to be expressed and worked through.

>> **Gaining perspective:** When facing challenges, it's normal to hyperfocus on the problems at hand. The downside is that people can become myopic in their thinking and be less open to support or finding creative solutions. It is imperative to take a little time out, to step back a bit in order to see a bigger picture, and remember that a future exists beyond this single point in time. Support the notion that without challenges, people don't change, grow stronger, improve, or grow. In this way, you can encourage them to embrace change.

>> **Looking for opportunities for learning and growth:** Once you have stepped back a bit, you can start looking for ways to learn and grow from the situation. Ask questions, look for guidance, and encourage self-reflection. Discuss as a family positives and strengths as well as what the possible weaknesses are that can be improved on. Stay the course during hard times and come together as a family to find meaning, discuss strategies, and make decisions. Brainstorm to look for ways to grow and help shift the mindset from one of victimization to one of victory.

>> **Seeking support:** You don't have to have all the answers. Show your family that it's okay to ask for help and to use other resources to better understand a given situation, your options, and ways to learn and grow. Join a support group, seek counseling, meet with other families who have been through similar situations, and speak to teachers and other adults who also spend time with your children.

Making spirituality a family affair

Cultivating a sense of spirituality in your home can help the family establish stronger bonds, build trust, maintain a durable self-identity, and be better able to handle hardships together. What exactly does this mean? Does it mean you attend religious services or pray together? Not necessarily. Spirituality relates to the profound belief that you belong to something greater that aligns you with a sense of belonging and purpose. (See Chapter 6.) You can cultivate spirituality through means other than religion, like engaging in a variety of meditation practices, deepening your relationship with nature, or connecting to awe, love, compassion, or gratitude.

All through my childhood, being home for Friday night dinner was a requirement. We had no choice in the matter. When I was younger, I did enjoy being with the family, lighting the candle, and enjoying our special meal, but as I grew older, I wanted to be with my friends, and I worried that I was going to miss out on all the fun. As I reflect back now, almost 40 years later, I can't recall a single evening out with my friends, though I do remember our rituals of Friday night dinner and the time I spent with my family. Though I never fully connected with the religious aspect of the dinner, I did come to appreciate the beauty of the ritual of blessing the food, showing gratitude for what we had, and commemorating the end of the week and the time for resting and reflecting. The time was filled with a lot of love, especially after I realized that I might as well enjoy myself while I was there and not with my friends.

Whatever you choose to do, I encourage you to find ways to be spiritual together. Here are some suggestions:

REMEMBER

>> **Turn awe and gratitude into rituals.** Create daily rituals of giving thanks and reflecting in awe about something you're grateful for. Before every meal, you can have members of the family talk about something they feel grateful for or say a blessing of gratitude for the food you're about to eat. You might also employ a ritual of counting blessings before going to sleep.

The more gratitude is practiced, the more it becomes habitual.

>> **Create a sacred space.** Somewhere in the home or the outside garden, designate a space where individuals can go to meditate, pray, contemplate, or simply sit in silence. Encourage all family members to contribute to designing this space so that everyone has the opportunity to add something of value and meaning.

>> **Breathe together.** Find moments to meditate together by doing a breath focus followed by contemplating awe, gratitude, compassion, or kindness. Consider making this a daily or weekly practice that the family does together.

>> **Explore and talk.** Take time to talk about beliefs and keep an open dialogue for people to express their feelings or opinions. Explore questions and ideas around what spirituality means and read spiritual literature together. Encourage your children to read books or watch shows with you on a variety of spiritual subjects.

>> **Go to services.** If the belief is shared, go to religious or spiritual services together regularly. Designate this time as one for sharing, praying, connecting with your community, and being grateful.

>> **Step out into nature.** Deepening your connection to nature as a family is another way to make spirituality a family affair. You can plant a garden together, go for walks in nature, or take camping trips. Spend time being mindful and pointing out the miracles of Mother Nature.

>> **Be altruistic.** As a family, you can volunteer together at a shelter, school, or nursing home or do something else within your community. Altruism is another form of spirituality that bonds you together not only as a family but also to your community.

Establishing Organization and Structure

Children need consistency and structure, and when you build in structure and organization into your lives, they're more likely to grow up feeling secure in themselves. You should also allow room for flexibility and change so that your family members learn to stay open and capable of navigating the unexpected. It takes establishing a strong sense of interconnectedness among family members, consistency in the home that is also flexible, and reaching out to networks of support.

Strengthening connectedness

Knowing that you belong to a loving family can help promote self-esteem, self-confidence, a positive outlook, and a resilient mindset — and this is especially true for children. Ensuring that everyone feels loved and valued more often than not takes being conscientious and making an effort. When stress and emotions run high, it isn't unusual to lose your temper, disregard someone else's opinion, or let go of self-care practices or healthy boundaries. Follow these simple actions to strengthen connectedness at home:

>> **Identify core values.** Companies define their core values, and as a family, you can too. These values serve as a foundation for other actions, behaviors, and decisions. You can create these core values as a family and identify what you admire about one another and the traits you hold dear. Establish a family motto and create signage, posters, or daily reminders of the values you live by as a family.

>> **Empathize and acknowledge.** Encourage empathy and acknowledge feelings when they're expressed. Consistently remind family members that thoughts, feelings, and beliefs are valid, even if not shared among everyone.

>> **Give a touch of love.** As social beings, humans crave a loving touch, and physical connection is vital for enhancing the feeling of belonging and being connected. Hug often, hold hands, and snuggle or express love through gentle touch with those individuals that you are close to (Note: The people you are close to refers to those individuals in your social circle whom you trust are taking precautions, wearing masks, and practicing safe social distancing).

- **Be fully present.** Model to your family how to be fully present and pay attention. Put away distractions and encourage everyone to focus and be present when someone is speaking.

- **Set loving boundaries.** Create rules and boundaries that reflect love and also respect for each individual and the needs of the family as a whole.

- **Make memories.** Share stories, jokes, and experiences, and make memories together that will stay with you for a lifetime.

- **Create rituals and celebrate.** Partake in family rituals that bond you together, and take time to celebrate and honor special moments, like birthdays or graduations or learning something new.

- **Practice teamwork.** Take on a project together that requires you to sweat and work together to complete the job.

- **Play together.** A sure way to enhance a sense of connection is through play and laughter. Play board games, sports, or any activity that gets the family together to have fun.

Creating structure with flexibility

Routines can be comforting for both children and adults because they provide consistency and set expectations. Routines are especially helpful when a family is navigating a major transition or hardship, as routines can ensure a sense of stability in the midst of change. They also provide individuals with a better sense of control and comfort, which is especially true for children. The key is not to be too rigid about routines and to allow a semblance of flexibility when life throws your family some curveballs. Structure can come in many forms. My recommendations are to

- **Institute routines.** You can have a set time for eating meals, going to sleep, doing homework, brushing teeth and washing up, celebrating the Sabbath or Sunday dinner, or attending game night or movie night. Establish these routines, and be consistent with the time of day or week.

- **Set expectations.** Set rules and establish consequences that are both positive (when expectations are met) and negative so that everyone knows what to expect and what is expected of them. Ensure that everyone is on the same page and understands what the rules are and why they're being established.

- **Be consistent.** Do as you say and follow through with routines, expectations, and consequences.

- **Model healthy behavior.** Don't say one thing and act in a different way. Model the behavior you want your family to follow.

>> **Engage in creative play.** Play is a way to enhance bonding and fun while also engaging family members to learn how to be flexible. You can have family members take turns making up new games, play a game of coming up with different uses for household items, play board or video games that require adaptive thinking, or play card games that operate on chance and strategy.

>> **Give responsibility.** Enable family members to make their own decisions every now and then, and assign them tasks that they're responsible for. Giving your children a variety of responsibilities that they're capable of doing helps them feel like they're contributing, supports their confidence, and gives them structure.

>> **Hold regular family meetings.** Life is constantly changing and is often busy. Set a time every week to hold a family meeting, even if it's only for 15 minutes to catch up, celebrate successes, review what is or isn't working, and assign tasks and responsibilities for the week.

Forming networks of support

Networks of support help people be more resilient, especially when the connections embody mutual trust, reliance, guidance, support, and mentorship. A child's resilience is especially influenced by the presence of reliable and supportive relationships, who help them feel secure while also guiding them to develop coping skills and learn to manage stress. Because children are influenced by everyone — family, teachers, peers, coaches, and so forth — you should ensure that you can trust that these people truly care about them, while also working toward building your own networks of support.

The people in your support networks may come from different places and serve different functions. For some, joining other groups or finding support comes easy. For others, figuring out whom to connect with can be challenging. The key is to think about your goals and find individuals and groups of people who can assist you to meet those goals. You can follow these general guidelines when looking to form your networks of support:

>> **Go wide.** Expand your network to include neighbors, other families, teachers, your children's friends, work colleagues, or counselors.

>> **Find people with shared interests.** Book clubs, sports groups, religious communities, and the neighborhood watch are examples of groups of people who may share interests that you or your children may also have.

>> **Get involved and help others.** Volunteer and encourage the children to join or do something on their own, whether it's for the school, church or temple — or even a bake sale to raise money for the neighborhood.

>> **Ask for help.** Be a model for the family by asking for help from other sources. You might join a support group or start one yourself or seek advice from a therapist, counselor, or teacher.

>> **Encourage children to ask for help.** Guide your children or family members to seek help from friends, counselors, and teachers when appropriate, gently encouraging them to learn to be more independent.

REFLECTION

Whom do you turn to in times of need? Can you name the different people who may be of support to your family? Do your children feel that they can turn to other people for help? Do you ask for help? Do you belong to a community?

Enhancing Communication

There's no such thing as a family without problems. Well, at least, I don't know of any families who experience no conflict in their lives, whether it comes from within the home or from the outside world. Families are made up of humans, which means people are bound to make mistakes, have misunderstandings and disagreements, or meet up with adversity in the outside world. For this reason, it's important to uphold love, honor, and respect in your home, as well as compassion and understanding, so that you can communicate effectively and work together as a team to solve problems and manage life's challenges.

Open, honest, compassionate, thoughtful, and clear communication is thus essential for building a resilient family. It enables family members to feel safe to express their emotions and differing opinions and be better able to resolve conflict and find solutions to difficult problems. Poor communication, on the other hand, often has the opposite effect, resulting in misunderstandings and usually more conflict.

Being clear and direct

My clients Joan and Michael had been married to one another for 18 years. They claimed that for 17 of those years, they rarely saw eye-to-eye and argued about everything. They had different coping styles, ways of addressing problems, and forms of expressing themselves. Whereas Joan was verbally quite expressive and open about her feelings and thoughts, Michael avoided talking about his feelings and tended to withdraw into himself. Joan tended to talk at length and sometimes in circles. She expressed affection verbally and through physical touch. Michael tended to speak with few words and suppressed negative feelings until pushed, at which point he usually exploded with anger. He expressed affection by buying gifts and through sexual intimacy. Both felt misunderstood by the other, and often arguments led to at least one person threatening divorce.

Working with both of them, I felt that the first step was to figure out whether they still loved one another and whether they remembered why they came together in the first place. Upon reflection, they both realized they still shared the same values and beliefs, still loved one another, and cared deeply about their two children. With this foundation established, I helped them work toward accepting and honoring one another's coping and expression styles, and we devised more effective ways for them to communicate. They were given guidance on how to be mindful, to regulate their emotions so that they could be connected with their needs and desires, and how to express themselves and speak clearly, succinctly, and compassionately. They're still working on it, but their children have reported a marked positive change that has brought the whole family closer.

Healthy communication occurs when your message is stated using simple language and is directed toward the person the message is intended for. For instance, if you're upset with your partner, express your concern clearly and directly to your partner rather than complain to someone else about it. The key is to regulate your emotions and speak without anger and disrespect. As such, being clear and direct is challenging when your emotions and stress level run high. That's why it's a good idea to incorporate techniques that encourage family members to learn how to self-regulate and stay calm. These are my recommendations to improve at communicating clearly and directly:

>> **Practice mindfulness.** Mindfulness helps calm emotions, enhances rational thinking, reduces stress and reactivity, and lowers impulsive behavior. Rather than think or even give in to your emotions, focus on being in the present moment nonjudgmentally. Appreciate how you're feeling, the experience you're having in your body, and how the other person might be feeling. You can work together to speak mindfully as well as listen. (See Chapter 9 for more on how to listen mindfully.) Learn mindfulness techniques as a family, and encourage using these techniques when communicating and especially when emotions may run high.

>> **Institute the pause.** Get family members into the habit of taking a pause before responding, so that they get into the practice of being thoughtful and clear with their words. This strategy is especially useful if a child or even a partner is upset or having an outburst or a meltdown, because it helps maintain a sense of calm.

TIP

A simple way to take a pause is to take five to ten deep breaths. You can count as you breathe in and out, using a counting sequence you prefer. I personally prefer counting to three as I breathe in and to six as I breathe out. Aside from calming you down, taking a pause also gives more space for each person to speak and be heard.

>> **Keep language clear.** When emotions run high and especially when there is conflict, communication can be vague. Keep language clear and specific. Avoid going off on tangents and stay to the point. Encourage family members to use their words in a clear fashion.

>> **Ask for clarity.** Rather than react, stay calm, ask questions, and seek clarification. Being curious also shows that you care about knowing more about the other person and their feelings and thoughts. Asking good questions is easier when you're actively listening and being mindful.

>> **Notice nonverbal cues.** Work together to be fully present without distractions, and pay attention to nonverbal messages. When you regulate your own emotions and quiet your thoughts, you can be more present and able to notice how someone is communicating nonverbally.

>> **Encourage honesty and respect.** By creating a sense of safety, trust, and respect, you encourage family members to be open and honest about their feelings and thoughts. Regularly have conversations about what it means to respect and acknowledge other people's perspectives and opinions.

>> **Talk frequently.** Take time to have meaningful conversations, whether it's at mealtime, a check-in during the day, or weekly family meetings. The more regularly you connect and communicate together, the more members of the family feel safe to express their opinions and feelings.

Regulating and expressing emotions

I have worked with many families who are quite adept at expressing their emotions. The problem is that the adults have a tendency to express their emotions without regulating them first, so when they're upset, their emotions are often expressed in a way that's confusing or hurtful to their children or spouses. When I work with these individuals, I guide them to connect with their emotions, feel them, understand them, and also calm them. Doing so enables them to better understand themselves and why they feel the way they do, examine limiting beliefs, and be better able to express themselves and their needs. Here are my recommendations for regulating and expressing emotions in the family:

>> **Let it flow.** If someone needs to cry or shout (or if you need to), let them do it. Avoid saying, "Don't," and be aware that your desire to use that word comes from your own distress and worry that things are getting out of control. When you say, "Don't cry," for example, it isn't helpful to the person who is crying to hear these words as they're being told not to do something that needs to be released. The key is to let it flow *out* but not *at*. If you need to shout, stand in the middle of the yard and shout, or punch a pillow. Get the energy out without directing it at a person.

>> **Talk about it.** Encourage family members to use words to express what they're feeling. You can practice talking about emotions, both positive and negative, during calm times by discussing characters on TV or in a book, asking questions about how these characters might be feeling, and discussing how they're expressing themselves. It's a good idea in general to talk about emotions and that it's possible to regulate them rather than have them control you.

>> **Model and teach self-control.** Show your family that it's possible to feel and express emotions in a way that is more controlled and constructive. If you want your family members to control their anger response, you want to show them how. Take a pause and a breath, be mindful, and use your words to clearly describe how you're feeling and why.

>> **Use creativity.** Expressing emotions doesn't have to be done verbally. It can be done through writing in a journal, drawing, painting, using toys, or doing another type of creative endeavor. Engaging in a creative activity to express emotions helps release stress levels as well as jumbled thoughts and feelings.

>> **Develop strategies.** Come up with strategies people can use when they're feeling out of control that bring calm, such as thinking about a happy memory, drawing a calming picture, taking a walk, or writing a story.

Solving problems together

A family that solves together stays together, through thick and thin. It's no different from a sports team or a team at the office (see Chapter 14) — when you work together, brainstorm, set goals, develop skills, and respect and value one another's opinions, your ability to be resilient during hard times as a family is assured. The secret is to work together to manage problems constructively and positively. You need to discover that conflict and obstacles are normal components of life and are challenges that can be managed and learned from rather than avoided. Follow these guidelines to improve at solving problems together:

>> **Take a step back.** When problems arise, the tendency is to hyperfocus on them, react, and fix. Sometimes, this isn't the best course of action, and you're better off stepping back to be better able to gain a bigger perspective and be able to respond rather than react. Stepping back also affords the opportunity to discuss the problem and allow other people to offer solutions, ideas, and feedback. Make a habit of stepping back to gain perspective. Take a pause and first establish whether there exists an immediate danger or threat to you or your family. If not, you know you have time to lower the stress response, think, discuss, and find a solution together.

» **Play solution-finding games.** Encourage family members to learn how to think creatively and solve problems by playing games that require individuals to come up with solutions. It can be board games or treasure hunts or having to build something from scratch.

» **Let them do it.** If you have a tendency to fix everything and make life easier for other people, stop. Let them take care of problems themselves, and support them with guidance and reassurance. Rather than give them answers, ask them questions to help them think and come up with their own ideas and solutions.

» **Address issues.** Avoid sweeping problems under the rug, and be proactive in addressing issues. Make sure that when any issues are brought up, it's done in a safe and open way, and perhaps consider setting a time and place when family members can voice concerns.

» **Define the problem.** Work together to get clarity and be as specific as possible in order to define the problem at hand. List who is involved, what the situation is, and how people are affected, and encourage accountability without shame or blame. Let people describe their role in the situation, if any, without shaming or blaming themselves or anyone else.

» **Uncover wants.** Once the problem is defined, work toward assessing what the goals are. Find out what is important to the people concerned, what it is they want or need, and what they might be worried about or afraid of.

» **Brainstorm.** Encourage family members to share ideas about possible solutions, and know that there is no right or wrong idea or good or bad idea. Gather as many ideas as you can. You can take turns suggesting ideas and writing down the thoughts.

» **Take a time out.** After brainstorming, it's always best to sleep on it, to give time for ideas to sit with each person for a while, let them mull it over, and take some time to gain more perspective. Take an hour or a day and then reconvene.

» **Evaluate the ideas.** Once you have finished sharing your ideas, evaluate them one-by-one. Look for the pros and the cons, what is relevant, and what is most appropriate. Honor all ideas and disagree respectfully, and then rate the ideas, ranking the best as number one.

» **Commit to trying solutions.** Having decided on a possible action plan, take the next steps to commit to seeing the solution through. Give each person something to be responsible for, and agree on a way to track progress and check in to see whether it's working.

» **Get guidance.** You don't have to have all the answers, so you can also brainstorm on whom you can turn to for guidance, support, advice, and help.

5

The Part of Tens

Chapter **20**

Ten Tips to Help Your Kids Cope with Stress and Change

Studies show that teens and children are more stressed today than ever. Whether it's peer pressure, the stress from their highly scheduled lives, schoolwork, world events, or parental worries, kids today greatly benefit from learning the positive coping skills that will help them cultivate resilience. In this chapter, I offer you brief ways that you can support your children to better cope with stress and change. (For more on building family resilience, see Chapter 19.)

Taking a Pause and Calming the Worry

It's normal and natural to want to protect your children from harm. The problem is that your anxiety may rub off on them, causing them to feel more anxious about their world and the future. Constant worry doesn't facilitate developing a more resilient mindset, or a belief that a positive outcome is possible when challenges are reckoned with. For your children to learn how to stay calm and confident, you have to model the behavior for them and then regulate your emotions, stay in the present moment, and remain calm and positive.

You can appreciate your child in the present moment, for example, rather than think about what they aren't doing correctly or what may happen later. Focus on what you can do right now that can support your child to feel more confident, calm, relaxed, or healthy. If you find this step difficult, that's okay: Pause for a deep breath and regulate your emotions. When the emotional charge is lowered, you're better able to stay calm and objective. Your ability to reason, stay present, and problem-solve will also improve.

TIP

When you find yourself worrying, take a pause and ask yourself questions that will help you better evaluate your fears and separate facts from fiction. Ask yourself how likely it is that the fears are realistic or will come true, whether you're jumping to conclusions, and how much is coming from your imagination. Ask yourself what the source of your worry is: Is it really about your child, or is it related to your own insecurities and self-limiting beliefs. (See Chapter 11 for further information on self-limiting beliefs.) Ask what kind of support you or your child might need and what resources you can draw on.

Take a pause and focus on what you can control. Think about what you want for your child in a positive sense — and if you're worrying, you may want to focus on the feeling of being secure and strong, for both you and your child. What does feeling strong and secure feel like? What does it look like seeing your child secure and strong? This visualization will help calm your anxiety while also guiding you to take the next positive steps that will support feeling secure and strong. Taking care of yourself will help give you more bandwidth to be present and calm.

Being a Role Model

The better your own coping skills, the more likely your kids will pick up on your behaviors and mannerisms. You don't have to be perfect all the time — you just have to work toward staying calm, being healthy, making responsible decisions, learning from your mistakes, and demonstrating positive behavior for your child to mimic. (See Chapter 19 for more details on being a role model for your family.) Here are some recommendations for being a role model:

» **Slow down.** Your children will absorb your reactions. If you panic, they will likely panic. Deliberately slow down: Slow down your speech and your breathing. Take a pause. Regulate your emotions and calm your mind when you feel upset. Slow down when it comes to your own schedule as well. Avoiding rushing from one activity to the next, give yourself plenty of time to reach destinations, and practice being mindful and fully present when you're with your kids.

>> **Practice self-care.** Your children will also look to you when it comes to self-care habits. Let them see you taking good care of yourself and making time for your needs. If they see you stay up late at night, they may not realize how important sleep is for them and their ability to cope, for instance. Get restful sleep, eat nutrient-rich foods, and make time for exercise, relaxation, and play. Let them see you taking care of your own well-being.

>> **Think positively.** Mirror for your children how to think positively and be more optimistic. Look for silver linings in challenging situations while also being realistic. Talk out your feelings, and show your kids how to shift negative thinking into more positive and less stress-provoking thoughts.

>> **Ask for help.** Show your children that it's okay to ask for help and seek advice, not because you feel helpless but rather because it's your way of getting stronger and gaining support and more information. Explain to them that asking for help from other people who have more resources helps you better manage challenges.

>> **Be approachable.** Many people who are distressed either shut down or lash out, making them unapproachable and therefore less amenable to getting help or connecting with others when they're truly in need. Allow your children to see that you're still approachable, even when you're faced with a lot of stress. Show them that it's possible to feel negative feelings, express them, and talk about them.

Maintaining Open Channels of Communication

Children and adults alike feel better when they have the opportunity to talk about their problems. Children may not realize, however, that talking about their feelings or a difficult situation may help them feel better. It's therefore important not to minimize emotions or feelings and to provide a safe space for them to express themselves. Some children are ready and willing to talk, and others need some coaxing. Whatever the case, you want to maintain open channels of communication.

Often, to calm their own fears and in the belief that they're helping, someone might tell a child, "Don't worry," or "Don't cry," or "Don't be upset." Making these statements to children shuts them down and invalidates their experience. It also prevents them from learning how to manage their emotions or stress. To keep communication channels open, validate kids' feelings, let them know that feelings are normal, and encourage them to express themselves and talk.

When your children talk, really listen to them. Put away any distractions and be fully present. Pay attention to nonverbal messages, and sit quietly with them for as long as necessary until they're ready to talk. You may choose a time when everyone is more relaxed, like at mealtimes or just before bedtime.

REMEMBER

When you do sit down to talk the feelings through, work with your child or children to put a label on the feelings. Ask questions and let them talk it out, guiding you both to figure out exactly what they may be stressed or upset about. If words fail, it may be that your child cannot find words to fully express themselves yet. Encourage them to draw a picture showing how they're feeling or write it out and then discuss it together.

Teaching Others How to Self-Calm

You may want to start teaching your children how to self-calm with basic relaxation exercises as soon as they're old enough to understand the meaning of the word *breathe*. Whether you're guiding a child to slow their breaths and breathe more deeply or you take them to yoga classes or have them listen to guided imagery, the goal is to teach your child techniques to self-calm that they can use on their own during times of stress or anxiety. Here are some tips:

» **Teach a breath focus.** Teach them to direct their focus on counting 1-2-3 as they breathe in and to count 1-2-3-4-5-6 as they breathe out. Count with them initially and then have them count on their own. (You can use any counting sequence that works for you.)

» **Picture a happy place.** Guide your child to think of a place where they feel happy and carefree, and imagine that they're happy there — relaxed and enjoying themselves.

» **Listen to guided meditations.** My clients tell me that they have given my guided-meditation audio CDs to their children, who loved listening to them, especially before going to sleep. Audio CDs are useful to have because your children can play them on their own as they're instructed to use their imaginations, take deep breaths, or stretch their bodies.

» **Engage the senses.** Direct your child to close their eyes and engage the senses in noticing their surroundings. Ask them to focus on what they smell, taste, feel, or hear. You can also instruct them to imagine a beautiful beach or park and then ask them to describe what they feel, hear, see, smell, or taste. This exercise gets them into the practice of mindfulness.

- >> **Do some yoga.** Many yoga classes ae offered for kids as well as for parents and kids, and studies show that yoga can reduce stress in children. Yoga is not only helpful in creating relaxation but also serves as a way to release energy through movement.

- >> **Blow off steam.** Encourage your child to recognize tension as it builds up and to engage in some kind of physical movement or exercise to blow off steam. They can do yoga, jump rope, dance to a favorite song, or play on the swings.

Facing Fears Together

There are times to shield your children and, as they grow older, times to support your children to shield themselves. As your children develop, you can help them learn how to face and overcome fears, how to evaluate situations, and how to better understand that failure and setbacks can be opportunities for learning and growth. You do so by facing fears together and giving them tools that they can use to manage adversity throughout their lives. Together, discuss positives and negatives, pros and cons, and more constructive or positive ways of perceiving the situation. Help them understand that making a mistake, failing, being unpopular, or failing to get what they want are situations that can be turned around for the better.

You can show your kids that anxiety doesn't last, and have them connect to their body to understand how the stress response works. Talk about the physical sensations and the emotional feelings, and have them write or draw to describe their experience. Show them how to recognize how the body expresses stress and fear, and how it's possible to change the feeling by using self-calming techniques.

TIP

When your child is able to see that they have control to change how they feel, you can then talk about the situation and ways to address the problems. Together, you can determine that it's possible to turn the situation around and set small goals that your child can manage.

Getting Organized

A big source of stress for many children is their inability to be organized. They may easily become overwhelmed by the demands of schoolwork, afterschool activities, or their social life and home responsibilities. Helping them build skills that enable them to get better organized helps them feel less stressed, and it gives them tools that will be useful to them as adults. Support your children by

>> **Creating routines and rituals:** Organization and structure through the creation of routines and rituals can help your children feel more secure. Try to stick to routines as much as possible during the week and on weekends. This includes making room for play and free time.

>> **Setting the tone in the morning:** Mornings tend to be hectic for most families and can be a source of stress for everyone. Try to plan ahead so that mornings can be organized and calm, by preparing lunches and laying out clothing the night before, as well as making sure homework is done, phones are charging, and backpacks are packed and ready to go.

>> **Keeping a planner:** Encourage your children to keep a planner on hand where they can write down their homework expectations, daily activities, and schedules. Sometimes, hanging a large calendar on the kitchen wall is helpful, where everyone can keep track of the schedule. You can help your child review the planner and figure out the highest priorities.

>> **Checking in regularly:** Being organized is challenging for everyone, so check in daily to see whether your child feels comfortable with their schedule or is feeling overwhelmed in any way.

>> **Allowing for free time:** As you stay attuned to your child's struggles or feelings of being overwhelmed, look for ways to establish more balance in their day. Perhaps they're overscheduled and need some play time. See what can be removed from their schedule and look at ways that they can feel free of obligations and just be the children that they are.

Unplugging and Descheduling

Kids need to have time to be kids. They need to play, feel free, run around, scream at the top of their lungs, and just have fun. They also need time to learn how to just be, rest, and relax. Unfortunately, in today's modern world, many children are overscheduled, overcommitted, glued to the screen, or forced to sit in class-rooms for long hours without recess.

Between school, homework, and afterschool activities, there's often little time for children to decompress, relax, play, or even sleep. Help lower your child's stress level by decreasing the daily demands put on them. Refrain from putting too many activities in their schedule so that they can have some downtime. Build in time every day for your child to play with their friends. Find out what your child loves to do, and encourage that activity as long as it's safe and encourages play. Make sure there's no pressure, no lessons, and no expected end-goals.

Though your child may prefer their play time to be on the computer or smartphone, keep screen time limited because too much screen time can add to anxiety and depression. You may want to set specific times in the day for your child to be completely unplugged from the screen, phone, or schoolwork. Get them out in nature where they can roam free, become more creative, and blow off steam, alone or with friends.

Learning to Embrace Change

For many children, anxiety stems from starting new things and worrying that they might do something wrong. You can support your children by helping them learn how to prepare for, and ultimately embrace, change. Here are some suggestions:

» **Get informed.** Show your child how to prepare for change by doing research ahead of time. If they're nervous about starting a new school, for example, you can visit the school and check it out, arrange to meet a child or two who may be in the same class, and meet the teacher ahead of time. Whatever the new endeavor, talk about it, use a search engine together to find more information, speak to people who may be involved, and connect with other parents and children.

» **Review expectations.** Often, your child's anxiety stems from the fear that they won't meet given expectations. Find out what your child feels is expected of them, and work to relax their fears by letting them know that they are only expected to try their best. Be clear about your own expectations. Set reasonable goals together, and break down the larger goals into smaller ones that your child feels they can manage.

» **Talk about making mistakes.** Make a habit of reviewing the day together and including wins and failures in the discussion. When talking about the slip-ups or failures, work together to find ways to learn, improve, and take next steps. This practice shows your child how to recover from mistakes, move forward, and let go of any fear around messing up.

» **Celebrate bravery.** The more your child feels that they're successful, the more confidence they build to meet future challenges and changes. Find ways to praise them for their accomplishments, especially when they have attempted a new endeavor. Hugs, stars on the calendar, their favorite dinner, or a meaningful event often does the trick.

Solving Problems Together

Many people have the tendency to swoop in and fix situations so that they can prevent others from worrying or suffering. Swooping in and fixing situations for your child, however, doesn't support them to learn how to problem-solve on their own. Solving problems together, on the other hand, teaches your child skills that they can use later as an adult. Together, you can

>> **Calm and express.** Discuss with your child what they perceive as the problem. Work with them to calm their emotions, show them that you understand and that you're listening, and encourage them to voice their feelings.

>> **Identify problems.** Problems often seem overwhelming and become less so when you talk it out and break everything down into smaller parts. As your child talks about their feeling, identify the problems. For example, your child may be upset because they're anxious about failing the science test. After your child feels calmer, have them complete a science problem with you and see that they do actually understand the material. You then discover that the child's anxiety is coming only from the worry about making a mistake.

>> **Break the problem down into goals.** Identifying the problem or problems then guides you to set manageable goals that can help solve the problems. Going with the preceding example, the goals may be finding ways to create calm, improving self-confidence, changing perspective around making mistakes, or looking at ways to make each science problem appear easier or less difficult.

>> **Brainstorm solutions.** Help your child brainstorm and come up with some solutions for each goal. You can offer up some solutions as well, and ask your child what they think.

>> **Take a time-out.** As with adults, it's always a good idea to take a time-out, and think about something else to step back for a bit and gain perspective. Let your child play a game, run around outdoors, or call a friend. Make sure this break is timed, and ensure that you're both back to problem-solving when the time is up.

>> **Choose solutions.** Take a look at your list of solutions and help your child pick one that they think might work best. Agree on a course of action.

Finding Support

It takes a village to help raise a resilient and happy child. You don't have to do it all on your own, in other words. Kids benefit from having other adult role models and getting advice from trusted adults. They also benefit from having other kids to learn from and talk to. You as a parent also benefit from being supported and having others share the load. Support can come from teachers, family friends, and counselors and can be a great source of help and relief.

REMEMBER

There is nothing wrong with asking for help. Asking also shows your child that it's okay to do so, should they need to in the future.

Perhaps your family is facing a particular challenge, and meeting with a counselor who specializes in this field may be helpful. Your child's teachers also usually spend more time with them than you do. Use them as a resource, keep them in the loop regarding your efforts, and see whether there are ways you can jointly help your child.

Your network of support will also include parents who have children of the same age or who have had the same experience. Seek their advice, and if they're trusted by your child, encourage your child to speak with them as well. As your children grow older and form their own social bonds, support them to reach out to their peers for help as well.

Chapter **21**

Ten Tips for Using Nature to Become Resilient

Science shows that exposure to nature improves attention, energy, memory, mood, and cognition. Your ancestors didn't need science to know this to be true. Their lives were intricately intertwined with nature, and they not only had to figure out ways to survive in harsh conditions but also look to nature for wisdom and healing. In this chapter, I offer you ways to reconnect with nature that will help boost your resilience.

Using Green for Therapy

Personally, spending too much time in front of the screen leaves me with brain fog and fatigue. Conversely, being out in nature leaves me feeling alert and invigorated, so my focus is improved, as are my abilities to concentrate, and for good reason: According to new research, spending time outdoors in nature improves your mood, vitality, and even immunity. Scientists have found that nature can help wounds heal, hospital stays to lessen, pain to decrease, and anxiety to abate.

Studies all over the world are also showing that the closer you live to some greenery, the better your health and the lower your stress level.

REMEMBER

Twenty minutes in nature is all it takes to access its benefits, whether you take a walk, hike, picnic, or fall asleep. Nature is loaded with unseen elements like negative ions and phytoncides — chemicals that stimulate or relax your brain and may even benefit your immune system as they lower your stress response. When you're outside, exposed to the beauty of nature, its variability, and its smells and sounds, the brain automatically shifts into a positive mental state, as does the body. So, if your mood is faltering or your energy is low, get some therapy by spending time in nature. If you can, aim for at least 20 minutes a day.

Enhancing Spirituality

Connecting with nature is also a great way to connect with spirituality. Spending time in nature can enhance your sense of awe and hope, showing you how life thrives despite adversity and why you never need to give up. It shows you that new flowers bloom after a frozen winter, that baby turtles survive threats and make it to the water, and that spider webs weave new webs after one might be destroyed. You're reminded how life persists despite challenges and that nature maintains its beauty, strength, and stubbornness as it reshapes itself. Scientists also say that when you spend time in nature, it's akin to putting a drop of morphine into your brain, which gives you a feeling of pleasure and of being high and connected.

Take time to walk or sit in your favorite place in nature and find awe all around you. Stand on top of a mountain and notice the wind blowing against your face or the sun warming your skin. Let nature fill your soul, and you will notice a palpable sense of connecting to something bigger than just you. You might notice that you feel stronger, more powerful, and more supported by the universe. You might even find that you feel more inspired while also humbled.

Clearing Your Head

It has been shown that people who walk in the forest versus an urban environment have significant improvements in cognition after the walk, and that students who have an unobstructed view to nature outperform their peers who do not have this view on standardized measures of attention. As for children with ADHD, greenness of play areas has been associated with milder symptoms of attention deficit, and windowless indoor play areas have been associated with more severe symptoms.

In addition, other unseen elements — like the small, negatively charged ions that are found inside pine forests, after a rainfall, near waterfalls or beaches where the waves pound on the surf — have been shown to aid in reducing stress and anxiety and in improving cognitive performance and immunity. These negative ions are quickly depleted in polluted environments, and in enclosed and air conditioned rooms, and especially in rooms that have electronic devices such as computers, photocopiers, and televisions, which now fill almost every home and office.

You would therefore benefit from taking regular nature-time breaks to clear your head. Green space can include neighborhood parks, gardens, or even just grassy areas, so you don't have to drive to a nearby forest or mountaintop. Research your own neighborhood and find where the parks are and then spend some time there. You will find that you're better able to focus, and you'll feel more energized.

Exercising Green

For many people, exercise is a chore. Even so, it seems that being outdoors makes exercise easier. Whether you're jogging or walking, doing so out in nature versus indoors has been associated with more energy, less fatigue, and less pain and negative thinking. Studies are also now showing that exercise compliance is more likely when it takes place outdoors. For athletes, this is also true. Researchers at Texas State University, for example, found that athletes' performances improved when they were surrounded by more green space.

When you exercise outdoors, you gain the benefits of being in nature and of being able to enjoy the process a little more. For instance, jogging in the woods results in faster 1,800-meter completion times and, in the psychological realm, more satisfaction, more enjoyment, and less frustration when compared to the open laps. Jogging in the woods decreases perceptions of fatigue and physical symptoms that might otherwise interfere with exercise adherence and outdoor running versus the treadmill at an equivalent duration. It also is associated with less fatigue, fewer anxious thoughts, lower hostility, more positive mental thoughts, and an overall feeling of invigoration.

You may notice that when you exercise outdoors, you're less likely to notice cramping, fatigue, or negative thoughts. It doesn't matter what you do — as long as you do it. You can walk along the beach or in a park, take a bike ride, play a game, toss a Frisbee, or go for a jog. Exercise by itself enhances your resilience. Exercising in nature provides you with triple the benefit because you also gain from the unseen elements of nature that are improving your immune system and lowering stress levels while also exercising longer and harder because you feel more energized.

Practicing Mindfulness

My favorite place to practice mindfulness is in nature. I find that it's easier to engage all my senses in the experience of being in nature, and when I do, I achieve a state of calm and clarity more easily. To remind myself how powerful and resilient I can be, I often walk in nature and admire the evidence of resilience all around me. I notice how the branches of trees bend without breaking, to relieve the weight of snow, and break as they grow older and become less resilient. I notice bulbs of flowers peeking their heads out of the soil or hawks that fly overhead looking for their next meal.

Taking a mindful walk is easy to do yourself: Just leave behind your mobile phone as well as your camera, get yourself to a place in nature, and walk aimlessly. The goal is to have no expectations or goals in mind and to simply allow your body to guide you where it wants to go.

Cultivating a Garden

In addition to being able to gather your own herbs and vegetables without going to the store, cultivating your own garden has a myriad of benefits that can boost your resilience. It's an outdoor activity, after all, so it means being outside and soaking up some much needed vitamin D. In addition, according to research that tracked more than 2800 people over the age of 60 for 16 years, gardening can also reduce the incidence of dementia. Pulling weeds and tilling the soil also counts as exercise, and you probably won't notice how hard you're working either, because you'll be immersed in the activity of gardening. Studies also show that this activity can boost your mood, encourage you to eat healthier foods, lower stress levels, and improve self-esteem.

If you don't have one already, you might want to cultivate your own garden. Start small so that you're more likely to keep at it, and plant flowers you love and foods you like to eat. Find a location in your yard that has good sunlight and access to water. Make sure you have good soil and that it's blended with nutrients. If you don't have a yard or space to cultivate your own garden, you can join a neighborhood or community garden program, which has the added benefit of socializing and creating new friendships. You can also have a windowsill garden, as long as it's an area that draws plenty of sunlight.

Eating with the Seasons

Everyone has different bodies, and they respond differently to the environment. For you, it's beneficial to be mindful and to pay attention to how you feel as the seasons change. Get acquainted with your body and how it responds to a variety foods or activities during different times of the day, week, and year.

Pay attention to what is growing locally, and try to eat the organic foods coming from your local farmers during those seasons. During warm months when you're outdoors and sweating, you need foods that hydrate — like cucumbers, watermelon, berries, melon, and peaches — which are also great sources of vitamins, minerals, and antioxidants. As the days grow shorter and cooler, you'll want more warming foods, like soups, stews, whole grains, and fats from avocado and nuts. You also may want to add more citrus fruits to gain vitamin C to support your immune system when colds are more frequent.

In general, think about bringing nature into your body, especially if you can't get out into nature regularly. Eat foods that grow from the earth and shop in the outside perimeters of the grocery store, buying fruits and vegetables, nuts and seeds, lean and hormone-free protein, and wholesome grains. Even better, plant your own vegetables if you can — you'll gain the combined benefits of eating healthy, spending time in nature, getting some exercise, and eating what is seasonally available.

Bringing Nature into Your Home

Believe it or not, when you bring nature into your home or office, you benefit from it even if you don't get outdoors. Studies show that adding elements of nature into your home, workplace, school, and even hospital can lower stress, reduce blood pressure, hasten healing, and increase productivity and general well-being. (See Chapter 17 for more detail on bringing nature and harmony into your living space.) In short, bringing nature indoors can have a wonderfully positive impact on how you feel.

You can bring plants into a room and enhance the feel of nature indoors. Put a plant in your office or wherever you spend a lot of time. Studies show that having a plant in a room can improve cognition and energy and even decrease pain. In this latter case, studies found that placing a plant in a hospital room reduced hospital stays, decreased the need for pain medication, and reduced the negative comments nurses made on their patients' charts.

You can open your blinds so that you have a view of nature and let the light in, and you can open the windows to let in fresh air. Countless studies show that individuals heal faster in hospitals and have more energy and better cognitive abilities at work, when they have a view of nature instead of the urban concrete jungle. If possible, spend the majority of your time when in your home or office in the room that provides you with views of greenery. If this isn't possible, you can hang photos of landscapes of nature and add a photo you may have taken in nature — perhaps showing a sunset, mountains, or a forest — as a screen saver on your computer or smartphone. You can also bring in nature's smells by way of essential oil diffusers, candles, or aromatherapy of lavender, rosemary, or eucalyptus.

TIP

One of my favorite ways to bring nature into the home is to add to your family, if you can, by getting a pet. This act of selflessness and care has been shown to raise oxytocin levels and other feel-good neurotransmitters, reduce stress, and improve healing. Whether it's a dog, cat, fish, or hamster, make the addition to your family, and get closer to the rest of the animal kingdom.

Using Nature to Relax and Play

Multiple studies confirm that an individual who is immersed in nature, looking at nature, or thinking of nature experiences better recovery from stress, less activity in the amygdala (the fear center in the brain), lower levels of stress hormones like cortisol, and reductions in blood pressure, heart rate, and muscle tension.

Why not unwind and relax by taking the time to lie on a blanket in the grass or on a hammock under the shade or spend a relaxing afternoon on the beach? Let nature remind you to slow down, be present, practice mindfulness, and enjoy the beauty around you. If you can't get outdoors, you can listen to guided meditations that involve scenes of nature. Feel-good chemicals will flow through your brain and body because you're meditating *and* because you're igniting memories of being in nature.

Nature can also remind you how to play because of the myriad of opportunities it offers you to be active. You can play catch with your children or play tennis with adults. Play in the ocean or in the sandbox. Pretend that you're going on an adventure in your backyard, or gather up your possessions and travel on a real adventure.

REMEMBER

Allowing yourself to relax and play like a child does wonders to lower your stress levels and put a smile on your face.

Enjoying a Getaway

When is the last time you "unplugged" from the world and allowed yourself to relax in nature? Aside from the myriad of health benefits that spending time in nature offers you, getting away into nature and away from the routine and unhealthy habits of your life can give you the kick-start you need to get back on the road to healthy-and-happy. It's true for me as well, because even though I lead a generally healthy life, I can also spend too much time at the computer screen, working or staying connected, which brings my mood down over time and keeps me from sleeping. Getting away, relaxing with dear friends or family or even alone, and spending time being in nature meditating, eating healthy, and sleeping deeply always gets me rested, renewed, and back on track.

Index

A

acceptance
  about, 76–77
  as an option for managing emotions, 66
  for developing social bonds, 205–206
  as a healthy boundary quality, 92
  of reality, 96
  relationships and, 199
  spiritual people and, 72
  of yourself, 86
accountability
  as a belief, 78
  as a characteristic of a trusted leader, 250
  for improving conscious communication, 94
  relationships and, 198
  showing respect with, 91
  striving for, 96
acknowledgement
  for cultivating empathy, 95
  for developing social bonds, 205–206
  for strengthening connectedness, 313
action, taking, 179–185
active listening
  for assessing trust and reliance, 199
  for cultivating empathy, 95
  for improving conscious communication, 93
adaptability
  as a characteristic of resilient, cohesive
    communities, 101
  as a characteristic of resilient leaders, 102
  emotions and, 63
adaptive coping habits, 11, 28–29, 30
adrenalin, 23
adventures, 169, 210
aging process, 37
aligning core values, 222–224
allostasis, 22

allowing love in, 189–191
altruism, spirituality and, 313
"always" word, 151
analyzing insights for decision-making, 141–144
antioxidants, 266
appreciation, 72, 188–189
approachability
  as a characteristic of a trusted leader, 250
  children and, 325
art of listening, 113–114
articulation, 142
assumptions
  avoiding, for cultivating empathy, 95
  challenging, 159–160
attention, focusing for listening, 113
attentive listening, relationships and, 198
attitude
  changing to optimism, 165–169
  choosing your, 292
  shifting to gratitude, 167–168
attributes, positive, 226
awareness exercise, 156–159
awe. *See* gratitude and awe

B

balance
  choosing, 295–300
  showing respect with, 91
  as a way to build trust, 89
behaviors, healthy, 73
beliefs
  limiting, 149–150
  power of, 27–28
  as a requirement for commitment, 87
  sharing, 304
  in your worth, 175

best friend, being your own, 86

blessings, counting your, 163

blood vessels, stress response and, 23

body, listening to your, 121–125

body scan, 122–124

bonded team, 100

bonds, strengthening by sharing, 208–211

bone density, 43

boundaries, healthy
  as a characteristic of relationships, 194, 198–199
  as a characteristic of resilient, cohesive communities, 101
  for cultivating empathy, 95
  establishing, 91–92
  self-worth and, 175
  setting, 299
  for strengthening connectedness, 314

brain
  about, 36
  activating whole, 143–144
  reframing, as a step in improving mental toughness, 161
  stress response and, 24

brainstorming, in goal alignment, 223

break, taking a, 144, 296

breath focus, 326

breath(ing)
  experimenting with your, 116–118
  mindful, 119
  spirituality and, 312

Brown, Stuart, 270–271

C

calmness
  as an action step in evaluating feelings, 65
  as a characteristic of a trusted leader, 250
  emotions, 67–68
  establishing, 115–121
  stress response, 67–68

Cannon, Walter (physiologist), 23

carbohydrates, complex, 42

cardiovascular system, stress response and, 24

catastrophizing, with victim mentality, 14

celebrating
  family members, 309
  relationships and, 198
  resilient communities and, 219
  wins, 278, 293
  yourself, 181

celebration expression, as a characteristic of resilient, cohesive communities, 101

challenges
  of assumptions, 159–160
  embracing, 240–243
  in MTQ48 Psychometric Tool, 53, 56–57
  seeing as opportunities, 291–292

change, embracing, 51, 240–243, 294, 329

Cheat Sheet (website), 3

childhood development, as a determinant for resilience, 9–10

children, stress and, 323–331

clarification
  for improving conscious communication, 93
  of objectives, 143

clarity
  for enhancing communication, 316–318
  family resilience and, 305
  as a healthy boundary quality, 92

clean slate, 242

clearing the mind, 244–245, 334–335

coach, being your own, 168–169

co-creation
  as a characteristic of resilient leaders, 102
  of your life, 148–149

cognitive empathy, 94

collaboration
  as a characteristic of resilient leaders, 102
  in shared values, 104

commanding, as a characteristic of resilient leaders, 102

commitment
  for assessing trust and reliance, 200
  as a characteristic of relationships, 194, 196–197
  choosing, 86–88

determining level of, 196–197

fostering with community, 99

making a, 86

in MTQ48 Psychometric Tool, 53, 55–56

to shared goals, 216

to shared goals, as a characteristic of resilient, cohesive communities, 100

communication

as a characteristic of relationships, 200–201

as a characteristic of resilient, cohesive communities, 101

conscious, 93–94

with curiosity, 202–203

effective, 218, 227–230

enhancing, 316–320

expectations, 96

improving, 227–230

maintaining open channels of, 325–326

with presence, 202–203

showing respect with, 90

styles, 230

vision, 248–249

communication skills, in needs assessment, 225

communicative, as a characteristic of resilient leaders, 102

community leadership pillar

ability to improvise, 106–107

about, 20, 97–98

building trust, 105–106

finding motivation, 107–108

group resilience and cohesion, 100–102

having fun, 108

individual resilience and, 98–99

sharing values, 104

showing respect, 104–105

stepping into, 102–103

comparisons, to others, 57

compassion

cultivating, 293

listening with, 125–127

showing, 81–82, 84

spiritual people and, 72

compassion meditation, 126–127

compassionate empathy, 94

compensatory behavior, as a characteristic of resilient, cohesive communities, 101

competency

as a characteristic of resilient leaders, 102

developing, 58

reviewing, 226

in shared values, 104

complex carbohydrates, for nutrient-rich diet, 42

conclusions, jumping to, as a stress signal, 115

confidence, in MTQ48 Psychometric Tool, 53, 57–58

confirming, communication and, 229

connectedness

as a characteristic of a trusted leader, 250

as a characteristic of resilient leaders, 102

family resilience and, 304

connections

for changing attitude to optimism, 166–167

with love and awe, 165

making, 144

spiritual people and, 72

strengthening, 313–314

with support, 186–187

conscientious communication style, 230

conscious choices, 180–181

conscious communication, 93–94

consistency

for assessing trust and reliance, 199

as a characteristic of a trusted leader, 249

for communicating your vision, 248

for creating structure, 314

family resilience and, 305, 308

as a way to build trust, 89

contribution

as a characteristic of resilient, cohesive communities, 101

enhancing sense of purpose with, 76

equal, 96, 217

control, in MTQ48 Psychometric Tool, 53–55

conversations, for listening and taking care, 260

F

failures
    embracing, 294–295
    viewing as opportunities, 51
fairness
    as a characteristic of a trusted leader, 251
    as a characteristic of resilient, cohesive communities, 101, 219
    as a characteristic of resilient leaders, 102
    establishing guidelines for, 231–232
family meetings, for creating structure, 315
family resilience
    about, 303
    adopting shared beliefs, 308–313
    developing core framework, 304–305
    enhancing communication, 316–320
    establishing organization and structure, 313–316
    setting an example, 305–308
fasting, intermittent, 266
fats, healthy, 42
fears
    facing, 327
    for listening and taking care, 260
    of risk, 241
    sharing, 203, 209
feedback, inviting
    about, 228
    as a characteristic of a trusted leader, 250
    for communicating your vision, 248
    for improving conscious communication, 93
feeling lucky, 80–81
feeling shame *vs.* accountable scenario, 155–156
feelings, evaluating, 64–65
feng shui, 283–287
fight-or-flight, 23–24, 62
fire, for feng shui, 285–286
fitness
    prioritizing, 257–263
    resilience and, 33–34
fittest, survival of the, 35–36
5-minute morning meditation, 252
fixed mindset, growth mindset *vs.*, 51–52

flexibility
    creating structure with, 314–315
    emotions and, 63
    family resilience and, 304–305
    time management and, 280
flow, going with the, 243, 318
focus
    as a characteristic of a trusted leader, 250
    redirecting, 294
    as a requirement for commitment, 87
forceful backup, as a characteristic of resilient, cohesive communities, 101
framework, developing core, 304–305
free radicals, 37
freeing up your mind, 276–278
fruits, for nutrient-rich diet, 42
frustration, as a sign of learned helplessness, 15
fun, having, 108, 188
functional foods, 41
functional movement, 267–271
furniture, for feng shui, 284
the future, visualizing, 245–246

G

gardens, 336
gastrointestinal tract, stress response and, 23
Gelb, Michael
    How to Think Like Leonardo De Vinci, 138
genes, as a determinant for resilience, 9
getaways, 339
giving
    back, 307
    to others, enhancing sense of purpose with, 76
    receiving and, 95–96
goals
    attainability of, 58
    community, 221–222
    defining, 246–247
    getting buy-in on, 221–222
    matching values with, 224, 225–226
    setting, 298

I

"I can do that, but___" phrase, 152

"I can't" phrase, 150–151

icons, explained, 2

identifying
  as an option for managing emotions, 65
  core values, 313

immune system
  fueling your, 37
  stress response and, 24

impatience, as a stress signal, 115

imperfection, accepting, 205

improvisation, ability for, 106–107

'in their shoes,' being, for cultivating empathy, 95

inclusivity
  as a characteristic of resilient, cohesive communities, 101
  establishing guidelines for, 231–232
  resilient communities and, 219

influence, sphere of, 235–237

influence communication style, 230

insensitivity, as a stress signal, 115

insight
  about, 129–130
  analyzing for decision-making, 141–144
  curiosity, 136–139
  emotions, 139–141
  gaining wisdom, 144–145
  intuition, 133–136
  journey to, 130–132
  quieting the mind, 132–133

inspiration
  as a characteristic of resilient leaders, 102
  enhancing sense of purpose with, 76
  finding, 162

insulted vs. eager scenario, 155

integration, as a characteristic of resilient, cohesive communities, 101

interest, as a characteristic of relationships, 194

intermittent fasting, 266

interruptions, as a stress signal, 115

intrinsic factors, 107

intuition
  about, 133–134
  clearing static, 134–135
  tuning in mindfully, 135–136

inventory, maintaining, 182–183

investment
  as a requirement for commitment, 87
  in time, 207–208

J

joy
  as a belief, 78
  enjoying, 84

judgment, emotions and, 63

justice, as a characteristic of resilient, cohesive communities, 101

K

kindness
  as a belief, 78
  for developing social bonds, 206

knowing your core values, 86

knowledge of resources, as a characteristic of resilient leaders, 102

L

leadership
  as a characteristic of resilient, cohesive communities, 101
  styles, 234–240

learned helplessness, 14–15

learning
  being open to, 31–32
  as a belief, 78
  commitment to, 84
  enhancing with community, 99
  family resilience and, 311

lessons, finding, 162

letting it go, as an option for managing emotions, 66

life
  co-creating your, 148–149
  getting a, 299–300
  happier, as a benefit of organizing, 274
  mystery and process of, 76–77
light sleep, 39
lighting, feng shui and, 284
limiting beliefs, 149–150
listening
  about, 111–112
  with all your senses, 119–120
  art of, 113–114
  for building trust and reliance, 204
  as a characteristic of a trusted leader, 249
  with compassion, 125–127
  for developing social bonds, 204, 205–206
  establishing calm, 115–121
  for evaluating communication and empathy, 200
  showing respect with, 90
  stress signals, 114–115
  tuning in to the senses, 112–113
  to your body, 121–125
lists
  creating for freeing up your mind, 277
  prioritizing, 279
load sharing, 96
lost, getting, 242
love
  allowing it in, 189–191
  choosing, 70
  connecting with, 165
  embracing, 272
  for listening and taking care, 260
  self, 184–185, 307
  for strengthening connectedness, 313
  unconditional, 309
loving kindness
  expressing, 78–79
  spiritual people and, 72
loving-kindness meditation, 79
lucky, feeling, 80–81
lunge, as a function movement, 268

M

Maier, Steven, 15
maladaptive coping habits, 11, 29
meaning
  finding, 294, 310–311
  gleaning from hardship, 162–165
meditation
  compassion, 126–127
  as a component of physical hardness, 45–46
  5-minute morning, 252
  guided, 326
  loving-kindness, 79
  mindfulness, 45
  movement, 46
  spiritual people and, 72
  in work life, 296–297
Mediterranean diet, 41
meetings, giving purpose and direction to, 228–229
mental health
  problems, as a sign of learned helplessness, 15
  spirituality and, 73
mental toughness and clarity pillar
  about, 18–19, 49, 160–162
  accessing, 58–60
  developing, 52–58
  fixed mindset *vs.* growth mindset, 51–52
  resilient mindset, 50–51
metabolic conditioning, 186
metabolic flexibility, 263–265
metabolic system, stress response and, 24
metabolism, improving, 263–267
metal, for feng shui, 286
metta, 79
microbiome, 266
milestones, clarity in, 226–227
mind
  clearing the, 244–245, 334–335
  freeing up your, 276–278
  opening the, 244–245
  quieting the, 54, 113, 132–133, 187, 272
  stress response and, 24

physical exercises, 267
physical hardness
  assembling components of, 38–48
  meditating, 45–46
  nature, aligning with, 46–48
  nutrient-rich diet, 40–43
  as one of six pillars of resilience, 18
  physical activity, 43–44
  relaxing, 45–46
  sleep, 38–40
physical space, decluttering, 281–283
physical vitality and flexibility pillar
  about, 33, 257
  brain and, 36
  components of physical hardness, 38–48
  evaluating, 260–263
  fitness, 33–34
  functional movement, 267–271
  immune system, 37
  improving metabolism, 263–267
  prioritizing fitness, 257–263
  recovery, 271–272
  sickness, 34–35
  survival of the fittest, 35–36
Pisano, Gary, 100
placebo effect, 27
planning, as a characteristic of resilient, cohesive
    communities, 101
plants, 47, 284
playing
  about, 270–271
  for creating structure, 315
  in nature, 338
  for strengthening connectedness, 314
positive culture, in shared values, 104
positive detachment, 68–69
positive expectation, 26–27, 28
positivity
  as a characteristic of resilience, 74
  children and, 325
  family resilience and, 307

powerlessness, with victim mentality, 13
practicing
  gratitude, 253
  mindfulness, 336
  self-awareness, 179–180
  self-care, 86
prayer, spiritual people and, 72
presence
  communicating with, 202–203
  for evaluating communication and empathy, 200
priorities, setting, 299
prioritizing
  fitness, 257–263
  in goal alignment, 224
  lists, 279
proactivity, for fostering optimism, 292
problem-solving
  children and, 330
  family resilience and, 305, 319–320
process of life, 76–77
procrastination, as a sign of learned
    helplessness, 15
productivity, as a benefit of organizing, 274
progressive muscle relaxation
  about, 46
  as a technique for controlling emotions, 67–68
projecting, as a stress signal, 115
prosocial, being, as a characteristic of
    resilience, 74
protein, for nutrient-rich diet, 42
psychological outlook, as a determinant for
    resilience, 10–11
pull, as a functional movement, 269
pupils, stress response and, 23
purpose
  as a characteristic of resilience, 74
  community, 221–222
  connecting with, 55
  searching for, 75–76
  in shared values, 104
  spiritual people and, 72
  as a step in improving mental toughness, 161

push, as a functional movement, 268–269

putting yourself down, with victim mentality, 13

Q

quality relationships pillar
  about, 83
  building trust, 88–89
  choosing to commit, 86–88
  establishing healthy boundaries, 91–92
  expressing empathy, 94–95
  giving and receiving, 95–96
  improving conscious communication, 93–94
  journey of self-discovery, 84
  showing respect, 90–91
  with yourself, 85–86
quality time, with family, 309
quieting
  the mind, 113, 132–133, 272
  your mind, 54, 187
quieting breath, 116

R

reality, accepting, 96
reappraisal, 67, 68–69, 163
receiving
  about, 84
  giving and, 95–96
receptivity, curiosity and, 138–139
reciprocity, as a characteristic of relationships, 194, 201
recovery, 271–272
redirection
  as an option for managing emotions, 66
  of focus, 294
reflection
  as an action step in evaluating feelings, 65
  for evaluating communication and empathy, 200
  for improving conscious communication, 93
  personal, 222–223
  rejection and, 294
  taking time for, 86

Reflection icon, 2
regulating emotions, 54, 318–319
rejection, reflection and, 294
relationships
  about, 173, 193–194
  allowing love in, 189–191
  believing in your worth, 175
  better, as a benefit of organizing, 274
  building lasting social bonds, 202–208
  connecting resilience with self-worth, 174
  creating quality, 193–211
  emotions and, 64
  evaluating, 195–201
  evaluating your self-value, 177–179
  noting self-criticism, 176–177
  strengthening bonds by sharing, 208–211
  taking action, 179–185
  taking care of yourself, 185–189
  with yourself, 85–86
relaxing
  as a component of physical hardness, 45–46
  curiosity and, 138
  in nature, 338
  techniques for, 67–68
reliance
  building, 203–204
  as a characteristic of relationships, 194, 199–200
  as a characteristic of resilient, cohesive communities, 101
  encouraging with community, 99
religion, compared with spirituality, 71–72
REM sleep, 39
Remember icon, 2
remembering
  showing respect with, 91
  victories, 164
reminders, setting, 296–297
repeating
  for communicating your vision, 248
  for listening, 113
reproductive system, stress response and, 24
research, 143

resilience. *See also specific types and topics*
about, 7
community and individual, 98–99
connecting with self-worth, 174
determinants of, 8–12
fitness and, 33–34
mindset, 50–51, 147
nature and, 333–339
six pillars of resilience, 17–20
spirituality and, 73
victim cycle, 16–17
what it's not, 12–16
who it's for, 7–8
resilient community
about, 213
creating foundation for, 220–232
determining your people, 213–214
evaluating, 214–220
resilient leaders
about, 233
being trusted, 249–251
characteristics of, 233–234
creating your vision, 244–249
embracing challenges/change, 240–243
self-awareness, 251–253
self-care, 251–253
style of leadership, 234–240
resistance training, 186
resources
combining, 217
knowledge of, as a characteristic of resilient leaders, 102
shared, as a characteristic of resilient, cohesive communities, 101
respect
as a characteristic of relationships, 194, 198–199
for enhancing communication, 318
in shared values, 104
showing, 90–91, 96, 104–105
of yourself, 86

respiratory system, stress response and, 24
responsibilities
clarity in, 226–227
for creating structure, 315
delegating, 279, 299
resting, 189
reward, as a requirement for commitment, 87
risk taking
fear of, 241
as a way to build trust, 88–89
rituals, for strengthening connectedness, 314
role models, for children, 324–325
roles
assigning people to, 224–227
clarity in, 226–227
clarity of, as a characteristic of resilient, cohesive communities, 100
in needs assessment, 225
routines
children and, 328
for creating structure, 314
getting out of, 243
Rusch, Heather, 8–9

S

sacred space, 312
sacrifice
as a requirement for commitment, 87
willingness to, 56
satisfaction, as a characteristic of resilience, 74
scanning the body, 122–124
seasonal eating, 337
selective hearing, as a stress signal, 115
self
accepting your, 183
uniqueness of, 183
self-awareness
as a characteristic of resilient leaders, 102
enhancing, 69

thoughts, forgetting, for listening, 113

time
 investment in, 207–208
 management of, 278–281

time pie exercise, 260–261

timed distractions, 280–281, 297

Tip icon, 2

transparency
 as a characteristic of a trusted leader, 249
 in communication, 232

true, staying, for communicating your vision, 248

trust
 building, 88–89, 105–106, 203–204
 as a characteristic of relationships, 194,
  199–200
 increasing with community, 99
 spiritual people and, 72

trusted leaders
 characteristics of, 249–251
 resilient communities and, 219–220

truthfulness
 for assessing trust and reliance, 200
 seeking, 130–132
 as a way to build trust, 89

tuning in
 mindfully, 135–136
 to the senses, 112–113

Turner, Ian, 53

U

unassuming, being, for evaluating communication
 and empathy, 200–201

uncertainty, embracing, 56

uncomfortable, becoming uncomfortable
 being, 241

unconditional love, 309

uncover, as an action step in evaluating
 feelings, 65

understanding
 being open to, 31–32
 enhancing sense of purpose with, 76

uniqueness, of self, 183

unplugging, 297–298, 328–329

V

validation
 as an action step in evaluating feelings, 65
 relationships and, 198
 showing respect with, 90

value(s)
 about, 293
 as a belief, 78
 in everyone, 84, 307
 matching with goals, 224, 225–226
 relationships and, 198–199
 shared, as a characteristic of resilient, cohesive
  communities, 100
 sharing, 104, 215–216

vegetables, for nutrient-rich diet, 42

victim cycle, breaking the, 16–17

victim mentality, 13–14

victories, remembering, 164

view, of nature, 48

vision
 communicating, 248–249
 creating your, 244–249
 of the future, 245–246
 maintaining your, 184

vitality self-assessment, 261–263

vulnerability
 for assessing trust and reliance, 199
 as a belief, 78
 as a way to build trust, 89

W

wakefulness, 39

walking, 120–121, 186

watching your words, 150–1523

water, in feng shui, 284, 287

well-being, spirituality and, 73

wellness retreat, 48

wholeness, as a healthy boundary quality, 92

About the Author

Eva Selhub, MD — or Dr. Eva, as her clients like to call her — has, for over 25 years, been practicing and teaching mind body medicine and methods to tap into our innate human ability to be resilient. She is the founder of Resilience Experts, LLC, a company that provides inspirational and informative coaching and consulting specializing in helping individuals and corporations alike achieve optimal wellness, resilience, innovation, and leadership. Dr. Eva's goal: to keep people out of the hospitals and fully engaged and thriving in life, even in the face of adversity!

Dr. Eva is an internationally recognized expert, physician, speaker, executive leadership and performance coach, and consultant in the fields of stress, resilience, integrative medicine, and working with the natural environment to achieve maximum health and well-being. As an author, a speaker, and a coach, she uses her powerful gift to translate complex information into practical and usable knowledge that any individual can access. Dr. Eva has previously authored four other books, including *The Love Response, Your Brain on Nature, Your Health Destiny*, and *The Stress Management Handbook*.

Board certified in internal medicine, Dr. Eva served as an instructor of medicine at Harvard Medical School and as a clinical associate of the world-renowned Benson Henry Institute for Mind-Body Medicine at Massachusetts General Hospital for close to 20 years, serving as their medical director for 6 of those years. She has been published in medical journals and featured in national publications, including the *New York Times, USA Today, Self, Shape, Fitness*, and *Journal of Woman's Health*, and has appeared on radio and television in connection with her work, including on *The Dr. Oz Show*.

Offering unique programs for individuals and companies that promote executive health and organizational well-being, Dr. Eva combines her clinical expertise and years of scientific research in neuroplasticity and stress with an in-depth practical study of meditation, spirituality, exercise physiology, and nutrition. Her method of teaching is energizing, personal, insightful, compassionate, and straight to the point. She doesn't mess around, yet she does it with love! Dr. Eva brings in humor along with personal experiences that move her audiences while also enabling them to tap into their own personal journeys, making the learning experience memorable and effective. She gives them the realistic picture behind statistical figures and scientific findings while blending in optimism mixed with great storytelling and actionable ideas to latch on to.

For more information on Dr. Eva's workshops, coaching, and consulting, visit her websites at www.drselhub.com and www.drselhubcorporate.com.

Author's Acknowledgments

I'd like to express my appreciation to Tracy Boggier, for having the insight to ask me to write this book, and to Tim Gallan, Becky Whitney, and the entire Wiley team for the clear direction and editing. I would also like to thank all the colleagues and teachers who have supported and guided me along the way to enable me to be able to step out of "medicine" and explore other facets of life, business, and spirituality. Thanks to all the great writers, meditation teachers, and fearless thought leaders whose work has inspired and informed this book. Lastly, thank you to all of my patients and clients, who have taught me how to teach, learn, and grow.

Dedication

This book is dedicated to family, including my parents, Jacob and Shirley; my siblings and sister in-law, Julie, Eliya, and Laura; and my niece and nephew, Maia and Ezra. They fill my heart with love and inspiration and are my "reason why."

Publisher's Acknowledgments

Acquisitions Editor: Tracy Boggier

Project Editor: Tim Gallan

Copy Editor: Becky Whitney

Production Editor: Tamilmani Varadharaj

Cover Image: © AlexSava/iStock /Getty Images

Take dummies with you everywhere you go!

Whether you are excited about e-books, want more from the web, must have your mobile apps, or are swept up in social media, dummies makes everything easier.

Find us online!

Leverage the power

Dummies is the global leader in the reference category and one of the most trusted and highly regarded brands in the world. No longer just focused on books, customers now have access to the dummies content they need in the format they want. Together we'll craft a solution that engages your customers, stands out from the competition, and helps you meet your goals.

Advertising & Sponsorships

Connect with an engaged audience on a powerful multimedia site, and position your message alongside expert how-to content. Dummies.com is a one-stop shop for free, online information and know-how curated by a team of experts.

- Targeted ads
- Video
- Email Marketing

- Microsites
- Sweepstakes sponsorship

20 MILLION PAGE VIEWS EVERY SINGLE MONTH

15 MILLION UNIQUE VISITORS PER MONTH

43% OF ALL VISITORS ACCESS THE SITE VIA THEIR MOBILE DEVICES

700,000 NEWSLETTER SUBSCRIPTIONS TO THE INBOXES OF

300,000 UNIQUE INDIVIDUALS EVERY WEEK

# of dummies

Custom Publishing

Reach a global audience in any language by creating a solution that will differentiate you from competitors, amplify your message, and encourage customers to make a buying decision.

- Apps
- Books
- eBooks
- Video
- Audio
- Webinars

Brand Licensing & Content

Leverage the strength of the world's most popular reference brand to reach new audiences and channels of distribution.

For more information, visit **dummies.com/biz**

PERSONAL ENRICHMENT

Staying Sharp
9781119187790
USA $26.00
CAN $31.99
UK £19.99

Facebook
9781119179030
USA $21.99
CAN $25.99
UK £16.99

Guitar
9781119293354
USA $24.99
CAN $29.99
UK £17.99

Investing
9781119293347
USA $22.99
CAN $27.99
UK £16.99

Beekeeping
9781119310068
USA $22.99
CAN $27.99
UK £16.99

Digital Photography
9781119235606
USA $24.99
CAN $29.99
UK £17.99

Meditation
9781119251163
USA $24.99
CAN $29.99
UK £17.99

Pregnancy
9781119235491
USA $26.99
CAN $31.99
UK £19.99

Samsung Galaxy S7
9781119279952
USA $24.99
CAN $29.99
UK £17.99

iPhone
9781119283133
USA $24.99
CAN $29.99
UK £17.99

Crocheting
9781119287117
USA $24.99
CAN $29.99
UK £16.99

Nutrition
9781119130246
USA $22.99
CAN $27.99
UK £16.99

PROFESSIONAL DEVELOPMENT

Windows 10
9781119311041
USA $24.99
CAN $29.99
UK £17.99

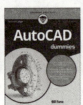

AutoCAD
9781119255796
USA $39.99
CAN $47.99
UK £27.99

Excel 2016
9781119293439
USA $26.99
CAN $31.99
UK £19.99

QuickBooks 2017
9781119281467
USA $26.99
CAN $31.99
UK £19.99

macOS Sierra
9781119280651
USA $29.99
CAN $35.99
UK £21.99

LinkedIn
9781119251132
USA $24.99
CAN $29.99
UK £17.99

Windows 10 All-in-One
9781119310563
USA $34.00
CAN $41.99
UK £24.99

SharePoint 2016
9781119181705
USA $29.99
CAN $35.99
UK £21.99

Fundamental Analysis
9781119263593
USA $26.99
CAN $31.99
UK £19.99

Networking
9781119257769
USA $29.99
CAN $35.99
UK £21.99

Office 2016
9781119293477
USA $26.99
CAN $31.99
UK £19.99

Office 365
9781119265313
USA $24.99
CAN $29.99
UK £17.99

Salesforce.com
9781119239314
USA $29.99
CAN $35.99
UK £21.99

Coding
9781119293323
USA $29.99
CAN $35.99
UK £21.99

dummies.com

dummies
A Wiley Brand

Learning Made Easy

ACADEMIC

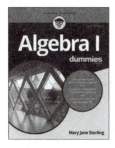

9781119293576
USA $19.99
CAN $23.99
UK £15.99

9781119293637
USA $19.99
CAN $23.99
UK £15.99

9781119293491
USA $19.99
CAN $23.99
UK £15.99

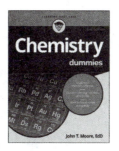

9781119293460
USA $19.99
CAN $23.99
UK £15.99

9781119293590
USA $19.99
CAN $23.99
UK £15.99

9781119215844
USA $26.99
CAN $31.99
UK £19.99

9781119293378
USA $22.99
CAN $27.99
UK £16.99

9781119293521
USA $19.99
CAN $23.99
UK £15.99

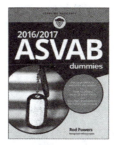

9781119239178
USA $18.99
CAN $22.99
UK £14.99

9781119263883
USA $26.99
CAN $31.99
UK £19.99

Available Everywhere Books Are Sold

dummies.com

Small books for big imaginations

GETTING STARTED WITH **Coding**

Get Creative with Code!

Camille McCue, PhD

9781119177173
USA $9.99
CAN $9.99
UK £8.99

MODDING **Minecraft™**

Build Your Own Minecraft Mods!

Sarah Guthals, PhD
Stephen Foster, PhD
Lindsey Handley, PhD

9781119177272
USA $9.99
CAN $9.99
UK £8.99

MAKING **YouTube®** VIDEOS

Star in Your Own Video!

Nick Willoughby

9781119177241
USA $9.99
CAN $9.99
UK £8.99

DESIGNING **Digital Games**

Create Games with Scratch™!

Derek Breen

9781119177210
USA $9.99
CAN $9.99
UK £8.99

GETTING STARTED WITH **Raspberry Pi®**

Program Your Raspberry Pi!

Richard Wentk

9781119262657
USA $9.99
CAN $9.99
UK £6.99

EXPERIMENTING WITH **Science**

Think, Test, and Learn!

9781119291336
USA $9.99
CAN $9.99
UK £6.99

CREATING **Digital Animations**

Animate Stories with Scratch™!

Derek Breen

9781119233527
USA $9.99
CAN $9.99
UK £6.99

GETTING STARTED WITH **Engineering**

Think Like an Engineer!

9781119291220
USA $9.99
CAN $9.99
UK £6.99

WRITING **Computer Code**

Learn the Language of Computers!

9781119177302
USA $9.99
CAN $9.99
UK £8.99

Unleash Their Creativity

dummies.com

dummies®
A Wiley Brand